ACTS
for
EVERYONE

PART 2
CHAPTERS 13–28

N. T.
WRIGHT

WJK WESTMINSTER
JOHN KNOX PRESS
LOUISVILLE · KENTUCKY

Copyright © 2008 Nicholas Thomas Wright

First published in 2008 in Great Britain by
Society for Promoting Christian Knowledge
36 Causton Street
London SW1P 4ST

and in the United States of America by
Westminster John Knox Press
100 Witherspoon Street
Louisville, KY 40202

All rights reserved. No part of this book may be reproduced or
transmitted in any form or by any means, electronic or mechanical,
including photocopying, recording, or by any information storage and
retrieval system, without permission in writing from the Society for
Promoting Christian Knowledge, 36 Causton Street, London SW1P 4ST.

09 10 11 12 13 14 15 16 17 — 10 9 8 7 6 5 4 3 2

British Library Cataloguing-in-Publication Data
A catalogue record for this book is available from the British Library.

ISBN: 978-0-281-05546-3 (U.K. edition)

United States Library of Congress Cataloging-in-Publication Data is
on file at the Library of Congress, Washington, D.C.

ISBN: 978-0-664-22796-8 (U.S. edition)

Maps by Pantek Arts Ltd, Maidstone, Kent, UK.

Typeset by Graphicraft Ltd, Hong Kong
Printed in Great Britain at
Ashford Colour Press
Reprinted in the United States
of America by Versa

CONTENTS

INTRODUCTION

On the very first occasion when someone stood up in public to tell people about Jesus, he made it very clear: this message is for *everyone*.

It was a great day – sometimes called the birthday of the church. The great wind of God's spirit had swept through Jesus' followers and filled them with a new joy and a sense of God's presence and power. Their leader, Peter, who only a few weeks before had been crying like a baby because he'd lied and cursed and denied even knowing Jesus, found himself on his feet explaining to a huge crowd that something had happened which had changed the world for ever. What God had done for him, Peter, he was beginning to do for the whole world: new life, forgiveness, new hope and power were opening up like spring flowers after a long winter. A new age had begun in which the living God was going to do new things in the world – beginning then and there with the individuals who were listening to him. 'This promise is for *you*', he said, 'and for your children, and for everyone who is far away' (Acts 2.39). It wasn't just for the person standing next to you. It was for everyone.

Within a remarkably short time this came true to such an extent that the young movement spread throughout much of the known world. And one way in which the *everyone* promise worked out was through the writings of the early Christian leaders. These short works – mostly letters and stories about Jesus – were widely circulated and eagerly read. They were never intended for either a religious or intellectual elite. From the very beginning they were meant for everyone.

That is as true today as it was then. Of course, it matters that some people give time and care to the historical evidence, the meaning of the original words (the early Christians wrote in Greek), and the exact and particular force of what different writers were saying about God, Jesus, the world and themselves.

This series is based quite closely on that sort of work. But the point of it all is that the message can get out to everyone, especially to people who wouldn't normally read a book with footnotes and Greek words in it. That's the sort of person for whom these books are written. And that's why there's a glossary, in the back, of the key words that you can't really get along without, with a simple description of what they mean. Whenever you see a word in **bold type** in the text, you can go to the back and remind yourself what's going on.

There are of course many translations of the New Testament available today. The one I offer here is designed for the same kind of reader: one who mightn't necessarily understand the more formal, sometimes even ponderous, tones of some of the standard ones. I have of course tried to keep as close to the original as I can. But my main aim has been to be sure that the words can speak not just to some people, but to everyone.

The book of Acts, which I quoted a moment ago, is full of the energy and excitement of the early Christians as they found God doing new things all over the place and learned to take the good news of Jesus around the world. It's also full of the puzzles and problems that churches faced then and face today – crises over leadership, money, ethnic divisions, theology and ethics, not to mention serious clashes with political and religious authorities. It's comforting to know that 'normal church life', even in the time of the first apostles, was neither trouble-free nor plain sailing, just as it's encouraging to know that even in the midst of all their difficulties the early church was able to take the gospel forward in such dynamic ways. Actually, 'plain sailing' reminds us that this is the book where more journeys take place, including several across the sea, than anywhere else in the Bible – with the last journey, in particular, including a terrific storm and a dramatic shipwreck. There isn't a dull page in Acts. But, equally importantly, the whole book reminds us that whatever 'journey' we are making, in our own lives, our spirituality, our following of Jesus, and our work for his kingdom, his spirit will guide us too, and make us fruitful in his service. So here it is: Acts for everyone!

To
John Pritchard and Mark Bryant
Fellow-workers for the kingdom of God

The Eastern Mediterranean in the First Century AD

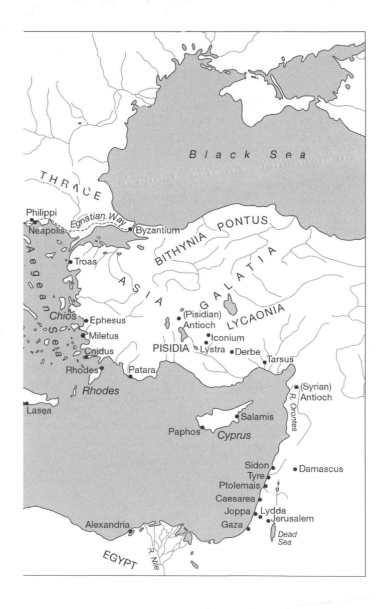

ACTS 13.1–12

Mission and Magic

[1]In the church at Antioch there were prophets and teachers: Barnabas, Symeon called Niger, Lucius of Cyrene, Manaen from the court of Herod the Tetrarch, and Saul. [2]As they were worshipping the Lord and fasting, the holy spirit said, 'Set apart Barnabas and Saul for the work to which I have called them.' [3]So they fasted and prayed; and then they laid their hands on them and sent them off.

[4]So off they went, sent out by the holy spirit, and arrived at Seleucia. From there they set sail to Cyprus, [5]and when they arrived in Salamis they announced God's word in the Jewish synagogues. John was with them as their assistant. [6]They went through the whole of the island, all the way to Paphos. There they found a magician, a Jewish false prophet named Bar-Jesus. [7]He was with the governor, Sergius Paulus, who was an intelligent man. He called Barnabas and Saul and asked to hear the word of God. [8]The magician Elymas (that is the translation of his name) was opposing them, and doing his best to turn the governor away from the faith. [9]But Saul, also named Paul, looked intently at him, filled with the holy spirit.

[10]'You're full of trickery and every kind of villainy!' he said. 'You're a son of the devil! You're an enemy of everything that's upright! When are you going to stop twisting the paths that God has made straight? [11]Now see here: the Lord's hand will be upon you, and you will be blind for a while; you won't even be able to see the sun!'

At once mist and darkness fell on him, and he went about looking for someone to lead him by the hand. [12]When the governor saw what had happened, he believed, since he was astonished at the teaching of the Lord.

Jim was full of enthusiasm when he left college. From his earliest memories he had been passionate about justice, about fairness, about people respecting one another and being able to live together in harmony. He had always admired the police (in England, this used to be quite easy) and had seen himself as a pillar of the community, helping society to get along, warning those who were messing about, and himself gaining respect all round.

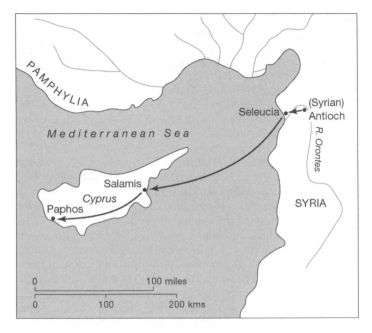

Acts 13.1ff

On his first day in the police station, an older officer came up to him.

'Now then, young man,' he said. 'Let's not have any of that "grand ideal" stuff round here. We don't want anyone making a fuss where there's no need. We'll tell you who to go after and who to turn a blind eye to. If we all just blundered ahead with this crazy notion of justice, we'd never get anywhere! People are watching, you know. Think of your family, think of your pension. You'll learn.'

And Jim realized he had a choice. Compromise or confrontation. A safe passage to mediocrity, or a dangerous route to getting the job done.

Many Christians in the Western world today simply can't bear to think of confrontation (except, of course, with 'those wicked fundamentalists'!). There really isn't such a thing as serious wickedness, so they think, or if there is it's confined

2

to a small number of truly evil people, while everyone else just gets on and should be accepted and affirmed as they stand. Christian mission then consists of helping people to do a little bit better where they already are, rather than the radical transformation of life that, as we have seen, was happening all around the place in the early chapters of Acts. And so, when we come to this great turning-point in Luke's story, the start of the extraordinary triple journey that would take Paul right across Turkey and Greece and back again, and then again once more, and finally off to Rome itself, we would much prefer the story to be one of gentle persuasion rather than confrontation. We would have liked it better if Paul had gone about telling people the simple message of Jesus and finding that many people were happy to accept it and live by it.

But life is seldom that straightforward, and people who try to pretend it is often end up simply pulling the wool over their own eyes. It's a murky world out there, and though the choice of compromise is always available in every profession (not least in the church), there is in fact no real choice. What's the point in trying to swim with one foot on the bottom of the pool? You're either up for the real thing or you might as well pack it all in. And Saul and Barnabas were up for the real thing.

They had to be, after that send-off. Luke introduces 'the church in Antioch' with something of a flourish of trumpets; Antioch was on the way to becoming a second major centre of Christian **faith** after Jerusalem itself, and its leadership team was well known, with Barnabas and Saul among them. We get a fascinating glimpse of their regular devotional life: fasting and prayer surrounding the worship of the Lord, waiting for the **spirit** to give fresh direction. Whether they had been expecting something like this, we don't know. But to be told, suddenly, that two of the main leaders were wanted elsewhere must have come as something of a blow. (At the time of writing, I have just lost a close colleague who has been called to new ministry, and I am feeling the loss quite keenly.) But there are times, when you have been praying and waiting on God, when a new and unexpected **word** comes in such a way that you have no choice but to obey. And it's just as well that this is how things happen, because when you then run into problems, and especially confrontation, it would be all too easy to think, 'Oh no, we shouldn't have come.' But the answer, again and again, is, Yes, you should have come; and it is precisely because the **gospel** needs to make inroads into enemy territory that you need that constant support of fasting and prayer. (One might speculate and suggest that, since the **holy spirit** hadn't mentioned John Mark, whom Barnabas and Saul took with them [as in verse 5], we shouldn't be surprised that he got cold feet early on in the trip and went back home; but this may be stretching the point.)

We are not told that the spirit specified Cyprus as their initial destination, though Luke omits many details and it's quite possible that the direction was clear. In any case, Barnabas came from that island himself and it was a natural first port of call. There seem to have been Christian missionaries at work there already (see 11.19), but we should never imagine that a few quick visits and a few early converts meant that a whole town, still less an entire island, had been 'evangelized'. There was still plenty to do, and Barnabas and Saul were not simply going to try to persuade one or two people. They were going to take the **message** to the heart of the Jewish community on the island, and then to the heart of its **Gentile** community. They sailed from Seleucia, the port of Antioch (Antioch, like Rome, sat a few miles up river from the sea), took the short crossing to Salamis, at the east end of Cyprus, and travelled along the main road round the south of the island until they came to the capital, Paphos, at the western end.

Straight away they established a pattern which would be repeated in place after place. People have sometimes imagined that, because Paul styled himself 'apostle to the Gentiles', that meant he didn't bother any more with his fellow Jews, but nothing could be further from the truth. In Romans 1.16 he describes the gospel as being 'to the Jew first, and also, equally, for the Greek' ('Greek' here means, basically, 'non-Jewish'); and that describes, to a T, his practice as set out in Acts. Luke doesn't tell us what they said in the synagogues in Salamis and elsewhere, because he is saving that for when they get to the Turkish mainland, and because he has something sharp and important to report. When Barnabas and Saul arrived in

Paphos, they met two people in particular: the Roman governor, and a local magician.

Both of these are important, as well as in themselves, for what they signify, for Luke and for us. We have already seen that Luke is very much aware of the larger Roman world for which he is writing, and though Roman officials in his book sometimes do the wrong thing for the wrong reasons he wants everyone to be aware that he will give credit where credit is due, and is not prejudiced, or eager to regard all officials, and especially all Romans, as automatically a danger to God's world and God's people. This is not unimportant for us to remember in our own world, where political polarization easily leads people into simplistic analyses and diagnoses of complex social problems, and to a readiness to dismiss out of hand all authorities and anyone in power, whether locally or globally. In this case, the fact that Sergius Paulus had heard about Barnabas and Saul indicates well enough the kind of impact they had been making in his territory. The fact that he wanted to give them a fair hearing – and ended up apparently believing their message – is a wonderful start for their work.

But there is no advance for the gospel without opposition. Indeed, so clear is this truth that sometimes, paradoxically, it's only when an apparent disaster threatens, or when the church is suddenly up against confrontation and has to pray its way through, that you can be quite sure you're on the right track. On this occasion the gospel was invading territory which was under enemy occupation, and the enemy was determined to fight back. The enemy in question was the power of magic, which has already come up in Acts 8 and will recur in chapter 19. We who live in the curious split-level world, between modern scepticism on the one hand and the rampant culture of horoscopes and many other kinds of attempted raids on the supernatural on the other, would do well not to give a superior smile at this point. There are more things in **heaven** and on earth than are dreamed of in modern Western philosophies, and some of those things are very dangerous.

The confrontation comes to a head as the Jewish false prophet Bar-Jesus, also known as Elymas (Luke says this is a 'translation', but it's clear he really means 'alternative name'), tries to persuade the governor not to listen to what the apostles are saying. But now it is the turn of Paul to do what Peter had done in chapter 8. Notice the 'looking intently' in verse 9, a feature we've observed before. Sometimes, in a context of prayer, it is possible to see right into someone's heart, even if we would rather not. When that happens, the only thing to do is to take the risk and say what you see. And what Paul saw was ugly indeed, though not (alas) uncommon: a deep-rooted opposition to truth and goodness, a heart-level commitment to deceit and villainy and, as a result, an implacable opposition to the **good news** about Jesus. Paul reacts sharply, declaring God's judgment on him in the form of temporary blindness (which he himself had suffered, of course, in chapter 9; did Paul hope that in Elymas's case, as in his own, this would lead to **repentance** and to embracing the gospel?). The result is that the governor believed the gospel. Luke says that he was astonished at the 'teaching of the Lord'; this clearly doesn't just mean the theological content of what was being said, but the power which it conveyed.

One obvious lesson from all this is that when a new work of God is going ahead, you can expect opposition, difficulty, problems and confrontation. That is normal. How God will help you through (and how long he will take about it!) is another matter. *That* he will, if we continue in prayer, faith and trust, is a given.

One final note. Luke switches in this passage from the name 'Saul' to the name 'Paul', which he will now continue to use. 'Saul' was a Hebrew name, most famously used for the first Israelite king, whose noble and tragic story is told in 1 Samuel. Paul seems to be aware of this; he, like that king a thousand years earlier, was from the tribe of Benjamin, and on one occasion he quotes, in reference to himself, a passage about the choice of Saul as king (Romans 11.2, quoting 1 Samuel 12.22). Paul also mentions the king in Acts 13.21, in the speech we are about to hear. But the name 'Saul' didn't play well in the wider non-Jewish world. Its Greek form, 'Saulos', was an adjective that described someone walking or behaving in an effeminate way: 'mincing' might be our closest equivalent. It was, to put it delicately, not a word that would help people to forget the messenger and concentrate on the message. So, like many Jews going out into the Greek world, Paul used a regular Greek name, whether because it was another name he had had all along, which is quite possible, or because it was close to his own real name, just as some immigrants change their names into something more recognizable in the new country. One thing was certain. Paul was serious about getting the message out to the wider world. When you even change your own name, you show that you really mean business, even if it will lead you into confrontation.

ACTS 13.13–25

Address in Antioch

[13]Paul and his companions set off from Paphos and came to Perga in Pamphylia. John, however, left them and went back to Jerusalem. [14]But they came through from Perga and arrived in Antioch of Pisidia, where they went into the synagogue on the sabbath day and sat down. [15]After the reading of the law and the prophets, the ruler of the synagogue sent word to them.

'My brothers,' he said, 'if you have any word of exhortation for the people, let us hear it.'

[16]So Paul stood up and motioned with his hand for attention.

'Fellow Israelites,' he said, 'and the god-fearers among you: listen. [17]The God of this people Israel chose our ancestors, and he raised the people up to greatness during their stay in the land of Egypt. Then he led them out from there with his hand lifted high, [18]and for about forty years he put up with them in the desert. [19]He drove out seven nations from the land of Canaan, and gave them the land as their inheritance [20]for about four hundred and fifty years. After that, he gave them judges, up until Samuel the prophet. [21]After that, they asked for a king, and God gave them Saul the son of Kish, a man from the tribe of Benjamin. He ruled for forty years, [22]and after God had removed him he raised up for them David as king. He is the one to whom God bore witness when he said, "I have found David, son of Jesse, a man after my own heart; he will accomplish all my purpose."

²³'From this man's offspring, in accordance with his promise, God has produced a saviour for Israel: Jesus! ²⁴Before he appeared, John had announced a baptism of repentance for the whole people of Israel. ²⁵As John was finishing his course, he said, "What do you suppose I am? I am not the one. But look: someone is coming after me, and I am not worthy to untie the sandals on his feet."'

I sat in the small meeting room, intrigued at what I was hearing. I had been invited to a presentation organized by local councillors and businessmen in a particular area. They had a project, and they wanted support for it. There was an old factory, covering several acres, which the owners had abandoned. Now the council, together with local interest groups, wanted to develop the site in quite a new way, to make it a tourist attraction, to bring in visitors and, they hoped, new income for a deprived area.

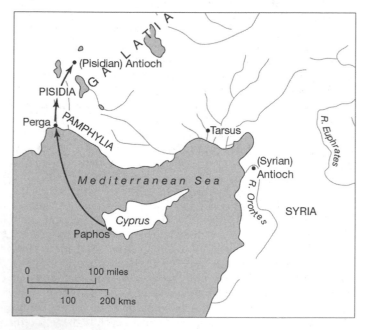

Acts 13.13–25

But they didn't start with the project. They began some-where very different. They talked about the town, and about its history. They showed slides of how things used to be at the height of prosperity. They talked about the people who had grown up in the area, about how they had given their lives to working in the old factory, about the community spirit and the sense of place and history. They did everything, in fact, to demonstrate what a splendid community this had been, and should be . . . and could be. Only then, when they had done everything to demonstrate what a rich culture and heritage the area had, did they start, very carefully, to talk about the new plan. They stressed its continuity with what had happened in the past. They showed how the new innovations would fit in. They knew perfectly well that what they had come up with was quite different from anything that had happened before, but they wanted us on board and knew that simply to slap the proposal on the table would invite instant rejection. As I write, the proposal is still under discussion.

It's good sense; and of course it's what Paul does again and again, as he effortlessly now takes the lead where before it was Barnabas leading and him following. Perhaps, now that they are in Turkey, which was Paul's home territory (Pisidian Antioch is about 200 miles west of Tarsus, and further inland), Paul feels himself more at ease. This is a typical diaspora synagogue; he knows how these people tick, the stories and songs they are familiar with, how to get the point across. We will see a few chapters from now that when he is faced with different audiences – most noticeably in Athens in Acts 17 – he takes a very different line in order to achieve the same effect. But here he launches in to the history his audience knew and the hopes they already cherished.

Paul had an easy platform to do this, because it was cus-tomary in synagogues to allow visitors to give a fresh word of exhortation, following the reading from the law and the prophets. Indeed, some have suggested that Paul and Barnabas (John Mark has already left by this stage, as we see in verse 13) wore clothes which signified their status as qualified Jewish teachers, rather like someone showing up in an academic gown or a clerical collar; but this may be far-fetched. The important point is that the instant **fellowship** of Jewish people around the world, and the ready acceptance of previously unknown visitors to public worship, provided a natural context for Paul to announce the **good news**, as he was committed to doing, 'to the Jew first'. (He also mentions 'god-fearers'; these were **Gentiles** who attended the synagogue, and worshipped the God of Israel, but who had not yet become proselytes and hence full members of the community.)

His approach was obvious. Like Stephen in chapter 7, he tells the story of Israel, bringing out particular points. But whereas Stephen had concentrated on Abraham, Joseph and Moses, Paul makes his way swiftly through the early years to arrive at the monarchy of Saul and David. What he says about the early period, though, is enough to establish the fact that God's method of operation is to choose his people, to prepare them, to lead them through one stage after another, and then, finally, to give them 'the man after my own heart' as king. In other words, perhaps the main point of verses 17–20 is to stress that God's purposes normally take a while to unfold, to get to the place where the ultimate purpose can be revealed. Unlike some in our own day who see the Israelite monarchy merely as a dangerously ambiguous flirtation with the wrong sort of power, Paul is quite clear: this was God's will, and God was delighted to have arrived at the choice of King David after such a long time.

Now of course Paul would have been the first to agree that David, though he may have been 'the man after God's own heart' (verse 22, quoting a combination of Psalm 89.20 and 1 Samuel 13.14), was also himself a man with deep and tragic faults and failings. Paul, indeed, cites David as a classic penitent, dependent on God's grace for **forgiveness** (Romans 4.6–8). But the point is not that the story stopped at David, but that in working with Israel for several hundred years to produce the king who would establish the pattern of someone ruling over God's people with justice and truth (that seems to be what 'after God's own heart' is getting at), God was establishing a further pattern as well: the notion of waiting for the true king, the ultimate king, 'great David's greater son'.

And so, as soon as he gets to David in his story, Paul moves on. In the next section of the address he will explain, in line with Peter's sermon in Acts 2, how it is that things which David himself said or sang must be taken as referring, not to David himself, but to the descendant in whom they would be fulfilled. Here he simply declares, slicing through a thousand years of further waiting, that now at last God has produced for Israel the one who will rescue them. Notice, he says for *Israel*. Paul believes, of course, that what God has done in Jesus he has done for the whole world, but he makes it very clear, throughout this address, that the first stage is always to see Jesus in relation to Israel itself. He speaks, as one might to a synagogue audience, of 'this people Israel' (verse 17), and the whole point of the address is not that this is a model for how one might speak to just any audience, but that this is what has to be said to God's people themselves. What God promised to our ancestors he has now fulfilled. The good news which bursts out of this for the Gentiles is exactly that: the good news that the creator God has fulfilled his **covenant** promises with Israel, promises which always envisaged blessing for the world. It is fatally easy for the church to tell the story of Jesus while simply ignoring the entire story of Israel. That is the way to produce a shallow, sub-biblical and ultimately dangerous theology.

Notice, too, that Paul refers to Jesus, right off the top, as 'saviour' or 'rescuer'. He hasn't said what Israel needed rescuing from. Later on he will talk about 'forgiveness of sins', but every Jew in the first century knew that all was not well on several levels; that Israel, though God's people, were not living in freedom, were not being much of a light to the nations, and were often finding it difficult to keep their own law, whether because of pressure from pagan society or laziness within the Jewish community. All was not well: when would God's purposes finally come true, when would Israel be rescued from her continuing plight? That is the implied question, a corporate as well as an individual problem, to which Paul offers the solution of Jesus the Saviour. It is vital, of course, that Jesus is a descendant of David; this was well known in the early church, and Paul refers to it at the foundation of his '**gospel**' statement in his greatest letter (Romans 1.3). Hidden in the long years of gestation, the promise of a coming **Messiah** contained, not just a message for Israel, but good news for the whole world, as Psalms like 2, 72 and 89 had always insisted. But the **message** had to come to Israel first.

It is interesting to find **John the Baptist** playing such a prominent role in verses 24 and 25, corresponding of course to the place he has in all four gospels. It is as though one could hardly expect the Messiah to come unannounced, without Israel being prepared. And John, according to Paul here, was doing two things in particular. He was getting people to repent, to turn back from everything which would hinder them from joining in the new work of God's **kingdom**. And he was pointing ahead to the one who was coming. Paul is setting up a system of signposts, from David a thousand years before to John a mere 15 or so years earlier. And all the signposts point to one person: Jesus the Messiah, the Rescuer. Paul's strategy is a challenge to us all, to understand our audience well enough to know how to tell them the story in a way they will find compelling, how to set up signposts in a language they can read.

ACTS 13.26–43

The Messianic Challenge

[26]'My brothers and sisters,' Paul continued, 'children of Abraham's family, and those here who fear God: it is to us that the word of this salvation has been sent! [27]The people who live in Jerusalem, and their rulers, didn't recognize him, and they fulfilled the words of the prophets which are read to them every sabbath by condemning him. [28]Even though they found no reason to condemn him to death, they asked Pilate to have him killed. [29]When they had completed everything that had been written about him in prophecy, they took him down from the cross and put him in a tomb. [30]But God raised him from the dead, [31]and he was seen for several days by those who had come with him from Galilee to Jerusalem. They are now his witnesses to the people.

[32]'We are here now to bring you the good news which was promised to our ancestors, [33]that God has fulfilled this promise

to us, their children, by raising Jesus. This corresponds, indeed, to what is written in the second Psalm:

'You are my son; this day I have begotten you.

[34]'That he raised him from the dead, never more to return to corruption, conforms to what was written:

'I will give you the holy and faithful mercies of David.

[35]'Because, as it says in another place,

'You will not hand over your holy one to see corruption.

[36]'Now David served his own generation, and in the purposes of God he fell asleep and was gathered to his fathers. He did experience corruption. [37]But the one God raised up did not experience corruption. [38]So let it be known to you, my brothers and sisters, that forgiveness of sins is announced through him, and that everything which could not be set right under the law of Moses [39]can now be set right for all who believe.

[40]'Beware, then, lest what the prophets foretold comes true of you:

[41]'Look out, you scoffers – be amazed, and disappear!
I am doing something in your days, a work which you
   wouldn't believe
Even if someone were to explain it to you.'

[42]As Paul and Barnabas were leaving, they begged them to come back the next sabbath and tell them more about these things. [43]Many of the Jews and devout proselytes followed them once the synagogue was dismissed. They spoke to them some more, and urged them to remain in God's grace.

At the time I am writing this there is a massive global debate taking place. Led by senior figures in science and government, people everywhere are asking whether the world and its atmosphere are really warming up at the alarming rate that they seem to be doing, whether this is in fact caused by human agency as many people think and, if so – since the dangers from this warming are massive – what can be done about it.

This is a hugely important debate, and it carries a note of urgency. If it is indeed true that global warming and its attendant dangers are being caused by things we are doing, particularly by how we run our industries, then we must act swiftly. If we do nothing, the moment will pass, and the dramatic changes to our world will happen, with loss of life and livelihood and huge risks for social and cultural stability, leading potentially to massive displacement of people, to food and water shortages, and to the violence and war that desperate people resort to when everything is at stake. Fortunately (in my view) the churches around the world seem now to be in the forefront of this movement, as is only right.

There are no doubt many turns and twists, and not all the arguments advanced for the emerging consensus are as good as they should be. But few doubt that the situation is urgent and must be addressed at once. This is something strange and new in the Western world, where the prevailing philosophy most of us have imbibed is that we've more or less got everything right with our modern democracy, our business, commerce and industry, and that, if we just have more of the same and remain calm and sensible, a bright future is assured for us, our children and our world. The message is, This May Not Be the Case, and we need to do something about it urgently.

That is the kind of urgency which Paul now injects into his address. This isn't simply a history lesson with a new ending. It is a history lesson which is rapidly turning into a warning: something new is happening under your very noses, and unless you join in you will miss out! God is doing a new thing, the new thing which he had long planned and promised. When that happens, it isn't just something you might think about in long winter evenings and discuss over a drink with your friends, like the question of which is the best rock group in the last 30 years, or what to do about crime, or why the price of beetroot has dropped. This is more like someone rushing into a hotel bar and shouting that the river is rising, there are just a few boats left, and if you don't want to swim for it you'd better get on board right now.

Because the **resurrection** of Jesus, which is the main subject of this second half of Paul's address, has introduced a new note of urgency into everything. Jesus is risen, so new creation has begun. Jesus is risen, so God has at last fulfilled his promises to Abraham, Isaac and Jacob, to Moses, David and the prophets. Especially, here, David: Paul, like Peter in Acts 2, goes for the Psalms and for the teasing but pregnant things they have to say. Psalm 2, quoted in verse 33, speaks of the new birth of God's own son, the **Messiah** who is to rule and judge the nations. Psalm 16, quoted in verse 35, speaks here, as Peter said it did in 2.27, of an extraordinary promise: that this Davidic figure, though he might die, would not experience the normal corruption and dissolution of the body that takes place after death. How on earth can that be?

Well, in David's case it didn't happen. He died, was buried, and decayed. But – and this is a strong indication, if any such were needed, of what Luke, like the rest of the New Testament, thought 'the resurrection' was all about – Jesus did not experience corruption. He was raised up after being thoroughly dead and buried, so that his body did not decay. This, declares Paul, is the sure sign that he is indeed the one promised to David and through David, the one through whom God is bringing in the new world order for which he called Israel into being in the first place.

Paul also quotes a passage which was not in Peter's address in Acts 2, a passage which is of great interest for various reasons. 'I will give you the holy and faithful mercies of David.' As those words stand, this is a prophecy that what God promised to David, the sacred **words** to which God would be faithful, are now being fulfilled in Jesus. But the verse comes from Isaiah 55.3, which in context – and Paul knew his scriptures, not least Isaiah, very well indeed – belongs with the wonderful promise of new **life** breaking out for the whole world on the basis of the achievement of the Servant in chapter 53 and the consequent renewal of the **covenant** in chapter 54. 'Ho, everyone who is thirsty!' shouts the prophet, 'Come to the waters! Come and drink! It's all free! And it's for everybody!' And the point about the fulfilment of the promises to David in Isaiah 55.3 is that the promise is now being thrown open to all and sundry. No longer just for one man, or one family, but for all people. There is no contradiction here. As Paul would insist, it is *because* God has been faithful to his promise in and through Jesus that the **message** can now go out to all the world. He is the Messiah ('**Christ**'), and those who follow him are Messiah-people ('Christians'). And, on this basis, Isaiah 55 continues with the wonderful, world-changing promise of the fresh word of God going out to renew, heal and transform the entire created universe.

With that message of resurrection and renewal as the focal point of his message, Paul needs to do two other things. First, as the lead-up to the explanation of resurrection, he needs to explain how it was, granted that Jesus was indeed the true heir of David, that the people of Jerusalem, especially their leaders, missed the point and didn't recognize him. Here he touches, briefly but tellingly, on a deep and dark mystery which it will take all of Romans 9—11 to address in full. The Jerusalemites and their leaders, he says, didn't understand the scriptures that were read to them **sabbath** by sabbath, *but they fulfilled those scriptures by condemning him.* It isn't just that the scriptures spoke of the coming Messiah, and they failed to understand them. The scriptures spoke of the coming Messiah *being rejected by his people* and, all unwittingly, they fulfilled precisely those prophecies. This is a twist in the story which takes us down, deep down, to the mystery of God's call of Israel in the first place: when God wanted to save the world, he called a people whom he knew to be part of the problem, as well as being, from then on, the bearers of the solution. This is one of the hardest things Paul has to say, but it can't be avoided. All, Jew and **Gentile** alike, must be humbled before God if they are to receive his rescue and new creation as what it is, a gift of grace and not a favour automatically reserved for a special few.

But this is at once balanced, at the end of the address, by the open and eager invitation. The new world which God is creating through the death and resurrection of Jesus is all about '**forgiveness** of sins'. At every level. Your sins and mine. The wickedness, the folly, the failing, the rebellion; the shameful, dirty, lying, cheating, glittering, sophisticated, flashy, corporate, international, global, local, personal, individual sins – the whole lot. All dealt with. The **law** of Moses enabled you, says Paul (verses 38–39) to get rid of a good deal of sin, to be declared 'in the right' in relation to them. But there were all kinds of other things still muddying the waters, and they can now all be sorted out. Nothing need stand in God's record against you any more. You can be 'justified', declared to be in the right, forgiven, a full and free member of God's people.

16

That is the immediate effect of the **good news** that Jesus is risen as the Messiah, **God's son**.

Accepting this is, of course, quite a challenge. That's why there's a warning attached, again taken from the prophets, this time Habakkuk 1.5, the chapter before the same prophet declares, as Paul just has, that there will be a way of justification open to all on the basis of **faith** (Habakkuk 2.4). Watch out in case you miss out. No wonder they followed Paul and Barnabas down the street and asked to hear some more. No wonder, too, that Paul and Barnabas urged them to continue in God's grace. The whole address was about grace: the great story of God's amazing mercy to the world, to the human race, to Israel, now coming to its climax in Jesus. Stick with the story, they say. Learn it, live in it, live from it. Don't imagine you can possess it. Let it possess you.

ACTS 13.44–52

A Light to the Gentiles

⁴⁴On the next sabbath, almost the whole city came together to hear the word of the Lord. ⁴⁵But when the Jews saw the crowds, they were filled with righteous indignation, and spoke blasphemous words against what Paul was saying.

⁴⁶Paul and Barnabas grew very bold.

'God's word had to be spoken to you first,' they declared. 'But since you are rejecting it, and judging yourselves unworthy of the life of God's new age, look! We are turning to the Gentiles! ⁴⁷This is what the Lord has commanded, you see:

'I have set you for a light to the nations,
So that you can be salvation-bringers to the end of the earth.'

⁴⁸When the Gentiles heard this, they were thrilled, and they praised the word of the Lord. All those who were marked out for the life of God's new age became believers. ⁴⁹And the word of the Lord spread through the whole land.

⁵⁰But the Jews incited the devout aristocratic women and the leading men of the city. They stirred up persecution against Paul and Barnabas, and drove them out of their district. ⁵¹They, however, shook the dust off their feet and went on to Iconium. ⁵²The disciples were filled with joy and with the holy spirit.

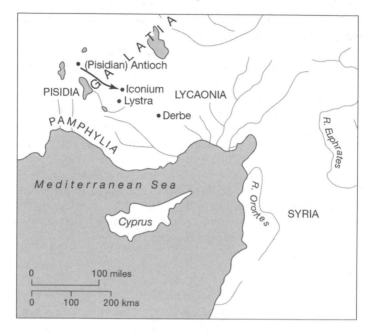

Acts 13.51

Everyone who works with words – the poet, the journalist, the philosopher, the translator, the theologian – knows it all too well. We use a word one day and it seems perfectly all right. It does the job. The next day we are told it now means something different, or is now regarded as impolite. Often words do what T. S. Eliot said they do, cracking and sometimes breaking under the burden and tension we put on them, slipping, sliding, perishing and decaying just when we wanted to rely on them. This happens particularly when there is an embarrassing or unpleasant social reality for which any name is going to be tricky: witness the slipping and sliding between 'negro', 'nigger', 'black' and 'African-American' (and many more) in the United States over the last two or three generations. Sometimes the words crack, break or decay with imprecision when the reality is so great that it can hardly be conceived: reviewers who really like a novel, a film or a concert quickly run short of adjectives to say that this wasn't just 'great', 'beautiful', 'powerful' or whatever – those have been said so often, and this was different! – but something more. And sometimes the words stay the same, in traditional contexts, while the meaning moves on, slowly, silently, unnoticed until it's almost too late. The word which meant one thing is now used, without anyone realizing it, for almost the exact opposite. (People have often pointed out that the euphemism for 'strike', namely 'industrial action', is exactly wrong, since what is happening is 'industrial inaction'.)

Something like this latter move – a word staying in place while popular perception changes – has happened in the Western church in relation to '**resurrection**'. At the beginning, as we have seen, it clearly and unambiguously referred to someone being bodily alive again after being bodily dead. But years of imprecision have meant that many people today, when they *say* 'resurrection', actually *think* 'disembodied immortality'.

Something very similar to this, and for the same reason, has happened to a well-worn phrase which trips off the tongue so easily: '**eternal life**'. What do *you* think of at once when you hear that phrase? Chances are, if you are part of a church within, or influenced by, the Western church of the nineteenth and twentieth centuries, you will think of a final state which is beyond space and time: an 'eternity' in which, as one hymn puts it, 'time shall be no more', and space and matter as well.

But the phrase which has so often been translated 'eternal life' actually means 'the life of the age'. No wonder, you may think, we don't put it like that; nobody would have a clue what we were talking about. But Jews of Paul's day and many other times would know exactly what was meant. For them, there were two 'ages', or 'periods of world history': the **present age** and the **age to come**. And the '**life**' of the 'age to come' is the state to which all devout Jews would aspire. Indeed, we know of debates among Jews of Paul's day and thereafter as to precisely who will inherit this life, the life of 'the age to come'. But the point is: nobody, thinking within the framework of thought which this phrase reflects, imagined that this 'age' would be 'eternal' in our sense – timeless, spaceless, matterless. It will be a whole new period of history, when everything will be put right at last. It will be the 'great restoration' we met in

Acts 3.21. Everything will be different; but it will still be a world like ours, only much, much more so, more solid, more throbbing with life and energy, because the curse of corruption and death itself will have been banished, making it 'eternal' in that sense but not in our usual ones. It is our inability, in the Western thought of recent centuries, to conceive of such a world (is it actually inability? or is it unwillingness?) that has made it so hard to speak of some of the foundational beliefs of the early Christians.

Because, when Paul and the others spoke of 'eternal life', they didn't mean something (as we say) 'purely spiritual'. The life of the coming age had already begun when Jesus came out of the tomb on Easter morning, and will be complete when God does for the whole world what he did for Jesus that day. And all those who share in that Easter life in the present are assured of a full share in it in the future. That is what it means to be part of 'the life of the coming age' now, and on that great day.

And that is what verses 46 and 48 are talking about, heavy as they are with both warning and joy. If you turn away from this **message**, declares Paul to the synagogue audience, then you are declaring that you don't see yourselves as belonging to God's coming new age! How can you do that? This is your ancestral hope, your dream, your future – and you're rejecting it! While, at the same time, the **Gentiles**, who had not been looking for a 'coming new age' or the special kind of life that is proper to it, were discovering it. They celebrated the fact that, according to the scriptures Paul was now quoting, God's new age, his rescue from corruption and decay and all that thwarts truly human existence, was open freely and equally to them. Paul says something closely parallel to this in Romans 9.30–33.

At the heart of this passage stands one of the great biblical witnesses to the turn-around which was taking place in the first generation of Christian **faith**. As so often, it is from the central section of the book of Isaiah, the passage which speaks of God's **word** doing new things, working through the strange ministry of the Servant to restore Israel *and thereby* to send out the message of **salvation** to the whole world. The poem which Luke's readers heard (Luke 2.32) on the lips of old Simeon in the **Temple**, as he welcomed the baby Jesus, come back to mind:

A light to lighten the Gentiles
And the glory of your people Israel.

The point, which we go on emphasizing because it is so important throughout Luke's work, as indeed throughout Paul's, is that *within* the hope of Israel there always lay the promise – sometimes buried under the rubble of anger against the wicked and blaspheming pagan nations who were oppressing them, but always available to be rediscovered, dusted down and put once more to good use – the promise that when God did for Israel what Israel longed for him to do, then the Gentiles would come into the picture. Abraham had been called so that in him all the families of the earth might be blessed. Israel at Sinai was called to be a nation of **priests**. David was celebrated, in hope rather than actuality, as the king whose dominion would eventually stretch to the ends of the earth. And Isaiah specifically said that the work of the servant, the one who embodies Israel and puts God's plan for Israel into effect, will not merely be to restore the tribes of Israel, but to be a light to the nations.

It is at this point where, without too much reflection, we can see why many of the Jews who heard this message in the first century rejected it angrily. It must have sounded to them like a compromise. All these years they had been maintaining their Jewish distinctness, keeping themselves clean from the impure, pagan lifestyle of the wider world. They had been true to the commandments which marked them out from the world full of idols all around them. They had suffered many things, mockery, social ostracism, sometimes physical abuse or even death, to be true to this heritage and this calling. And now – all these pagans surrounding them were going to come flooding in to *their* world, without so much as a by-your-leave? This was blasphemous nonsense! And the 'righteous indignation' which welled up in them, deeply understandable as it was – and corresponding exactly to the reaction of the young Saul of Tarsus only a few years before – was, again, this thing called 'zeal' (Acts 13.45). Not 'envy' or 'jealousy', as some translations have it, but 'zeal', righteous indignation, zeal for their God and his **law**: the thing Paul himself confesses to in Galatians 1.14, Philippians 3.6 and (by implication) Romans 10.2.

And it was this 'zeal', in Antioch as in so many other places later on, that led to the trouble which caused Paul and Barnabas to leave town in a hurry. Jesus had spoken of **apostles** wiping the dust off their feet when a town refused their message of peace (Luke 10.11). That is what they did now, faced with leading local people coming out in support of those of the synagogue community who had been stirred up to anger. The **gospel** doesn't leave things intact. At the end of this first major missionary visit, we have three distinct groups: the angry and aggressive people who don't want to know; the joyful, **spirit**-filled local people who had believed the message; and the two apostles, escaping persecution and scurrying on to the next town.

Oh, and the word of God (Acts 13.48), which, though 'attacked by voices of temptation', is doing its own work as usual.

ACTS 14.1–7

Iconium

[1]What happened in Iconium was much the same. They went into the Jewish synagogue and spoke, with the result that a large crowd, both of Jews and of Greeks, came to faith. [2]But the unbelieving Jews stirred up and poisoned the minds of the Gentiles against the brothers. [3]They stayed there a long time, speaking boldly on behalf of the Lord, who bore them witness to the word of his grace by giving signs and wonders which were done at their hands.

[4]But the inhabitants of the city were divided. Some were with the Jews, and some with the apostles. [5]But then the Gentiles and Jews, with their rulers, made an attempt to ill-treat them and stone them. [6]They got wind of it, however, and fled to Lystra and Derbe, cities of Lycaonia, and to the surrounding countryside. [7]There they went on announcing the good news.

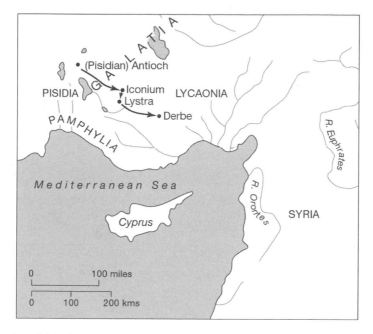

Acts 14.1–7

I once knew a young man who suffered seriously from depression. He was grappling with all kinds of issues, memories, buried fears, imagined guilt (and some real guilt, too). He had, on my recommendation, been to see one or two doctors, because his condition was becoming clinical. But, he told me, he got frustrated with the medication he'd been prescribed, and which he had taken for a while.

'All the highs and lows disappeared,' he complained. 'OK, I don't like the lows. In fact, they're terrible. But the highs went as well. I just felt like a cow, mooching around, never getting excited about anything. I can't live like that. It's just not me.'

And he came off the medication and went on working with a counsellor who, through patience, wisdom and prayer, brought him steadily through the worst.

Now for all I know they may have improved the medication since then. I'm not an expert in that area. Sometimes medica-

23

tion may be the only way to help someone out of the deepest part of a depression so that they can begin to work on the real issues. But that notion stuck with me, of doing away with the highs and the lows. And I find myself thinking of it as I read a passage like this and compare it with what I know of ordinary church life in today's Western world.

Those of us in what we like to think of as 'mainstream' denominations – Roman Catholic, Anglican, Methodist, Reformed, and some others – are, by and large, respectable. All right, we are not as socially acceptable, in many places, as we once were. But there are two things you won't find much of in our ordinary day-by-day life. You won't find much in the way of persecution. Nobody is stirring up and poisoning people's minds against us (well, they do sometimes, but not as sharply as they might). And you won't find much in the way of signs and wonders. Nobody is running and jumping about the streets showing that God has healed them (well, they do sometimes, but we are normally so afraid of 'extremism', and of charlatans claiming to be healers when all they're interested in is money, that we tend to fight shy of even the possibility of healing).

And I can't help reflecting that we have become like my young friend on medication. The lows have gone, but so have the highs. What is the medication that we have taken which has made us the ecclesiastical equivalent of a herd of cows, mooing and mooching to and fro, doing nobody any harm, but never getting excited either? Nobody much gets healed, and nobody much gets stoned.

Let's ask the question this way. We have already looked at the impact Paul's **message** had on the synagogue in Antioch. It is not unlike the impact Peter's similar message had on his hearers in Jerusalem on the **day of Pentecost** itself: some were thrilled, others very angry. We have seen that the main message that emerges for us out of all that is that the ancient promises of God were being fulfilled in and through Jesus, as **Messiah**, for Israel and thence for the whole world. Israel – Jews both in Judaea and Palestine and all around the world – had to hear about it as soon as possible; these were *their* promises that had been fulfilled! But part of the message was precisely that the fulfilment was a complete fulfilment in the sense that the *underlying* purpose of the promises, that *through* Israel God would bless the whole world, was now being accomplished. The synagogue communities were being invited to embrace a fulfilment of their own long-cherished hopes, which necessarily meant a relativization of their own 'special' sense. When the postman has delivered all the letters, he is no longer the special person he once was as he walks down the street, not because there was anything wrong with being the postman, but precisely because it was his job, and he's finished it.

Now, once we've got our minds round that, and watched in passages like the present one as the same pattern unwinds once again, we can address the question: how might we, in today's mainstream churches, go about a more apostolic witness to our wider community? Is there, shall we say, a less depressing way of living and speaking the **gospel** than the one in which many find themselves caught?

For a start, it's important to make sure we really are announcing, and living by, the gospel itself – the full message about Jesus as the risen **son of God**, fulfilling God's ancient promises for the benefit of the whole world, offering **forgiveness** of sins (not just a comforting, cosseting spirituality) and the hope of God's new world (not just pie in the sky when you die). If we really sort that out, that's one step in the right direction.

For another thing, we need to pray more seriously, perhaps with fasting. As we have seen, the genuine gospel is bound to confront other power-structures, other thought-systems. We will need all the spiritual resources we can muster.

But, when those are in place, what is the equivalent, for us, of what Paul and Barnabas were doing when they went into the local synagogues? (I am assuming that most of my readers are not themselves Jewish; there is a very specific question to be addressed in that context, and it isn't what I'm talking about here.)

The synagogue wasn't just a place of worship. It was the main community centre for Jews in each locality, the place where they came together to address and settle all kinds of issues. The equivalent in many towns and cities wouldn't necessarily be a 'religious' building, but what we often call 'the public square' – which might literally be just that, a public square, but might well be a network of council chambers, government offices, town halls, health services, police stations and all the other paraphernalia of contemporary civic life. And the message wouldn't be simply a 'religious' one about God, heard in terms of private spirituality and an escapist '**heaven**' to hope for hereafter, with some odd moral codes thrown in for the present. It would be, for our world and our day, what Paul's message to the synagogue always was: that for which you have longed is here, but it doesn't look like you thought it would.

But what is our society longing for? Peace; justice; freedom; a voice and a vote which will count; health. Around and above all of those, love. Inside and through all of those: to satisfy the hunger of the heart, a hunger which no amount of money, fine houses, fast cars, luxury vacations and love affairs will ever begin to reach. And the task of the church, though it certainly goes much wider and deeper than this, at least includes the following: that we should, in prayer and with wisdom, be able to tell the story of our world, our increasingly neo-pagan society, in terms of the long history of promises we have clung onto and pledges we have made and broken. We should be prepared to think it all through so we can tell the story that people know is *their* story, the one they always knew they wanted to hear. And we have to tell it so that, like Paul telling the story of Israel, it ends with Jesus, not artificially or like a conjuror pulling a rabbit out of a hat, but so that he appears as what and who he is: the truly human one, the one in whom are hidden all the treasures of wisdom and knowledge, the living bread through whom all our hungers are satisfied.

And of course it's no good at all simply trying to *say* it. We have to live it. We have to create, and sustain, communities where this life is being lived in such a way that when we speak of it we are obviously telling the truth. That is the hard part. As long as our churches are places where we struggle to sustain an hour or two's public worship per week, with 'real life' only minimally affected by it, we will indeed end up like a bunch of vaguely religious cows in a field, mooing on Sunday mornings and chewing the cud the rest of the time. No highs and no lows. But if we really worked at trying to be for our world what the **apostles** were for their Jewish world, things might change. The gospel might come alive. Vested interests would be challenged, and they would bite back. But we would be on the map once more: the map which Luke is offering us, even as the apostles hurry on once more to the next cities and districts, ready for more highs and more lows in the cause of God's **kingdom**.

ACTS 14.8–20

Confusion in Lystra

⁸There was a man sitting in Lystra who was unable to use his feet. He had been lame from his mother's womb, and had never walked. ⁹He heard Paul speaking. When Paul looked hard at him, and saw that he had faith to be made well, ¹⁰he said with a loud voice,

'Stand up straight on your feet!'

Up he jumped, and walked about.

¹¹When the crowds saw what Paul had done, they shouted loudly in the Lycaonian language,

'The gods have come down to us in human form!'

¹²They called Barnabas 'Zeus', and Paul, because he was the main speaker, 'Hermes'. ¹³The priest of Zeus, whose temple was just outside the city, brought oxen and garlands to the city gates. There was a crowd with him, and he was all ready to offer sacrifice.

¹⁴But when the apostles, Paul and Barnabas, heard of it, they tore their clothes and rushed into the crowd.

¹⁵'Men, men,' they shouted, 'what on earth are you doing? We are just ordinary humans, with the same nature as you, and we are bringing you the wonderful message that you should turn away from these foolish things to the living God, the one who made heaven and earth and the sea and everything in them. ¹⁶In earlier generations he allowed all the nations to go their own ways, ¹⁷but even then he didn't leave himself without witness. He has done you good, giving you rain from heaven and times of fruitfulness, filling your bodies with food and your hearts with gladness.'

¹⁸Even by saying this, they only just restrained the crowds from offering them sacrifice. ¹⁹But some Jews arrived from

Antioch and Iconium, and persuaded the crowds to stone Paul. They dragged him outside the city, thinking he was dead. [20]The disciples gathered round him, however, and he got up and went into the city. The next day he and Barnabas went off to Derbe.

I have a sneaking sympathy for the medical profession.

Two or three generations ago, everybody knew that there were all kinds of diseases that the doctors couldn't cure. They would do their best with what was available. They would offer sympathy, wisdom, encouragement and sometimes actual cures for actual diseases. But often all they could do would be alleviate pain for a while, as the disease either ran its course and cleared up or finished the patient off altogether.

Now we all assume, in the Western world, that the doctor ought to be able to cure everything, more or less at once. We have believed the boast of a kind of scientific imperialism (not that anyone in the medical profession has said it, but it has crept into our consciousness unawares): that the time is rapidly approaching when nobody will have to suffer anything very much, that the doctors will be able to sort it all out, and that they should have it all completed by next Tuesday.

And then when the doctor, or the hospital, doesn't deliver the goods on time, we push them off the pedestal we've built for them and declare that they are useless, or fakes. We grumble when we can't get an appointment at once (or we pay a lot of money to make sure we can). We complain bitterly if someone goes to hospital with one disease and contracts a different one while they are in there – while in many countries, certainly in my own, we would grumble even more if our taxes were raised so that, like France and some other places, we could have the kind of hospitals we would all really like. One way or another, we make the doctors either gods or devils. We either divinize them or demonize them. It can't be much fun. (Not that anyone does that with clergy, now, do they?)

Paul and Barnabas go through this process in quick succession, and not without more touches of Luke's comedy. Here is Paul, doing one of the things he does best, healing a disabled man. And here, all of a sudden, is a great solemn procession, pagan religion at its most serious, with garlands of flowers and oxen all ready for a great celebratory **sacrifice**, exactly the kind of thing that Paul wanted to declare was irrelevant to worshipping the true God. There are ancient texts and inscriptions which speak of Zeus and Hermes arriving on earth and being entertained by an ordinary pair of mortals; there is some evidence to suggest that this old story belongs in the part of Turkey where Paul and Barnabas now found themselves. It may be that the townsfolk were, so to speak, always on the lookout in case it really happened one day. So Paul and Barnabas – who if they are anything in the pagan world are missionaries on behalf of the One True God, the God of Abraham, the God of Jewish monotheism who stands over against all pagan idols and declares that they are a load of empty nonsense – this Paul and Barnabas are not only faced with the full show of pagan worship, but they are themselves identified with the very gods they have come to debunk! It is remarkable what can happen to a **message** when the hearers insist on inserting it firmly into their own worldview.

But as soon as Paul and Barnabas have explained the mistake (which they do with difficulty (verse 18) because, once people are bent on having a ritual and a party and a celebration meal all rolled into one, which pagan sacrifices were, then they are going to be disappointed if you stop them) the mood of the crowd changes. If these people aren't Zeus and Hermes, who on earth are they? They must be imposters! At this point, Luke tells us, some Jews came from Antioch and Iconium, still righteously indignant at the message which flew in the face of *their* traditions – just at the point when Paul and Barnabas have been explaining that the message flies in the face of the *pagan* traditions as well. The result is inevitable: violence. What is remarkable is that Paul survived it. As the main speaker by this stage (which was why he was identified with Hermes, the messenger of the gods) he seems to have become the main target; though you might have thought that, if people reckoned Barnabas had been impersonating Zeus, that might not have been the most popular thing in town, either. We tend to think of 'stoning' as more or less automatically meaning 'killing', and of course often it did; but if all it means is that several people picked up middle-sized rocks and threw them at him, they might well stun him or hurt him badly without actually completing the job.

But the heart of the passage is of course the remarkable things that Paul and Barnabas say when they realize what the crowds are about to do. This passage (verses 15–18) is totally unlike what Paul said in the synagogue at Antioch, for the very good reason that there he was addressing devout and potentially suspicious Jews and here he was addressing, in haste and under pressure, devout and very muddled pagans. In fact, what he says to them could just as well have been said by a non-Christian Jewish missionary, and the same could be said for a good deal (not all) of the longer, more measured, address to pagans in Acts 17.

He begins with God the creator: the God who made the **heaven**, the earth, the sea and all that is in them. This foundational Jewish doctrine comes (to those who appreciate its significance) as a huge sigh of relief to those who have lived in a world of many gods and goddesses, each concerned with their own business, ready to do favours or lash out if annoyed, but above all eager to be placated by hapless humans. No, declares the Jewish tradition ancient and modern. There is one God, and he made the lot. He is responsible for all the good things in the world, and if you don't see that then you are guilty of ingratitude to one who loves you and cares for you. Crops and good weather, seedtime and harvest, are all signs of the goodness and love of this one true God.

What then can we say about the muddles and messes that humans have got themselves into? God is prepared to overlook all that, says Paul (verse 16; compare 17.30, and Romans 3.25). He has been preparing a long, slow plan to set the whole world right. It has taken all this time because the principal way the creator wishes to work in his world, in accordance with his original intention, is through human beings, and it was bound to take time to bring the people he chose to the right place (none of this is said, but all of it is I believe implied). Now, however, it's time to set things straight. Paul doesn't get a chance even to mention the name of Jesus. But if he had, without explaining the worldview within which Jesus and his identity, achievement and message make sense, they would no doubt have tried simply to fit him into their pagan thought-world, as indeed happened in Athens (Acts 17.18).

One of the things this passage highlights is the almost bottomless pit of potential misunderstandings that await anyone who tries to speak, and live out, the essentially Jewish message of the **gospel**, with its remarkable news of the one true creator God. There are so many barriers in the way, so much anger against the way the world is (often with people simultaneously blaming God for all the bad and declaring that they don't believe in him), so much distortion of what the message is, through bad teaching, or bad experience of church or synagogue. But the point of this whole narrative, in its larger framework, is precisely to show the explosive, if deeply confusing, effects of taking the message of Jesus out into the wider world. The journey of the gospel from Jerusalem 'to the ends of the earth' (1.8) is unstoppable, but uncomfortable. That comes with the territory.

ACTS 14.21–28

Opening the Door of Faith

²¹They preached in Derbe, and made many disciples. Then they returned to Lystra, Iconium and Antioch, ²²strengthening the hearts of the disciples, and urging them to remain in the faith. They warned them that getting into God's kingdom would mean going through considerable suffering. ²³In every church they appointed elders by laying hands on them. They fasted, prayed, and commended them to the Lord in whom they had believed.

²⁴They went through Pisidia and came to Pamphylia; ²⁵and when they had spoken the word in Perga they went down to Attalia. ²⁶From there they sailed to Antioch, which was where they had been commended to God's grace for the work which they had accomplished. ²⁷Once there, they called the church together, and told them all the things which God had done with them, and how he had opened a door of faith for the Gentiles. ²⁸They stayed there a long time with the disciples.

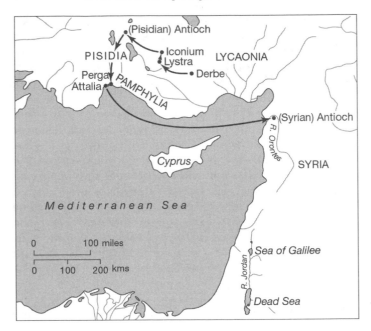

Acts 14.21–28

I stood at the back of the exhibition, and chatted with the artist. He was a local man, and we were glad to support him. We had even bought one of his paintings, a marvellous study of a bird in flight.

'What does it feel like,' I asked, 'seeing people buy these paintings which you've taken such a long time over, and watching them take them away knowing you'll probably never see them again?'

'Very strange,' he replied. 'It's like sending children off to college, only worse. You don't know what company they'll get into. You don't know whether people will look after them. With paintings, you don't know whether they will hang them somewhere special, or just shove them in an attic and forget them.'

I came home and prepared for the big event of the next week: two ordination services. And I realized that I was in

32

something of a similar position. I was about to lay hands on 20 or so people, all carefully selected, trained and prepared. We would spend several days in prayer together, and then join with enormous congregations to pray together for the ministry they would have. Then I would lay hands on them, smile for the cameras afterwards, and off they would go to their various parishes. Of course, I would see them again – quite frequently, I hope. But they are, in all sorts of senses, out of my hands.

If that was true for me, how much more was it true for Paul. We worry, today, about whether we are preparing people properly for ministry because the longest course we normally offer is still less than three years. (I am jealous of my Roman Catholic colleagues who still demand seven years from their students!) We worry about whether we've got the proper programme of post-ordination follow-up training so that new ministers receive proper support. We remind ourselves that the world out there (at least in the UK) is by no means as sympathetic to the church, and to clergy, as it used to be. The newly ordained will need encouragement on a regular basis, perhaps in the form of a mentor, a senior and experienced pastor who can be on hand to field questions, to head off silly ideas, to settle people down and point them in the right direction.

And all that Paul did was to come through town, a few days or weeks after his first preaching, to appoint 'elders', to fast and pray and lay hands on them, and then to move on. Apart from the odd letter, and a follow-up visit in a few years' time if they were lucky, that was it. They were on their own.

But they weren't, of course. The entire enterprise, the whole movement, everything about following Jesus from top to bottom, is built on the belief that Jesus is Lord over the church as well as the world, and that by his **spirit** he calls, he equips, he guides, he warns, he rebukes, he encourages. It's his business. And that is what the laying on of hands, with prayer and fasting, actually signifies. It isn't a method of control. Sometimes people imagine that the more ritual you have at that point the more you're setting up some kind of hierarchical system in which the people at the top have all the power and the people down below simply do what they're told. That may be how it works in some places, for all I know; it's certainly not what I believe, or what I try to practise. The whole point about the laying on of hands, with fasting and prayer, is, as Luke says in verse 23, to 'commend', or 'entrust' them 'to the Lord in whom they had come to believe'. Laying hands on people isn't a way of grabbing control over them; it's a way of relinquishing control, of declaring publicly that they are now responsible to the Lord himself for what they do. Of course, if they get into trouble in my world, it'll come back to me sooner or later. But ordination itself isn't about that. It's about the fact that the church belongs to Jesus, that ministers belong to Jesus, and that he is responsible for them.

This is in fact only the second mention of 'elders' in Acts, the first being in 11.30 with reference to the Jerusalem 'elders'. Luke makes no attempt to explain who they were; he assumes his readers will know, or guess. It is assumed that churches, even new and small ones, will need, and will have, local leadership, trained on the job. Of course, the encouragement and teaching of the **apostles**, as in verse 22, is foundational and vital. But, going back once more to 2.42, it is only one part of the whole. There is also the common life, the breaking of bread, and the prayers; and each church must look after those for itself, without departing from 'the apostles' teaching'.

Another theme is starting to become prominent in the story: 'the grace of God'. When Barnabas went to Antioch in 11.23, he rejoiced 'because he saw the grace of God', in other words, he saw that God was powerfully at work reaching people who had no qualifications, nothing to commend them, no social or cultural status, no pride of race or ancestry or moral achievement. Then in 13.43 Paul and Barnabas exhorted the believers in (Pisidian) Antioch 'to continue in the grace of God', that is, to continue a life of trusting the generosity of God rather than trying to grab back control, or pride of achievement, for oneself. Now, as they get back to (Syrian) Antioch (verse 26), Luke reminds us that that was where they had been 'commended to the grace of God' for the work they had completed: in other words, that the initial prayers of the church had been for the powerful, sovereign love of God to be at work in, through and around them, both guiding them and reaching out through their words, their life and their prayer to do new things in the world, works of healing of hearts and minds and bodies. In other words, 'grace' is not just a doctrine to be believed; it is a fact you can lean your weight on. That is precisely what ministry is about, including the ministry of planting churches and commissioning or ordaining new ministers in turn.

In particular, it is through this grace that God has 'opened a door of faith for the Gentiles'. Clearly Luke doesn't mean that until this particular mission no Gentiles had believed in Jesus. He himself has told us at length about the Ethiopian eunuch, at even more length about Cornelius, and more allusively about **Gentile** Christians in Antioch (11.19–26). What he seems to mean is that out there, in obviously Gentile territory, there were new communities being planted, some of which had no connection even to the synagogues; and that in these communities what counted was not who your parents were but the fact that you believed in Jesus. As Paul himself says, writing later to Rome: God will justify the **circumcised** by their **faith**, and the uncircumcised *through* their faith (Romans 3.30). He never loses the sense that Gentiles come *in from the outside* into the community of the people of God, so that even though the badge of membership they wear is identical to the badge which the Jewish Christians wear – that is, faith in Jesus as the crucified and risen **Messiah** and Lord – there is, for the Gentile Christian, a sense of entry into something totally new, while for the Jewish Christian there is a sense of the radical renewal of a family membership already possessed in theory.

Something of exactly this delicate sense, of absolute and complete equality of status within the church but different routes to get there, persists not only in Romans but also in Galatians; and, though the matter remains hugely controversial, I agree with those scholars who think that Galatians was written at around this moment in the story which Luke is telling, in other words, before the great Council of Acts 15. I am inclined to think – along with a good many archaeologists and historians – that the 'Galatians' addressed in the letter were precisely the churches of (Pisidian) Antioch, Iconium, Lystra and Derbe, and that the 'agitators' who had come in to disturb them by insisting on circumcision had done so fairly soon after Paul had left them behind. I am inclined to think that the 'long time' in verse 28 that Paul and Barnabas spent in Antioch was the time towards the end of which Peter came to Antioch (Galatians 2.11), after which certain people came from Jerusalem (Acts 15.1; Galatians 2.12) to teach something very different from what Paul had been teaching in southern Turkey. If that is so – and, actually, even if it isn't, but I think it works quite well – then we have to say that Luke's quiet emphasis on 'grace' at this point corresponds quite closely to Paul's insistence on 'grace' in Galatians. It was grace that was at stake throughout the controversy that now erupted. Was the gift of new **life** in the **gospel** to be dependent utterly on God's free gift, or did it have something to do with human qualifications, even qualifications which were themselves part of God's calling to his people?

The worrying thing, of course, is this: when Paul and Barnabas laid hands on the newly appointed elders, and then left them to it, that didn't mean they were automatically 'safe'. Indeed, it probably meant that that was when new times of testing would burst in on them. That is often how it works. But Paul meant what he said in verse 22: it is through much suffering that we shall enter God's **kingdom**. And sometimes the suffering comes in the form of terrible, church-dividing controversy.

ACTS 15.1–11

Is Circumcision Necessary?

[1]Some people came from Judaea to Antioch and, on arrival, began to teach the Christians that they could not be saved unless they were circumcised according to the custom of Moses. [2]This caused considerable uproar and dispute between them and Paul and Barnabas, and the church decided to send Paul and Barnabas, and some others from their fellowship, to the apostles and elders in Jerusalem, to try to sort out the problem. [3]So they were sent off by the church. They travelled through Phoenicia and Samaria, telling people as they went

about the conversion of the Gentiles. They brought great joy to the Christian communities.

[4]When they arrived in Jerusalem they were welcomed by the church, the apostles and the elders, and they told them all the things that God had done with them. [5]But some believers from the party of the Pharisees stood up.

'They must be circumcised,' they said, 'and you must tell them to keep the law of Moses.'

[6]The apostles and elders gathered together to see what to do about this matter. [7]After considerable argument, Peter got up.

'My brothers,' he said, 'you know that from our early days together God chose that it should be from my mouth that the Gentiles should hear the word of the gospel and believe. [8]And God, who knows the heart, bore them witness, by giving them the holy spirit just as he did to us. [9]He made no distinction between us and them, but he purified their hearts through faith. [10]So now, why are you putting God to the test, by placing a yoke on the disciples' neck which neither we nor our ancestors have been able to bear? [11]Rather, we believe that it is by the grace of the Lord Jesus that we shall be saved, just like them.'

'I thought we'd settled this!'

Dennis was furious. Halfway through the second week of term and it had happened again.

They had sat around the kitchen table, the five of them, in the old house they had rented for their second year at college. They all knew they needed to get on with their work; and they needed some house rules in place so they wouldn't keep getting angry with each other over points of disagreement. They had drawn up rotas for cooking and cleaning; that part was working fine. They had agreed an absolute ban on music after midnight, and that was fine too. But, partly because one of them was allergic to tobacco smoke and another had recently given up smoking and didn't want to be lured back into it again, they had agreed an absolute ban: no smoking in the house. The two smokers had agreed somewhat reluctantly, but they'd gone along with it. There was always the garden shed, or the lane at the end of the street.

And then, ten days in, Dennis (who was allergic) began to sneeze while sitting working at his desk one evening. Surely it

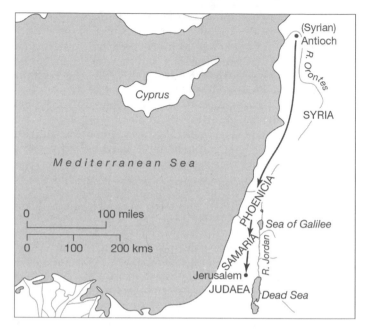

Acts 15.1–11

couldn't be . . . but they'd promised, hadn't they? How could they? And, sniffing the smell (and making himself sneeze some more), he got up from the desk, stormed out into the corridor, and let fly. 'I thought we'd settled this!'

Jim's door opened and he appeared, crestfallen and apologetic. You see, his father had come to visit, just for the evening; and he didn't want to go out; and he always had a smoke after supper; and he'd thought, perhaps, it would be all right . . .

But it wasn't. A blazing row, another kitchen table conference, lots of sullen stares, and a further and final agreement on the absolute ban.

Now, to be fair, and get a balance to things before we launch into Acts 15, we ought to tell a story that goes in the opposite direction. Let us go and visit Moira.

Moira is the cellist in a string quartet. She comes originally from Germany, where she was taught by a man who was taught by a man who had known Brahms personally, had played the Elgar concerto under the great man's baton and, in addition to substantial solo work, had performed in both quartets and orchestras across the world. Moira is, naturally, proud of this pedigree, and she does her best, through study and assiduous practice, to keep up her high standards. The public appreciate it; often, a cellist isn't the main star in a quartet but, though the violinists and viola player are excellent, many people, asked why they have come to the quartet's concert or bought the CD, will name her playing as the main reason. She carries with her a gentle but clear sense of the noble tradition of European music; she seems to breathe the air of the great concert-halls of Vienna, Milan, Paris and Berlin as they used to be before the disastrous wars of the twentieth century shook European culture to its foundations.

So when the quartet plays Beethoven, or Brahms, or Mozart, there is always a sense that she provides not just the ground bass for the music but the solid, substantial sense of *what the music is really all about*. She can feel in her bones the way the themes, the subjects, the harmonies and the rhythms flow this way and that, across the different movements and even between different quartets in the same set. She is, in short, a purist, and her colleagues and public value and love her as such.

So imagine Moira's reaction a few weeks ago when the leader of the quartet, a brilliant but very young violinist, came to the group excitedly with a new contract proposal. A well-known radio station wants them to branch out. They will play their favourite movements, or even parts of movements, from their Top Twenty quartets of all time. They will play them on the radio, they will make recordings of their selections, they will have special 'pop quartet' concerts in major venues. The radio station will splash advertising everywhere. There will be a phone-in so people can call and say which bits they like best, and then they can play them again, over and over! Tens of thousands of people who've never heard quartet music before will flood in. It's a whole new market! They want it, we can do it, they will pay good money . . .

And Moira is livid. How can they? How *can* they? Why don't they dress up in silly costumes and dance the can-can at the same time, then? Why don't they hum old Bavarian folk-songs while they're at it? What is this – a serious music outfit or a three-ring circus? You can't just rip movements out of quartets; you might as well pull 20 lines out of a Shakespeare play and have someone stand up on stage and recite it, as if *that* would make any sense. Or cut up the *Mona Lisa* and sell it in little squares as souvenirs! Brahms would be turning in his grave. Someone has to make a stand. If only her teacher, or *his* teacher, could hear this nonsense! He'd put them right! If the general public want to understand what real music is all about, people should put on proper concerts instead of this let-'em-all-come-anyway rubbish . . .

Moira, bless her, is a **Pharisee**. Of course she is. She understands tradition. She knows that you can cut a tree down in ten minutes but you can't grow another one in ten years. She knows that people have worked, slaved in poverty, struggled and even died in the effort to reach the very pinnacle of creative art. She knows that all around there are people who are only too ready to add saxophones to fifteenth-century ensembles, to turn a noble symphonic theme into an advertising jingle, to pretend that the important thing about Mozart was his sex life, to psychoanalyse Brahms *yet again* as though everyone didn't already know about his poor mother and as though that would add one iota to the sheer, heart-stopping beauty of his *German Requiem*. She speaks up for the rock on which the whole Western musical tradition stands, before someone blows it to pieces to sell it off in bits, stamped with pictures of famous composers. Had Moira been in Jerusalem, faced with the news from Antioch, not to mention Turkey, she would have been quite clear. **Circumcision** matters, because Moses said so, and that was a millennium and a half ago (and anyway it was given to Abraham in the first place, two thousand years ago) and people have died because of their determination to keep the laws and the customs. That is our identifying mark as God's people. It's a solemn sign of the **covenant**. It says so in the Bible. What will it be next – pulling down the **Temple**? Telling us we should all keep pigs and eat pork?

And Dennis, in my first story, is of course playing the part of Peter or Paul. Look: we had all this out before, at the time of the Cornelius business. It was quite clear that we had to decide what we did. We laid it down (11.30) as a fixed principle: 'God has granted Gentiles, too, **repentance** that leads to life', *without them needing to be circumcised*. Never mind the fact that, since then, pressure has grown, that people have arrived who say we have to do it anyway. It was agreed. That's where we should stand.

We can understand Dennis. We can understand Moira. We can understand Paul and Peter, and we can and should certainly understand the 'circumcision faction', who are here named more precisely as believing Pharisees (verse 5; Paul was himself of course a believer who had belonged to the Pharisaic party, but he would have claimed that he had thought through the implications of **faith** in Jesus as the crucified **Messiah** more fully than they had). But we must become very, very clear about one thing. Acts 15 is not simply a matter of 'tradition' versus 'innovation'. It cannot be used as a stick with which to beat anyone who resists any new proposal ('but look, in Acts 15 it was the traditionalists who were wrong!'). Acts 15 is about the reassertion and the working through of the principle already established in chapter 11, which concerns not a general or abstract point about tradition and innovation, but a very specific and concrete point which is central to the whole of early Christianity: *precisely because God has fulfilled his covenant with Israel in sending Jesus as Messiah, the covenant family is now thrown open to all, without distinction*. It isn't a matter, it can't be a matter, of belonging to one particular ethnic group, no matter how sacred, how chosen, how blessed with God's presence and entrusted with carrying his promise to the world. It is time for that promise to be delivered, not kept as a private possession. *This was what the 'tradition', at its best, was actually about all along.*

The Moiras of this world might say that this is a way of saying that the tradition, in order to be true to itself, must then self-destruct, and that this is absurd. Perhaps so. But that is surely why, writing only a few years later, Paul declared that the **gospel** of Jesus crucified and risen is not only foolishness to the Greeks, but a scandal to the Jews. He should know. He had been where Moira was. That was his world. But God had turned that world upside down. And Peter (whatever he had

41

said or done in Antioch a few weeks or months earlier) agreed. It was a matter, once more, of grace. 'It is by the grace of the Lord Jesus that both they and we shall be saved.' If it was a matter of ethnic identity, and of converts taking that on as of necessity, then grace would no longer be grace.

ACTS 15.12–21

The Judgment of James

¹²The whole company was silent, and listened to Barnabas and Paul describing the signs and wonders which God had done through them among the Gentiles. ¹³After they had finished, James replied.

'My dear brothers,' he said, 'listen to me. ¹⁴Symeon has explained how, at the beginning, God graciously favoured the Gentiles, to take from them a people for his own name. ¹⁵This, indeed, is in accordance with the words of the prophets, which say,

¹⁶'After this I will return, and will rebuild the tabernacle of
    David which had collapsed,
And I will build the ruins again, and set them straight,
¹⁷So that the rest of the human race may seek the Lord,
And all the nations upon whom my name has been called.
Thus says the Lord, who has made these things ¹⁸known
    from of old.

¹⁹'Therefore this is my judgment: we should not cause extra difficulties for those of the Gentiles who have turned to God. ²⁰Rather, we should send them a message, warning them to keep away from things that have been polluted by idols, from fornication, from what has been strangled, and from blood. ²¹Moses, after all, has from ancient times had people proclaiming him from city to city, since he is read in the synagogues sabbath after sabbath.'

One of the difficulties about living in the new European Union (I realize that this remark may be out of date as soon as it's written, since new proposals come forward every few weeks, but the general truth still stands) is that there are at least four different attitudes towards law, towards constitutional matters, and towards the responsibilities of citizens under the law and under constitutions, within Europe as a whole.

Running the risk of substantial caricature, we could label them like this. The Greeks and Italians may be glad that a new law has been passed. There ought to be a law on such matters. They themselves have no intention of keeping it, of course, but it's useful to have it on the statute books just in case. The Germans, however, coming from a strong philosophical tradition where things are thought out from first principles, pass laws and expect them to be enforced. How else can you run a society efficiently? The French . . . well, perhaps I had better not comment about the French. But we British: well, we tend to favour the attitude brilliantly summarized in a recent popular work of sociology: 'What do we want? Gradual change! When do we want it? In due course!'

How you keep those different attitudes to laws and con-stitutions together under one roof is something the politicians are still working at. The phrase 'sack of ferrets', which one of my friends sometimes uses to describe an awkward group of clergy, comes unbidden to mind. But we should note that often, when people discuss theological controversies, they assume a basically German approach: once something has been discussed, agreed and settled, that ought to be that. No ifs and buts, no clever exception clauses; if it's right it's right and we must put it into practice, no matter what anyone feels. And, without making any kind of a case for a Greek/Italian, or a British, solution (still less a French one) to the theological problem that faced the conference in Jerusalem, I think we need to loosen our grip on the somewhat rigid either/or approach which has so often been adopted. Basically, James and the conference as a whole were clear on two things. First, the **law** should not be imposed on **Gentile** converts. Second, they should be told that they had better keep some significant bits of it just in case. Get it? No? Well, let's come at it from the side and see what happens.

First, though, a word about this character James. We have met him only once before in this book: when Peter, about to go underground for a judicious time (12.17), tells the assembled church to tell James what has happened. He can't mean James the brother of John, because he's just been killed, and there seems no reason for him to single out James son of Alphaeus, one of the Twelve. He must mean this James, James the brother of Jesus himself.

James, like Jesus' other brothers, had not believed in him or followed him during Jesus' public career (John 7.5). But Jesus had appeared to him, in a special and separate occasion, after his **resurrection** (1 Corinthians 15.7). And James had become part of the young church; then a prominent member; then, perhaps after Peter's brush with disaster in Acts 12, the natural leader, even though he wasn't one of the Twelve. In fact, when Paul is describing his early visits to Jerusalem in Galatians, he refers to him as 'one of the so-called "pillars" ' (Galatians 2.9, referring back to 1.19 where the identification is explicit). And it is 'from James', according to Paul (though not Luke in Acts 15.1), that certain people came from Jerusalem to Antioch to insist on **circumcision** for Gentile converts (Galatians 2.12). James, by all accounts, became far and away the most prominent leader in the first generation of Christianity, standing at the centre of a worldwide movement (once we step back from the heavy concentration on Paul we find in Acts, this becomes clear), and quite probably the author of the New Testament letter that bears his name. As time went on he acquired a reputation, even among those Jews who resolutely refused to believe in Jesus, for great piety and devotion: one later legend says that he spent so much time on his knees, praying for his people, that his knees became hardened, like camel's knees. He was eventually killed by some zealots in AD 62. At least he did not live to see the awful days of the war, and the siege and destruction of his beloved city.

So James' judgment, summing up the debate and its results, is extremely important. He begins by picking up what Peter has said (referring to Peter as 'Symeon', which may be Luke's way of indicating that the debate was conducted in Aramaic), and emphasizing that what counts is the grace of God. But then, crucially, he cites a biblical passage which sums up so much of the theology both of Acts and of Paul: when the house of David has been re-established, then the Gentiles will come flocking in to share in the blessings that will follow. This passage, from the end of the prophet Amos (9.11–12), follows hard on the heels of a warning about God's judgment on his own people, a judgment so severe that Israel's own election is downgraded to be merely one example among many of what God has done with various peoples (9.7). But, once 'the house of David that has collapsed' is restored – and James, like all early Christians, believed as a first principle that that was what had happened through Jesus being established as **Messiah** by his resurrection – then not only will the nations come flocking in, but Israel itself will be restored (9.11–15). James goes for the centre of the passage, and draws the conclusion that the Gentiles are indeed welcome as they are, on the basis of God's grace and with **faith** in Jesus as their only badge of membership.

That, however, is the point at which the 'rigid application' school would say: That's been decided, so the Mosaic law is a dead duck, so let's hear no more of it. That is all very well. Two initial comments. First, there was nothing *wrong* with the Mosaic law itself. If it had been decided, after lengthy and biblically rooted discussion, that people had been behaving in a way that offended God or oppressed their neighbours, then a decree banning the behaviour in question would have been instant and without exception. When Paul says No to incest in 1 Corinthians 5, he doesn't mean, 'Well, not very much, anyway'; he means, 'None of that!' But saying that the Mosaic law doesn't apply to Gentiles isn't that kind of thing.

Second, it is important to consider the impact that the decision will have on the church as it spreads throughout the larger world, not least where it will be living side by side, and perhaps intermingled, with substantial Jewish communities who will be perplexed by it. What is it, this body which looks very Jewish from one angle but very un-Jewish from other angles? And so James and the others work out the double principle of *no needful circumcision* on the one hand and *no needless offence* on the other. I have to say, having spent half my adult life in the academy and the other half in the church, that this sounds much more like the kind of solution that emerges from real discussions in real churches, whereas the absolute line of 'This is the decision so that's that' sounds much more like the conclusion reached in a coffee-enhanced seminar room.

No needful circumcision. The Gentiles who have believed in Jesus do not have to be circumcised; that is, they do not have to become Jewish in order to become Christians. They are not second-class citizens. They are not in a separate category when it comes to **salvation** itself. Paul and Peter had got the result they wanted, and nothing was going to change that; the **Pharisees** could huff and puff (and they continued to do so, as we see in Acts 21), but this point stood.

But *no needless offence.* Every city and town in the world had Jewish inhabitants at this time, according to the historian Josephus. So, wherever you went, people would be used to hearing what the law of Moses said. And, precisely since the Christians claimed that in Jesus as Messiah the law and the prophets had been fulfilled, and because this claim was always going to be at best puzzling and at worst offensive, the Gentile Christians were to be encouraged not to offer needless slaps in the face to their as-yet-unbelieving Jewish neighbours. It would therefore be a great help if they would observe the most obvious point: to keep well away from pagan temples and from everything that went on in them. Though the interpretation of the decree remains controversial, it seems most likely that what James had in mind was the actual performance of the various rituals involved in pagan worship, including the drinking of blood, ritual prostitution and other orgiastic elements that – even if they were not practised in all pagan temples all of the time! – were assumed to be practised in at least some temples some of the time. This would have been the most obvious and (to Jews) offensive form of continuing pagan behaviour for any Christian to indulge in, and it is hardly asking a great deal for a follower of Jesus Christ to abstain from it.

In fact, all this looks strongly like a way of saying something to the Gentile Christians out in the wider world while really saying something to the Pharisees back home: 'Look, it's all right; admitting these Gentiles who have believed won't mean a total collapse into idolatry and immorality; it needn't result in chaos or church/synagogue disputes.' It wouldn't be the last time an agreed statement from a church body was designed more to send out signals than to become part of a code of law.

There are various puzzles left over after this decision, and we shall look at some of them again in the next section. What impresses me, and what I long to see in the church of today and tomorrow, is the realism with which the question is addressed, rather than the brittle absolutism that so many might prefer. And if anyone thinks that this is some kind of a compromise, it is not only a compromise which stands here in scripture itself, but is one which James himself argued on the basis of scripture. Let the reader understand.

ACTS 15.22–35

The Letter to the Churches

²²Then the apostles and elders, with the whole assembly, decided to send people from their number, Judas Barsabbas and Silas (men well thought of by the Christian community) to Antioch with Paul and Barnabas. ²³They sent a letter with them, which read as follows.

'The apostles and elders send greetings to our Gentile brothers and sisters in Antioch, Syria and Cilicia. ²⁴Since we have heard that some of our number (not, however, sent by us) have been saying things which have troubled you, causing you distress of heart, ²⁵we resolved unanimously that it would be best to send to you men whom we have chosen, together with our beloved Barnabas and Paul, ²⁶who have risked their lives for the name of the Messiah, the Lord Jesus. ²⁷So we have sent Judas and Silas, and they will tell you the same things face to face. ²⁸For it seemed good to the holy spirit and to us not to lay any burden on you beyond the following necessary things: ²⁹that you should abstain from what has been sacrificed to idols, from blood, from what has been strangled, and from fornication. If you keep yourselves from these, you will do well. Farewell.'

³⁰So they went off and came down to Antioch, where they gathered the people together and presented the letter. ³¹When they read it, they were delighted with the message it contained.

³²Judas and Silas, who were themselves prophets, said a good deal to encourage the brothers and sisters, and they gave them strength. ³³When they had spent some time there, they left the family in peace and returned to those who had sent them. ³⁵But Paul and Barnabas stayed on in Antioch, teaching and preaching the word of the Lord, with many others as well.

Yet again in the news there is a story of a 'leak' from government sources. Official documents may say one thing, but someone whispering round the corner to a friendly journalist has said another. One minister denies that there is a problem; another one is reported as having said we need a public enquiry to find out what's going on. How can you tell?

If we think we have problems, with all our electronic and print media rumbling away all the time, they had a parallel but different problem in the early church. When someone sends a letter, how can you be sure it really did come from them? This was something Paul had to face early on (or, if you want to read it like that, it was a problem which a forger cunningly anticipated): in the second letter to the Thessalonians he suggests that a letter might come from someone, pretending to be him, saying that 'the day of the Lord' had arrived. Don't believe it, he says. Look at my handwriting, and don't trust a letter without it (2 Thessalonians 2.2; 3.17). The question of where something had come from, especially an apparently official document or edict, was often a problem in the ancient world.

For many people, this problem was resolved quite simply: a trusted intermediary would carry the letter, and would himself or herself report on the sender's instructions and vouch for the authenticity of the content. Thus Phoebe is sent to Rome with Paul's greatest letter; Tychicus, himself originally from Colosse, is sent there with Colossians; and so on.

In the present case, with the official letter from James and the Jerusalem church, there was a pressing need to make sure that the letter got through and was properly heard and understood. We know from Galatians that people had been spreading rumours about Paul – that he was really a junior to the Jerusalem **apostles**, that he had muddled up the **message** he should have been preaching, that he normally taught that people should be **circumcised** but had simply missed out that bit of the message when he was in Galatia, and so on. That's why, in that letter, Paul has to spend such a long time explaining his personal movements and his meetings with the Jerusalem apostles, somewhat as Peter in Acts 11 had to give a blow-by-blow account of his visit to Cornelius. It is sad that people within the family of the church should be so suspicious of one another as to make this necessary, but if it was so more than once in the first 20 or 30 years of the Christian movement perhaps we should not be surprised if it has continued that way since.

In particular, the message from Jerusalem to Antioch was so important, and agreed so strongly with the basic position that Paul had been arguing, that it was vital for it not to be misunderstood. The church in Antioch needed to know, beyond all doubt, that Paul had not simply written this letter himself and passed it off as an official document. So James and the others choose two of their number who would be trusted on all sides: Judas ('Judas', i.e. 'Judah', the name of the great royal patriarch, was very common, which is why this Judas is distinguished in verse 22 by his second name, Barsabbas) and Silas. Judas and Silas will add the personal touch to a letter which is, frankly, a bit stiff and formal, more like a committee report than a personal message. And they will be able to add further teaching to make sure that nobody is in any doubt as to the mind of the church.

The document is very clear that Paul and Barnabas, so far from being seen in Jerusalem as trouble-makers, are very much *persona grata*. They are 'beloved', and they have risked their lives for the name of Jesus. They are not, in other words, to be marginalized or regarded as holding unorthodox opinions. In any case, the opening greeting demonstrates how matters stand. The **Gentile** believers in Antioch and the surrounding districts are 'brothers and sisters', members (in other words) of the same family as James and the others, even though they have not been circumcised. This already concedes the substantial point at issue. And then comes the disclaimer: the people who went to Antioch from Jerusalem may have come 'from us' in the sense that they were part of the Jerusalem church, but we did not send them or commission them to say what they said to you.

This seems to correspond directly to the problem mentioned in Galatians 2.12–13. There, Peter's vacillating behaviour, eating with Gentiles one minute and withdrawing the next, was precipitated by the arrival of some people 'from James'. If the letter was written before the Council, Paul would still not have known for sure whether they were saying what James had told them to say, or whether they were simply using his authority to say what they themselves had wanted to say. As Paul puts it sorrowfully, 'even Barnabas' – Barnabas, who had shared so much of his work precisely with Gentile converts, who had seen God's grace at work among Gentiles in Antioch, who had supported Paul through thick and thin – even Barnabas was carried along with this play-acting, this putting on of a mask of Jewish separatism on top of the reality, which was a single **fellowship** consisting of believing Jews and believing Gentiles united in Christ (Galatians 2.13).

The letter then gives the instructions which were mooted in James's speech. Gentile believers are not to be required to undergo circumcision; that is the meaning of the rather vague 'not to lay any burden on you' (from the very beginning, it seems, official church documents lapsed by some kind of inexorable law into abstractions!). And they, the Gentile believers, are requested to make sure that they stay well clear of the main areas in which pagan culture, particularly pagan temples and what went on there, would give offence to Jews, whether believers or not. The final flourish, 'if you abstain from these, you will do well', could sound a little grudging, but again it should be understood as 'official-ese'. The real meaning is: 'That's all we ask, and if that's in place we are delighted to regard you as full members of the family.' We should note that this doesn't mean, 'If you find it hard to comply with these, your very **salvation** is in doubt', but 'If you cannot comply, it would make things much, much harder for all of us on this side of the fence.'

The main problem remaining about this 'apostolic decree' is, of course: what happened to it afterwards? Why does Paul never refer to it – for instance in 1 Corinthians, where it might have seemed not just appropriate but very helpful to him, particularly in chapter 8? Part of the answer may be that, as in Galatians, Paul was anxious that believers in churches founded through his ministry should not see him as a kind of second-hand (or second-rate!) emissary from Jerusalem and its leaders. He was a primary **apostle** in his own right, and nobody should imagine that they could appeal over his head to a higher authority. (It is interesting to note how the question of dispersed and centralized authority, which has been a feature of debates in various parts of the church in recent years, was there from the beginning.) In addition, Paul's attitude to controversial questions in 'his' churches tended, where possible, to be not 'Here is the rule which you are to learn and keep', but 'Here is how to *think* as men and women in Christ.' Give a church a rule and you guide them for a day; teach a church to think and you guide them for life. So Paul, while urging the Corinthians not to go into pagan temples (1 Corinthians 10), does not refer to the decree. There are of course other ways of explaining this (for instance, as many think, that Luke's chronology is completely inside out and that the Council only took place much later, after most of Paul's letters had already been written). But the way I have approached it seems to me to make good sense historically, and in terms of what Paul, and Luke, actually wrote.

One final note. Those with sharp eyes will have spotted that there is no 'verse 34'. The earliest and best manuscripts of the New Testament have the text as we now see it. But there is a puzzle. Luke says (verse 33) that Judas and Silas returned to Jerusalem; but a few verses later (verse 40) Paul chooses Silas as his new companion. So did Silas go back to Jerusalem, or did he stay in Antioch? There is of course no necessary contradiction. Paul was quite capable of sending a message to call Silas back. But at some point at least two **scribes**, independently, decided to tidy things up, and wrote various things to the effect that Judas only returned to Jerusalem while Silas remained in Antioch. When the New Testament verse-numbering was done, this additional material was still in the text people were using, and was called verse 34. All contemporary translations now omit it.

Paul and Barnabas are back at base, continuing their work both of evangelism and of teaching the believers. The major problem has been addressed, discussed, and laid to rest. All seems well. But that is the very moment when we should learn to watch out for fresh storm clouds on the horizon.

ACTS 15.36–41

A Huge Row

[36]After some days, Paul said to Barnabas, 'Let's go back and visit the brothers and sisters in all the various cities where we preached the word of the Lord, and see how they are doing.'

[37]Barnabas wanted to take John, called Mark, along with them. [38]But Paul reckoned that it was not a good idea to take with them someone who had left them in Pamphylia and had not gone on with them to the rest of the work. [39]There was a huge row, which resulted in them splitting up. Barnabas took Mark and sailed off for Cyprus. [40]Paul chose Silas, and went off, having been commended by the church to the grace of the Lord. [41]They went through Syria and Cilicia, strengthening the churches.

There is no point beating about the bush with this one. There are times in church work when leaders, including bishops, really want to knock two people's heads together and tell them not to be so pig-brained (though actually most pigs wouldn't dream of behaving like this), and I imagine every generation of readers has felt like that about Paul and Barnabas at this point. In fact, if anyone suggests that Luke, writing this book, is trying to whitewash early church history, or make out that the **apostles** were fledged angels, they should think again. This is a shameful episode, and the fact that it stands in scripture should not make us afraid to say so. On the contrary, its scriptural status should be interpreted as a sign that the Bible itself is warning us against allowing such a thing to happen. When Paul writes, as he often does in his letters, about the dangers of anger, bursts of rage, and so on, he must many times have looked back on this incident and hung his head in shame.

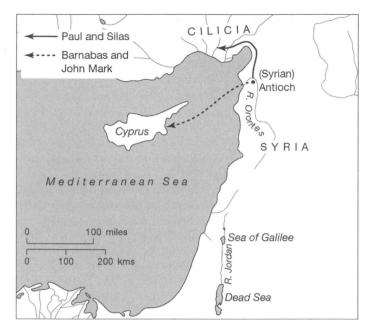

Acts 15.39–41

In case anyone supposes it wasn't after all as serious as all that, they need to have a look at the word at the beginning of verse 39, the word I have translated 'a huge row'. The word in Greek is *paroxysmos*, from which of course we get 'paroxysm'. When the word is used in a medical context it can mean 'convulsion' or refer to someone running a high fever. It carries overtones of severely heightened emotions, red and distorted faces, loud voices, things said that were better left unsaid. A sorry sight.

Part of the trouble is, as usual in this kind of thing, that both men were, in a sense, in the right. Paul was thinking back to what had happened in (Pisidian) Antioch, Iconium, Lystra and Derbe. John Mark hadn't even, as the Americans say, made it to first base in the Turkish leg of the trip; supposing a mob set on them again? Supposing stones and rocks were flying around once more? It would be much harder for him to run off back to Mum in Jerusalem once he was in the central uplands of southern Turkey. Paul knew he desperately needed people he could rely on totally, whatever happened (look at what he says about Timothy in Philippians 2.19–24!). Is it possible, as well, that there was a suggestion that Mark, a young Jerusalemite, might not have liked the fact that Paul seemed keen on moving out of strictly Jewish circles and into **Gentile** territory and Gentile evangelism?

At the same time, Barnabas – the 'son of encouragement', living up to his name as usual – could no doubt see that John Mark was only a youngster and that he'd simply panicked on the previous trip. He had probably now had a chance to settle down, and needed another opportunity to show he was up to it this time. I'd be prepared to bet that Barnabas had spent a quiet hour or two with John Mark during the visit to Jerusalem. They were after all cousins, according to Colossians 4.10 (quite a few people in the early church were related to one another). He had probably figured out that Mark had matured just a little bit, perhaps grown in his own spirituality as well. So of course he should have a second chance. And this would show the Jerusalem church that they, Paul and Barnabas, were wanting to cement the partnership between Antioch and Jerusalem which had been firmly and publicly established through the Council.

The worst rows, of course, happen when both people are in the right. We can all too easily imagine the scene. And, unfortunately, it has the memory of Galatians 2 falling like a shadow across it. Barnabas had apparently wobbled (when those wretched men came from Jerusalem) in his commitment to what Paul saw as a fundamental principle. Paul had been shocked; and even though they'd clearly made it up, and had gone together to Jerusalem and won a great victory for the point at issue, there may have been not just a shadow, but a dark cloud, in the back of Paul's mind as he thought ahead to the problems that might await them in Galatia. Would Barnabas wobble again – on this issue, or perhaps on some other? Would he be able to trust him?

For Barnabas himself – just to indulge further in the dangerous game of trying to think inside someone else's head at the distance of two thousand years and several major changes of culture – there would be anger as well. Paul, after all, had been his protégé. He had introduced him to the Jerusalem apostles when they had all been suspicious of him. He had fetched him from obscurity in Tarsus and given him the chance to become a famous preacher and teacher in Antioch. He had taken the lead in their first missionary expedition, and if Paul had more or less taken over as the chief speaker after that there was still a sense that Barnabas was a senior figure. Paul surely owed him something. Could he not bend on this point?

I doubt if there is a senior church leader anywhere who does not look at this scene and say, 'There but for the grace of God go I', or as it may be, 'There despite the grace of God went I.' It is all too easy to see. At the same time, we should note – since grace is after all one of Luke's great themes at this point in the book – that something fresh came out of it all. Two missionary journeys instead of one, with Barnabas and Mark going off to Barnabas' native Cyprus to consolidate the work there, and Paul taking Silas – a Roman citizen, as it happened, which was going to be important in ways neither of them could have imagined at that point – on a trip which turned out to be far more than a revisit to Syria and Cilicia, but instead a whole new venture into uncharted territory both geographical and theological. (Silas, by the way, is the same person as 'Silvanus' who appears in the two letters Paul wrote to Thessalonica, and who is also mentioned in 2 Corinthians 1.19. Whether or not he is the same as the 'Silvanus' mentioned in 1 Peter 5.12 it is impossible to say.) The God who makes human wrath to serve his praise has done it again (Psalm 76.10). That doesn't excuse sinful human wrath, of course. It simply shows once again what the **gospel message** itself massively demonstrates: that God can take the greatest human folly and sin and bring great good from it.

That is a humbling and necessary lesson for the church to learn in each generation. Luke could quite easily have found a less embarrassing way of explaining the new missionary pairings. I have a hunch that he told this shocking little story partly at least because he wanted this lesson to be heard and taken to heart.

ACTS 16.1–10

Timothy – and New Developments

¹Paul went on further, to Derbe and then Lystra. There was a disciple there by the name of Timothy, the son of a believing Jewish woman, but with a Greek father. ²The Christians in Lystra and Iconium spoke well of him. ³Paul wanted to have Timothy go with them, so he took him and circumcised him because of the Jews in those regions, since they all knew that his father was Greek. ⁴When they went through the cities, they handed on to them the decisions which had been taken by the apostles and elders at Jerusalem, so that they could observe them. ⁵The churches were strengthened in faith, and grew in number every day.

⁶They went through the region of Phrygia and Galatia, since the holy spirit had forbidden them to speak the word in the province of Asia. ⁷When they came to Mysia, they tried to go into Bithynia, but the spirit of Jesus didn't allow them to do so. ⁸So, passing by Mysia, they came down to Troas. ⁹Then a vision appeared to Paul in the night: a man from Macedonia was standing there, pleading with him, and saying, 'Come across to Macedonia and help us!' ¹⁰When he saw the vision, at once we set about finding a way to get across to Macedonia, concluding that God had called us to preach the good news to them.

A few weeks ago I had to choose a new close colleague to work with. It was difficult. There were some splendid people to choose from. Together with trusted friends and wise advisors, I prayed for God's guidance, I did as much homework as I could, I prayed some more. I called some key leaders together and we prayed for wisdom. We met some of the likely candidates. So much talent, so much giftedness, so many possibilities. We could see ourselves working with this person, with that person, with the other one too. Eventually the choice came back to me.

I went for a long walk, praying as I went. You can't rush these things, and I didn't have to. But, step by step, I found to my surprise that one particular person kept coming to my mind. I could see myself working with him. Praying with him. Laughing with him. Trusting him totally in the complexities of the work we're trying to do. I challenged myself. Was I just making it up? Was I just secretly hoping it would be him and forcing the issue? Back came the answer, No, this wasn't the case. There was something special about this, a matter of shared vocation. And if you pray for wisdom about a particular decision, and then find that your mind starts making itself up in a way you hadn't expected, you either go with it or you imply that you didn't really mean that prayer in the first place.

Now I have no idea whether Paul went through something like that before he chose Timothy as a travel companion and assistant, but I think it extremely likely. He may well have met Timothy and his family earlier. According to one of the letters to Timothy, both his mother and his grandmother were believers (2 Timothy 1.5), and there can't have been that many Christian families in Lystra, even by this stage. Paul knew he would need help of various kinds and at various stages, and after his previous experiences he knew he had to have someone he could totally trust. He had become convinced of that in Timothy's case. When, several years later, he mentioned Timothy in one of his most personal letters, in a passage we referred to earlier, it's clear he had been right (Philippians 2.19–24).

But there was a problem. And it's precisely at this point that some people have accused Paul of rank inconsistency. Paul's missionary methods, as we have seen, were to go in the first place, whenever he got to a new town, to the Jewish synagogue. That meant that he and his companions would have to be acceptable as fully-fledged Jews – not 'acceptable' in the sense of being 'acceptable to God', but able to move freely among the Jewish community without putting up the wrong kind of barrier at the wrong moment. Timothy was indeed Jewish: his mother was Jewish, and the primary qualification for Jewishness is through the mother's side (since, according to the pragmatic rabbinic thinking, long before DNA testing, you can never be absolutely sure about paternity but you can about maternity). But because Timothy's father was Greek, he hadn't had him **circumcised** when he was a baby. So Paul circumcised Timothy: not (I stress) because Timothy needed circumcision to become a full member of God's people, but because it was

Acts 16.1–10

going to be much easier to advance Paul's mission if his companions were all able to be seen as proper Jews. (Paul discusses this principle in 1 Corinthians 9.12, 19–23.)

This, then, is the opposite of what happened in relation to Titus in Galatians 2.1–5. Titus was a **Gentile**; some of the hardliners in Jerusalem wanted him to be circumcised before they would regard him as a proper member of the family; and Paul refused. We sometimes think it would be nice if life were not complicated, but it is, and the complexities matter. They are part of God's world and God's work.

So off they set, Paul, Silas and Timothy. But where were they to go next? A natural route would have been to continue westwards, eventually coming down the Lycus valley past Laodicea and the other towns there and emerging at the coast at Ephesus. But the **holy spirit** had told them they were not to preach the **word** in 'Asia', the Roman province which occupied the whole western end of modern Turkey. So they headed north, up through Galatia (Derbe, Lystra and the other towns on the first journey are in the south of Galatia), and then west into the region of Phrygia. It's quite some way; we are talking about a couple of hundred miles, depending on which route they took (which is a matter of considerable discussion, for the very good reason that no firm evidence exists). Two hundred miles on foot takes two or three weeks at the very least; what did the little company think they were doing, and where did they suppose they were going? This must have been something of a testing time for all of them, with Paul and Silas establishing a partnership, and Timothy, as the younger colleague, getting to know them but wondering what on earth he had let himself in for. It's one thing to trust God's guidance when it's actually quite obvious what to do next. It's something else entirely when you seem to be going on and on up a blind alley.

It got worse. They came to north-west Turkey, and concluded that maybe God wanted them to go into Bithynia, the Roman province that ran along the north edge of Turkey, on the south shore of the Black Sea. Wrong again: 'The spirit of Jesus', says Luke, 'didn't let them.' (How did they know? Was this a specific word of prophecy which one of them received? Or was it a deep, growing, internal conviction?) Well, there was only one way left: down to the coast at Troas. What are we doing here? Troas is in the province of Asia, and we've been told not to preach here. It seems that at this stage they had all been thinking of developing the work within Turkey, which was after all where two of them, Paul and Timothy, came from in the first place.

And then it happened. A vision at night. Paul sees a man from – Macedon! Northern Greece! Across the sea and into a totally new area! 'Come over and help us!' pleads the man. The weeks of walking and waiting, of wondering and praying, had led to this. They weren't going to do more primary evangelism in Turkey at all. They were off to Greece, crossing one of the great frontiers in the ancient, as in the modern world. This really would be breaking new ground.

And a new companion seems to have joined the party, too. Notice the 'we' in verse 10. Many people have tried to guess what this means. The most obvious solution is that the author of Acts has, at this point, joined Paul and his companions. Alternatively, the author has had access here, and in some other passages later on, to the journal of someone who had been with Paul. It is of course always possible to dream up more and more complex theories, and there has been no shortage of attempts. But the best solution, in my judgment, is also the simplest. At Troas, Paul and his companions met Luke, who came with them for the next part of the story.

ACTS 16.11–24

Preaching and Prison in Philippi

¹¹So we sailed away from Troas and made a straight course to Samothrace, and the next day to Neapolis. ¹²From there we went on to Philippi, a Roman colony which is the chief city of the district of Macedonia. We stayed in this city for some days.

¹³On the sabbath day we went outside the gate to a place by a river where we reckoned there was a place of prayer, and there we sat down. Some women had gathered, and we spoke to them. ¹⁴There was a woman called Lydia, a godfearer, who was a seller of purple from Thyatira. The Lord opened her heart to pay attention to what Paul was saying. ¹⁵She was baptized, with all her household.

'If you have judged me faithful to the Lord,' she begged us, 'please come and stay at my home.'

So she persuaded us.

¹⁶As we were going to the place of prayer we were met by a girl who had a spirit of divination. She and her oracles made a good living for her owners. ¹⁷She followed Paul and the rest of us.

'These men are servants of God Most High!' she would shout out. 'They are declaring to you the way of salvation!'

¹⁸She did this for many days. Eventually, Paul got fed up with it. He turned round and addressed the spirit.

'I command you in the name of Jesus the Messiah,' he said, 'come out of her!'

And it came out then and there.

¹⁹When the girl's owners saw that their hope of profit had vanished, they seized Paul and Silas, dragged them into the

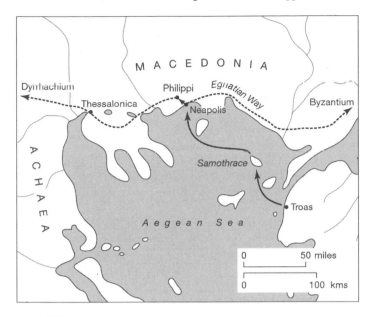

Acts 16.11–12

public square before the authorities, [20]and presented them to the magistrates.

'These men', they said, 'are throwing our city into an uproar! They are Jews, [21]and they are teaching customs which it's illegal for us Romans to accept or practise!'

[22]The crowd joined in the attack on them, and the magistrates had their clothes torn off them and gave orders for them to be beaten with rods. [23]When they had thoroughly beaten them, they threw them into prison, and gave orders to the jailer to guard them securely. [24]With that instruction, he put them into the innermost part of the prison, and fastened their feet in the stocks.

A friend of mine, a few years after being ordained, was sent to work in an inner suburb where, for a long time, vice had reigned unchecked. The police knew what was going on but were following a policy of containment rather than confrontation:

as long as it didn't spread, they could keep an eye on it without interfering. Drugs, sex and stolen goods of all sorts were readily available; petty and not-so-petty crime flourished. And my friend, perhaps with cheerful naivety and perhaps with a strong sense of God's call, began to preach the **gospel** in a way that that particular church hadn't experienced for many years.

His preaching had an impact. People on the street took notice. Some came to **faith**, and began to pray for the neighbourhood. More people came to believe the gospel. Addicts and prostitutes started to drop in to the church; people would pray with them and try to help them out of their damaging and dehumanizing lifestyles.

But then, before too long, the unofficial powers that ran the area began to take notice as well. Threatening letters started to arrive. Objects were hurled through the windows. And, more sinister still, my friend was struck down with a mysterious illness. For a while he was completely incapacitated. He was only healed through urgent and prolonged prayer. He realized, and the whole church had to take on board, that what he had done was to walk into a spiritual field of force and to challenge it. The dark powers that had run the place for many years, and had made a lot of money for a few people out of the misery of the many, were striking back. That is how it often happens. I don't wish to be melodramatic; many people go through an entire lifetime of faithful ministry without anything like this ever coming near them; but it does sometimes happen.

This is certainly what was going on in Philippi. Paul, Silas, Timothy and Luke (if it was him) had walked into territory where all kinds of forces, all sorts of powers, were at work, and three of them in particular come rushing together in this story. But first, we note Paul's regular pattern of evangelism.

After all, you couldn't just walk into the main street of a major city in the ancient world and begin preaching. The authorities would have you picked up in no time. You needed a base, a place from which to operate. And Paul's habit, for good theological reasons, had been as we have seen to begin where the local Jews were worshipping. That normally meant the synagogue.

The trouble was, there wasn't a synagogue at Philippi. Perhaps there weren't enough Jews in the area. What there was was a regular 'place of prayer', an informal location, down by a river outside the town. Somehow Paul and his friends got wind of Jews meeting there for prayer, and they went and joined them. It seemed to be mainly a group of women; perhaps, as with Timothy's family, it was a matter of Jewish women with Greek husbands. And not all of them were even actually Jewish; Lydia, who we meet here, was a godfearer, a **Gentile** who, as we've seen in other cases, had come to recognize in Judaism something powerfully attractive and wise which wasn't on offer in the normal hurly-burly of pagan ritual and belief. Lydia was a businesswoman, an independent figure, dealing in purple cloth; in other words, she was working at the top end of the market. She was the Karen Millen of northern Greece.

Luke tells the story of her **conversion** extremely simply. 'The Lord opened her heart to pay attention to' – in other words, to give assent to, to believe – 'what Paul was saying.' Sometimes that's how it happens, rather as with Cornelius in chapter 10. Here is someone who has been praying, seeking God, opening themselves to the possibility that this God might come seeking them. Perhaps, indeed, it was partly through Lydia's prayers that Paul had received his vision in Troas. Anyway, the **word** Paul preached was in Lydia's case tapping at a window that was already open. In came the light, into her heart came the **message** of the Lord, and she and her household were **baptized**. Then, realizing that Paul and his companions would be much better off in establishing a ministry if they were resident in someone's home than if they were staying in an inn somewhere, she insisted on inviting them to stay with her. She already had a 'household', and now had four more guests. This confirms the impression, from her profession, that she was a woman of considerable means.

But then the three malevolent powers took matters in hand. First, the strange spiritual forces, which seem to be stirred up by a new gospel work, just as in chapters 8 and 13. The ancient Greek world knew all about 'divination', and people regularly went to places like Delphi to ask the priestess of Apollo for advice on everything from getting married to making war. Sometimes it seems that the system was merely a matter of cynical folk making a profit out of simple souls, both the ones asking the question and the ones giving the 'answer'. But sometimes, as here, it seems to have been a case of someone, often a young woman, actually possessing some kind of prophetic **spirit**. And her 'minders' were, of course, making a tidy profit out of her.

And, like a compass needle swinging suddenly round to point to a new and powerful magnetic force, the unfortunate young woman found herself following Paul and Silas and yelling after them. (We are reminded of the way in which Jesus' appearance in various places precipitated similar outbursts, in e.g. Luke 4.33–37.) 'Slaves of God Most High!' she yells at them. 'That's what these men are! They're announcing **salvation!**'

Now that was true; but probably not in the sense either that she meant it, or that people would understand it. 'God Most High', to someone living in Philippi, wouldn't mean the God of Abraham, the One God of Jewish monotheism. It would mean either Zeus or whoever people thought of as the top god in the local pantheon. And 'salvation' wouldn't mean what it meant to a Jew or a Christian, entry into the world of God's new creation, overcoming corruption, sin and death. It would mean 'health' or 'prosperity' or 'rescue' from some kind of disaster, as we shall see later in Acts 16.30–31. In any case, this was the kind of publicity Paul could do without; he may well, in addition, have felt deeply sorry for the enslaved young woman herself. Eventually he turned round and, calling not on some nebulous 'Most High God' but on the name of Jesus, he commanded the spirit of prophecy to leave her. And it did.

Which, of course, brought the second malevolent force into play. The profit motive. The girl's minders were suddenly as bereft of business as a fisherman whose boat has just sunk. Not for the last time, when the gospel suddenly impacts someone's trade, they turn nasty.

And so they invoke the third force: religious and political prejudice. They dragged Paul and Silas before the magistrates. 'These men are Jews', they shouted (which was of course true), 'and they are advocating customs which *we Romans* ought not to adopt or observe' (which was of course half true). The point was this. Philippi was a Roman colony, and proud of it. The town stood on the main road you would take if you were travelling between Rome and almost anywhere in Turkey or further east. As a colony (settled by military veterans after the wars of the previous century), Philippi needed to keep up its Roman standards and culture. And these men . . . they aren't our sort. They're trying to change our customs. *They're anti-Roman!*

And that's enough. The combination of religion, money and politics is asking for trouble, and Paul and Silas got it. Stripped, flogged and jailed, they discovered what happens to those who challenge the powers of the world with the power of the Name of Jesus.

ACTS 16.25–34

Earthquake and Salvation

[25]Around midnight, Paul and Silas were praying and singing hymns to God, and the prisoners were listening to them. [26]Suddenly there was a huge earthquake, which shook the foundations of the prison. At once all the doors flew open, and everyone's chains became loose. [27]When the jailer woke up and saw the prison doors open, he drew his sword and was about to kill himself, supposing that the prisoners had escaped. [28]But Paul shouted at the top of his voice,

'Don't harm yourself! We're all still here!'

[29]The jailer called for lights and rushed in. Trembling all over, he fell down before Paul and Silas. [30]Then he brought them outside.

'Gentlemen,' he said, 'will you please tell me how I can get out of this mess?'

[31]'Believe in the Lord Jesus,' they replied, 'and you will be rescued – you and your household.'

[32]And they spoke the word of the Lord to him, with everyone who was in his house. [33]He took them, at that very hour of the night, and washed their wounds. Then at once he was baptized, and all his household with him. [34]Then he took them into his house, put food on the table, and rejoiced with his whole house that he had believed in God.

I remember old Bishop Stephen Neill, who was winning classical scholarships around the time my father was born, telling me how we should translate verse 30. He was used to hearing people quote the panic-stricken question of the Philippian jailer to Paul and Silas in the words of the old Authorized (King James) Version.

'Sirs,' says the jailer in that translation, 'what must I do to be saved?'

That was, of course, the question preachers wanted their congregations to ask, so that they could be ready with Paul's answer about believing in Jesus. So they naturally tended to invest the jailer's remarks with all the theological freight of a much later generation of conscience-stricken Westerners. In a long line from Augustine to Luther and beyond, not least to John Bunyan, for whom the question 'What must I do to be saved?' had been his own deeply personal cry before he discovered the truth of the **gospel**, they came with a strong sense that there was a **heaven** and a hell, that some would go to the former ('saved') and some to the latter ('not saved'), and that it was therefore more than a little important to be sure where one stood.

But of course the Philippian jailer knew none of this. In his pagan world there were all kinds of theories about the afterlife, but none of them was anything like so clear, or so precise, as the medieval heaven-and-hell scenario which dominated later Western thought. In any case, it was midnight; there had just been an earthquake; the prison he was in charge of had burst open; he was going to be held responsible for escaped prisoners, which would probably mean torture and death; he was on the point of committing suicide – and was he about to ask these strange visitors for a detailed exposition of justification by grace through **faith**?

No, of course not, said Bishop Neill. In any case, as we have seen, '**salvation**' in the ancient world didn't mean 'going to heaven when you die', and that is by no means how the New Testament writers use it. Jesus himself frequently speaks of someone being 'saved' when he means 'healed' (e.g. Luke 8.48: 'your faith has saved you', in other words, 'has made you well'). So 'saved' meant, simply, 'rescued', 'delivered' – from whatever problem, be it sickness, financial disaster, personal catastrophe, or anything else, might be threatening.

So the wise bishop recommended the form of words I have used here. It isn't the strictest word-for-word translation, but it catches the sense of the jailer's frantic question. 'Gentlemen, will you please tell me how I can get out of this mess?'

And of course he got more than he bargained for, just as people regularly do when they ask questions which everyone, from Jesus himself through to the youngest and most inexperienced evangelist, can take and deepen. Because of course it is a deepening, not a change of subject. It isn't that we hear one question and answer another (though Jesus himself, in John's **gospel** especially, sometimes sounds to us as though he's doing that). Rather, the Christian worldview sees the entire mess that the world is in, from the global facts of human rebellion, idolatry and sin, the corruption of human life and relationships, the pollution of our planet, the worldwide systems of economic exploitation, and so on, right through to *this* messy situation here and now, this sudden crisis, this person in desperate need or sorrow or fear, and *this* person whose own deliberate sin has raised a dark barrier between themselves and God – the Christian worldview sees all of this under the heading of 'the way the world currently is', as opposed to 'the way the world will be when Jesus is reigning as Lord – and the way it can become even here and now, because Jesus *is* already reigning as Lord, but his reign must spread through humans acknowledging that lordship.' That's why 'believe in the Lord Jesus' is always the answer to the question of how to be rescued, at whatever level and in whatever sense.

In other words, Paul and Silas address both the very specific question the jailer has asked *and* the deep, world-deep, heart-deep, God-deep question which, with practised eye, they can see lies beneath it. Something of the same to-and-fro between different levels of 'salvation' has already occurred way back near the start of the book: the disabled man at the Beautiful Gate was 'saved', but the explanation concerning the Name of Jesus involved the claim that in this name we must all be saved – including those who are not disabled or beggars (4.12).

Having made that clear, the confident appeal of Paul and Silas, that the jailer should 'believe in the Lord Jesus' so that he and his household may be saved, does of course stand as a classic summary of what the Christian **message**, the *evangel* or '**good news**', is all about. It isn't about getting in touch with one's inner spiritual self. It isn't about committing oneself to a life of worship, prayer and good works. It isn't even about believing in some particular theory of how precisely God deals with our sins in the death of Jesus. It is about recognizing, acknowledging and hailing *Jesus Christ as Lord* – the very thing which Paul declares triumphantly at the climax of the great poem in his letter to this very city (Philippians 2.10). 'If you confess with your lips Jesus as Lord', he wrote to the Romans (10.9), 'and believe in your heart that God raised him from the dead, you will be saved.' Everything else is contained within that – all the volumes of systematic and pastoral theology, all the worship and prayers and devotion and dogma, all the ethics and choices and personal dilemmas. The phrase 'Jesus is Lord' is what, from the earliest times, people said as they came for **baptism**, as the jailer and his household promptly did.

So how had it happened? Luke wants us to realize something about the earthquake. God's messengers are not protected from the sufferings that will come when their message challenges the easy, smug rule of political, economic or religious forces. But God is not mocked. Vindication will come. We would much prefer it if we could have the result without the process, the crown without the cross, but that is never the way in the **kingdom of God**, as Paul made clear to the people of Iconium and Antioch (Acts 14.22).

And there is a larger theme just beginning here, a theme which will steadily grow and swell throughout the book until it ends with a great question-mark as the book stops just before what might have been its final climax. This is the first time Paul has been brought before Roman magistrates. As we shall see, there is considerable irony in this, since he was himself a Roman citizen and should have been able to appeal to them for protection. Perhaps it was just as well that he should discover what it was like to be on the rough side of Roman justice before he could begin to explore its positive values. But from this point onwards the book makes its way not least through a succession of trial scenes, with Paul always the one in the dock, usually literally and sometimes (as in the Ephesus riot) metaphorically. It's easy to miss this, because the 'travelogue' aspect of the book is so striking, and so well done, that we can forget what is happening, again and again, when Paul stays still for long enough for someone to accuse him of something. But then it's always the same: accusations, threats, violence, intimidation and then vindication, whether by public statement of the authorities or by simple escape. What happens in Philippi puts down a marker. This is how it is going to be.

But that isn't a cause for gloom. It is a reason for celebration. The night-time feast in the jailer's house sets the pattern for the bizarre celebration of God's kingdom from that day to this. The world is turning the right way up at last, and what better way of showing it than a Roman jailer throwing a midnight party for two battered but rejoicing heralds of King Jesus?

ACTS 16.35–40

Publicly Vindicated

[35]When day broke, the magistrates send their officers with the message, 'Let those men go.' [36]The jailer passed on what they said to Paul.

'The magistrates have sent word that you should be released,' he said. 'So now you can leave and go in peace.'

[37]But Paul objected.

'We are Roman citizens!' he said. 'They didn't put us on trial, they beat us in public, they threw us into prison, and now they are sending us away secretly? No way! Let them come themselves and take us out.'

[38]The officers reported these words to the magistrates. When they heard that they were Roman citizens, they were afraid. [39]They went and apologized, brought them out of the prison, and requested that they leave the city. [40]So when they had left the prison they went to Lydia's house. There they saw and encouraged the brothers and sisters, and then they went on their way.

One of the most famous cases in ancient Roman law was the one brought by the young upstart barrister Cicero against the rich, aristocratic proconsul Gaius Verres.

Verres, like many Roman aristocrats of his generation, had discovered how to play the famous Roman system of democracy to his own advantage. Of course one had to go through the official motions of being elected to various offices of state – quaestor, praetor and so on. No problem: there were friends who could fix all that, who could buy or manipulate enough votes to get a candidate safely installed. Even the consulship itself, the senior position in Roman society, held for one year, wouldn't present too much of a problem. Likely candidates had things worked out months, sometimes years, in advance, and pressure would be brought to bear on people who threatened to upset this careful planning with silly ideas that they might like to put themselves forward to stand against the candidates who 'everybody knew' were going to get elected anyway.

Holding public office was important in itself, but it was the gateway to something even more important: money. After a year in office, the normal practice was for the newly retired 'proconsul', as they were called, to go off and govern one of the many Roman provinces. We have met several such provinces already in this book: Judaea, Syria, Cilicia, Asia, Galatia and Bithynia. We are currently in Macedonia, and will soon be in Achaea. All of them were run by people who had held leading magistracies back in Rome. We shall meet a couple of them in due course, in the final fateful scenes in Judaea.

Some governors, of course, did their best to rule their provinces with a measure of justice and wisdom. In fact, by Paul's day this had considerably improved from the time of Cicero, partly because of the very case I am mentioning. But in the first century BC it had become common practice for provincial governors to do on a massive scale what, notoriously, tax-collectors did on a small, local scale: make a handy profit for themselves by extortion. So Verres, after serving his term as a praetor, set off for Sicily, licking his lips at the prospect.

He went about it with systematic ruthlessness. Having discovered that with his official powers, and soldiers to enforce his will, he could do what he liked, he not only imposed heavy financial levies. He sequestered whole estates, stripped houses of art treasures, and grabbed anything he saw or heard of that sounded even moderately worth his notice. Shiploads of loot were sent back to his home in Rome. Anyone who objected, or who threatened to report him or prosecute him, was dealt with summarily and brutally.

That was where Verres made his main mistake. When rumours leaked out of what was going on, some frightened Sicilians appealed to the young barrister Cicero for his help. He was initially nervous. Verres had friends in high places, and attacking him wasn't the best way for Cicero himself to get on in the world. But the case got under his skin, and he investigated. What he found appalled him, and it appalled all of Rome when it came out in Cicero's devastating presentation of the evidence, once Verres, after a lot of squirming and legal wrangling, finally came to trial (in 70 BC). And the crucial point in the prosecution, the point which even Verres' friends and his many bribed supporters could see was going to topple their man, was the point at which Verres had crucified a man who had been trying to tell people what was going on. *And the man was a Roman citizen.* The great plea which had echoed round many nations, 'I'm a Roman citizen', had gone unregarded. Verres had had the man flogged and executed, and with his dying breath he had gone on declaring the citizenship because of which he should have been exempt. Verres left Rome before the trial ended and went into voluntary exile. Years later, he was put to death on the orders of Mark Antony, supposedly because Antony in turn fancied some of the art treasures Verres still possessed.

That story, of course, went round the world of Roman politics and governance as a stinging cautionary tale. *I'm a Roman citizen!* It was the ace up the sleeve, the card to play when you really needed to win the game. Whatever else magistrates knew about running their local towns or districts, they knew they shouldn't do what Verres had done. If news of such a thing got back to Rome . . . it didn't bear thinking about.

And that is more or less all we need to know by way of background to the present passage. *They were afraid when they heard that Paul and Silas were Roman citizens.* Paul milked the situation for all it was worth. He took the high moral ground – and the very high political ground. He demanded a public apology, and got it. They asked him to leave, and he took his time over it, going to Lydia's house first, knowing that nobody would dare come after him again. Having experienced the downside of Roman rule, Paul was determined to make the upside work for him as well if not better.

This passage, and others like it, have raised for many people the question of whether Paul was right, and whether Christians today are right, to use their civic status or rights in the service of the **gospel**. Ever since the high Middle Ages, when church and state were more or less identical in European society, people have questioned whether such an arrangement was ever a good thing. They have looked all the way back to the settlement of Constantine, under whom, at the start of the fourth century, the Roman Empire officially became 'Christian', and have asked whether that, too, was an awful mistake. Then, with the same anti-establishment zeal, this line of thought has been pushed back towards Paul. The Paul of the letters, people say, made several covert attacks on the Roman establishment, insisting in a variety of ways that if Jesus was Lord then Caesar, ultimately, wasn't. I agree, broadly, with that reading of Paul. So why does it make sense, here and later in the story, for Paul to pull the rabbit out of the hat, to get himself out of trouble by claiming Roman citizenship?

Some people think that Luke just made all this up, to advance a very different agenda to that which the real Paul embraced. I don't agree. Just as with the apostolic decree of the Jerusalem Council in the previous chapter, things are usually more complicated in real life than they seem in the neat, one-size-fits-all theories of the seminar room. *Of course* when Paul says 'Jesus is Lord' he meant, among many other things, 'and therefore Caesar isn't'. Psalm 2 was near the foundation of his whole theology. Passages like Isaiah 40—55, with their scathing denunciations of pagan rulers and their gods, had deeply informed his thinking and praying. But, as with the apostolic decree, he didn't want to end up being so theoretically correct that he was stuck in a prison cell being correct all by himself when he could be out there preaching the gospel. God had given him the extraordinary position of being a highly trained **Pharisee** and a Roman citizen, and had called him to do a job. Paul took it for granted that the tools God had given him were tools he should use.

This doesn't provide an easy template for all subsequent Christians to figure out how they should employ their political or civic status within their Christian vocation. That will vary from time to time, regime to regime, and vocation to vocation. It does suggest, once more, that we should avoid easy dogmatisms of this or that kind and, while holding firmly to the belief that Jesus is Lord and that through him God's **kingdom** is indeed coming on earth as in **heaven**, be ready for some surprises as to how that latter reality is brought to birth.

ACTS 17.1–9

Another King!

¹Paul and Silas travelled through Amphipolis and Apollonia, and came to Thessalonica, where there was a Jewish synagogue. ²Paul went there, as he usually did, and for three sabbaths he spoke to them, expounding the scriptures, ³interpreting and explaining that it was necessary for the Messiah to suffer and to rise from the dead, and that 'This Jesus, that I am announcing to you, is the Messiah'. ⁴Some of them were persuaded, and threw in their lot with Paul and Silas, including a large crowd of godfearing Greeks, together with quite a few of the leading women.

⁵But the Jews were righteously indignant. They took some villainous men from the market-place, drew a crowd, and threw the city into an uproar. They besieged Jason's house and searched for Paul and Silas, to bring them out to the mob. ⁶When they couldn't find them, they dragged Jason and some of the Christians before the town authorities.

'These are the people who are turning the world upside down!' they yelled. 'Now they've come here! ⁷Jason has had them in his house! They are all acting against the decrees of Caesar – and they're saying that there is another king, Jesus!'

⁸When they heard these words, the crowd and the authorities were both greatly agitated. ⁹They bound Jason and the others over, and then dismissed them.

Just north of where I am writing this, and visible from not far away, is the small but famous island of Lindisfarne, commonly known as 'Holy Island'. It was the first beachhead of Christian **faith** in England, long before the Romans sent Augustine from Rome to the south of England to annexe the flourishing native movement on behalf of the increasingly powerful Roman see. Lindisfarne was the island where, in the seventh century, men like Aidan and Cuthbert were bishops, and where missionaries like Chad and his brother Cedd were trained and sent out into the wild lands further south.

The thing that most people know about Lindisfarne, especially if they've tried to get there, is that twice a day it is cut off. At low tide you can walk across the old pilgrim path, or drive

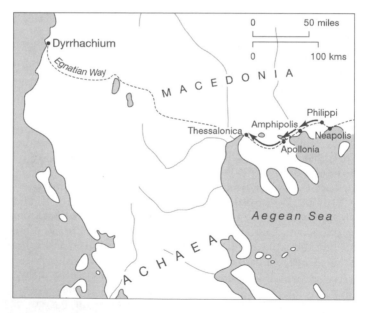

Acts 17.1

a car across the roadway that has now been built (until quite recently, if you wanted to drive over, you would hire a local taxi, whose driver would know where to find the more solid ground). But the tide comes sweeping in around the island, faster than people normally imagine, covering the road itself to a depth higher than a car, or a human being. Many people have been cut off over the years, and several drowned, through being caught in the middle.

Part of the problem, of course, is that precisely around the road, and the footpath across the sands, the tide comes in *from both directions*. It mainly washes in from the north, but at almost exactly the same time it comes round the small island and rushes in from the south. To be caught in the middle, even supposing you were a strong swimmer, doesn't just mean you'd have to go with the flow, ride it out, and hope to land up somewhere safe. You are likely to be thrown around by the double force and drowned before you can work out what's going on.

What we have here in Thessalonica, the large port (to this day) at the north-west corner of the Aegean Sea, is the coming together of the two tidal waves which we have seen, so far, sweeping separately up to Paul and his companions. On the one hand, we have threats and opposition from Jews, as in Pisidian Antioch. On the other, as in Philippi, we have pagans who whip up charges about laws, customs and religious questions to protect their economic and political status quo. What happens when the two waves meet in the middle and crash over Paul's head?

Answer: another riot. We ought to be getting used to this by now; though, since most people reading this have probably never seen, let alone been caught in the middle of, a real riot we ought to pause and think just how frightening that must be. Here things follow a very similar pattern to what we see in the **gospel** accounts of Jesus' trial: a Jewish charge, easily transformed into a pagan one. This time Paul and Silas are nowhere to be found, and they escape under cover of night, leaving behind a young, small church for whom Paul felt strong and warm pastoral love, as is revealed movingly in the letter we call 1 Thessalonians, written apparently just a few weeks after his departure.

Paul follows his normal practice in going to the synagogue; clearly Thessalonica had a larger Jewish community than Philippi. As in Pisidian Antioch and elsewhere, he expounded the scriptures; Luke obviously intends us to imagine addresses not unlike the one in Acts 13. But this time there is a new note, which we have not seen since the biblical exposition *par excellence* delivered by the risen Jesus on the road to Emmaus in Luke 24. Paul, says Luke, 'was interpreting and explaining that *it was necessary* for the **Messiah** to suffer and to rise again from the dead'. Perhaps Paul's own sufferings had driven him back again to contemplate not only the sufferings of Jesus but the **messianic** nature, the scripture-fulfilling nature, of those sufferings. Perhaps he always mentioned it and it's only now that Luke has drawn our special attention to it. One way or another, this forms an important part of his explanation to the Jews, since the fact of a crucified Messiah is the major road-block in the way of any devout Jew believing that Jesus was or could be God's anointed: how could God allow such a thing, how could God be honoured thereby, and how could God do, through such a Messiah, the messianic work of bringing peace and justice to the world, and rebuilding the **Temple**? Paul was only too well aware of those questions, and had good answers for them, but the answers always began, for him, with the scriptures. We can only guess at the passages he employed, but our guesses can be pretty accurate in view of his use of scripture in his letters on this topic: Isaiah 53, of course, but also Genesis 22 (Abraham's **sacrifice** of Isaac, referred to in Romans 8.32), Psalm 22 (read as a prayer of the Messiah), perhaps Zechariah's dark oracles of suffering and vindication.

But, as always, it wasn't simply a matter of a few proof-texts, though they would help. It was a matter of the entire plan of God, the whole sweep of the narrative, the story of Israel going into the dark tunnel of slavery in Egypt only to be rescued at the Passover, of David fleeing from Absalom only to be reinstalled after the great victory, of Jerusalem being destroyed and the nation carried away captive to Babylon, only to be brought back and rebuilt after a tribulation everyone had thought would be final . . . in other words, of a story whose main themes were all about suffering and vindication, disaster and reversal, death and **resurrection**. From there it was only a short step to the conclusion: if that's how the story works, and if that's what the messianic prophecies are shaped by, it really does appear that this Jesus, crucified and risen, truly is the Messiah.

That wasn't, of course, the way many in the synagogue community wanted to understand the story of Israel; and it certainly wasn't the template they had in mind for a Messiah, should God ever send one. Some were persuaded, as they usually were, and Luke tells us that a good many of the Greeks who had been worshipping in the synagogue embraced the gospel **message** as well. But, again as usual, there is what we might call the zeal factor: jealousy, righteous indignation, concern for the honour of God and the **law**. 'How can this man talk such nonsense? Doesn't he see that he is speaking blasphemously about God himself, suggesting such a thing? What happens to the great law of Moses if we start thinking this way – especially if, as he says, all these Greeks are welcome in the family without more ado?'

And so, with the best of motives, they do what 'zeal' was bound to do, and cause a disturbance. If something has to be done, it doesn't much matter who does it; so they enlist a bunch of ne'er-do-wells from the market-place (is Luke conscious of the irony of this, rejecting Paul but recruiting no-good pagan layabouts to help their zeal for God and his law work itself out?) and set the whole city in an uproar. At this point Luke introduces a character he seems to think we know, one Jason, whose house the mob attack. We haven't met him before, actually, and there is no telling (since it's not an uncommon name) whether this Jason is the same one we meet in Romans 16.21, someone who is with Paul when he's writing that great letter. But he seems both to be a local man and already marked out as a Christian. Since Paul has been in the city for three **sabbaths** it is perfectly possible both that Jason was converted early on in that time and that he has already been allowing his house to be used for meetings of believers, and as somewhere for Paul and his companions to stay.

It is Jason and some other local Christians who, this time, bear the brunt of the mob's anger. They weren't beaten or imprisoned. But to be dragged by a mob before the magistrates, accused of helping foment sedition, and then bound over to keep the peace is hardly the kind of thing you want to happen to you too often. No wonder, writing to them not long afterwards, Paul showed great sympathy for them in what they had suffered at the hands of their own neighbours and fellow townsfolk, and took care to place their sufferings on the larger map of the purposes of God (1 Thessalonians 2.14; 3.1–5).

But the real sting in the tail comes in what the mob said when accusing Jason and the others. Anyone who suggests that Luke was writing this book to show the authorities who might glance at it that Christianity was a peaceful movement which merely encouraged everyone to be good citizens should look at this pair of verses and think again. 'These people who have been turning the world upside down', they said, 'have come here.' Well, yes. Paul would probably, if pushed, say that they were turning the world the right way up, because it was currently upside down, but he would most likely have been quite pleased to see that people had at least understood that he wasn't just offering people a new religious experience, but announcing to the world that its creator was at last setting it all right. And, the charge goes on, 'all of them all acting against Caesar's decrees' – they don't say which ones, but the meaning seems to be in the final phrase – 'saying that there is another king, namely Jesus'.

Another king! Well, they really have got the message. Jesus is Lord and Caesar isn't; the fundamental 'decree' or 'dogma' of Caesar is that he and he alone is emperor. Northern Greece had been the site of the awful civil wars a century before, where Brutus and Cassius had fought it out with Antony and Octavian after the death of Julius Caesar, and then Antony and Octavian (Augustus) had fought it out for eventual mastery. A phrase like 'another king' sounded very much as though people were thinking of starting another civil war aimed at ousting the Emperor Claudius and installing another candidate. If all this took place, as seems likely, around AD 50, we should remind ourselves that less than two decades later no fewer than three emperors were hailed, in far-flung parts of the empire, as 'another king', and installed in quick succession, making up the 'year of the four emperors' of AD 69. These things were all too possible, and the charge all too believable.

So was Paul being a loyal Roman citizen, or wasn't he? It all depends on what sort of a 'king' you think he thought Jesus really was. It is easy to quote Jesus' famous saying, 'My kingdom is not of this world', but what John actually wrote was 'My kingdom is not *from* this world' (John 18.36), with the clear implication that, though derived of course from elsewhere, Jesus' **kingdom** was definitely *for* this world. And it is easy to show that the charge Luke reports against Jesus, that he was claiming to be a king (Luke 23.2), was, like the other accusations hurled around at the time, at best deeply misleading.

But when we stand back from the present incident and look at the whole sweep of Acts as it unfolds before our eyes, we begin to see a pattern emerging, a pattern which will grow and swell until it leaves us . . . wondering what on earth happened next. In Acts 1—12 Jesus is hailed as **Messiah**, king of the Jews, until eventually the present king of the Jews tries to do something about it but is struck down for his pagan arrogance. Now, from Acts 13 onwards, Jesus is being hailed as 'another king', 'lord of the world'; but there already is a 'lord of the world', and anyone who knows anything about tyrants, particularly ancient Roman ones, knows well that they don't take kindly to rivals on the stage. What is going to happen next?

But before this issue can be taken further, let alone resolved, there is fresh business to attend to. Fresh preaching and teaching await Paul and Silas a few miles west, in Beroea. But the lessons learnt in Thessalonica will stay with Paul, and must stay with us, as we journey on.

ACTS 17.10–21

Paul Reaches Athens

[10]The Christians in Thessalonica quickly sent Paul and Silas on, by night, to Beroea. When they got there, they went to the Jewish synagogue. [11]The people there were more generous in spirit than those in Thessalonica. They received the word with considerable eagerness, searching the scriptures day by day to

see if what they were hearing was indeed the case. [12]Many of them became believers, including some of the well-born Greek women, and quite a few men.

[13]But when the Jews from Thessalonica knew that the word of God had been proclaimed by Paul in Beroea, too, they came there as well, stirring up trouble and whipping up the crowd. [14]So the Christians quickly sent Paul away as far as the sea-coast, while Silas and Timothy remained behind. [15]Those who were conducting Paul brought him all the way to Athens, where he told them to tell Silas and Timothy to join him as soon as possible. Then they left him there.

[16]So Paul waited in Athens. While he was there, his spirit was stirred up as he saw the whole city simply full of idols. [17]He argued in the synagogue with the Jews and the godfearers, and in the market-place every day with those who happened to be there. [18]Some of the Epicurean and Stoic philosophers were disputing with him.

'What can this word-scatterer be on about?' some were saying.

'He seems to be proclaiming foreign divinities,' declared others – since he was preaching 'Jesus and Anastasis'. ('Anastasis' means 'resurrection'.) [19]So they took him up to the Areopagus.

'Are we able to know', they said, 'what this new teaching really is that you are talking about? [20]You are putting very strange ideas into our minds. We'd like to find out what it all means.'

[21]All the Athenians, and the foreigners who live there, spend their time simply and solely in telling and hearing the latest novelty.

There seems to be an increasing fashion in the sporting world, especially in sports that originated in Europe, for 'World Cup' contests, and similar events organized in geographical regions. Unless you are a very avid sports fan, these events seem to come tumbling over one another all the time: one minute it's football ('soccer'), another it's rugby, another it's cricket. The American sporting calendar doesn't look quite the same, but the annual round of American football, hockey, baseball and even golf seems to rattle by, too, with continual competitions to right and left.

When a team is playing in one of these multi-sided tourna-ments, the coaches know they have to be prepared to do battle

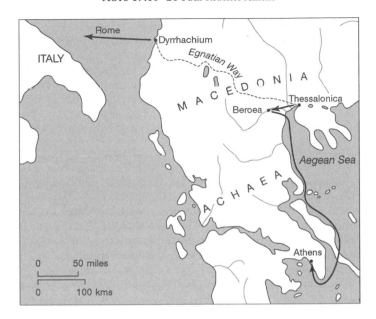

Acts 17.10–21

with many different types of opponent. In what we English call football, the Germans have a reputation for thoroughness, the Brazilians for outrageous flair, the Italians for a sense of style, and so on. It's no good getting ready for a game against Holland as though you were about to play Argentina. And so on.

Luke has shown us how the **gospel** matches up against two major opponents: the 'zealous' Jews, in synagogues around Turkey and now in northern Greece, and the economic and political forces of the Roman Empire. But there is an entire world of thought – and I mean 'world of thought' – which we haven't yet had on stage. This is the hugely important sphere of the prevailing ancient philosophies. They conditioned how thousands of 'ordinary people' saw the world, what they thought of as reasonable and unreasonable, what they thought about 'the gods', what they thought human life was for and how best you should live it. Millions who had never studied

81

'philosophy', who maybe even couldn't read or write for themselves, were nevertheless deeply influenced by the major currents of thought that were debated in the schools, just as plenty of people today who have never studied philosophy or economics are massively influenced by popular presentations in the media of large and complex ideas.

And now Luke is taking Paul to where he must meet the ancient philosophies head on: Athens. This is a different team. You can't just say what you say in the synagogue, or even what you said in a hurry in Lystra. This demands a different game plan, a different strategy. Luke is building us up for a big set piece, one of the classic scenes in the whole book. Athens is a major showdown between the new young **faith** and the old, established, tried and tested philosophies of the Western world, which still, in various modern guises, dominate people's thinking. Until we've thought through this confrontation, we are not ready for the global contest.

It is by no means clear that Paul intended to go to Athens (or, having done that, to go on to Corinth). Philippi stood on the Via Egnatia, the high road to Rome. From there you would naturally go west, through Thessalonica, across northern Greece, and take a boat across the narrow straits to Brindisi on the south-eastern coast (the 'heel') of Italy, and so on to Rome itself. What more natural, since Paul had been commanded by God to go to northern Greece, than that he should now go on, through north-west Macedonia, all the way along the road to the sea, and then – who knows? maybe on to Caesar's own city?

That might have been natural, but it wasn't, it seems, what the **holy spirit** had in mind. One day (we can see Paul musing about it in 19.21) but not yet. The reason he goes to Beroea, which is off the Via Egnatia to the south, is that the Thessalonian Christians bundled him off there as being more off the beaten track. And, once there, he seems to have been less than usual master of his own movements, with the local believers putting him on a boat to go, not west to the capital of the Roman world, but south to the ancient capital of the Greek one. Get the philosophy sorted out and the politics can follow in due course.

First, though, the welcome interlude at Beroea. What a relief to find some people who are actually prepared to say, in effect,

'Well, we hadn't ever thought of this sort of thing before; but let's have a look at the scriptures and see if it's true.' That is, again and again, all a preacher can really ask for: don't take it from me, we say, go home and study the scriptures for yourselves and see how it all fits together. But the (by now) inevitable happens, and zealous Jews arrive from Thessalonica, hot on Paul's trail. This time it is only Paul who is packed off, while the others stay, perhaps to help new believers become firmly established. From Beroea, which is somewhat inland, he is taken down to the coast and put on a ship, sailing round to Athens. There he was, alone, in the great intellectual capital of the ancient world.

And it was full – of idols. And ideas. And intellectual and cultural novelties of every kind. Luke's comment on the latter point (verse 21) is a bit sarcastic, since 'new' in the ancient world was one of the worst sneers you could offer, especially about an idea. 'Old' was best; everyone knew that. Mere novelty was ephemeral, here today and gone tomorrow. But if you were interested in temples, and idols, and every kind of religious cult, Athens was the place. It had everything – including some cultural symbols which would have strongly confirmed Paul's Jewish perception that idol-worship went closely hand in hand with sexual immorality. A glance at vase-paintings, statues, cult objects and so on in museums today leaves little to the imagination. Worship these gods, and your body (and everybody else's, too) becomes a toy. No question what a devout Jew would think about that.

Paul was not short of places to go and people to talk to. He did what he usually did in the synagogue, but we have no report of the reaction. More interesting to Luke at this point, he argues in the market-place, which in Athens was a market-place of ideas as well as of other commodities. And there it was that he met the great philosophical schools of the day, the Epicureans and Stoics.

Briefly, the Epicureans held a theory according to which the world and the gods were a long way away from one another, with little or no communication. The result was that one should get on with life as best one could, discovering how to gain maximum pleasure from a quiet, sedate existence. The Stoics, however, believed that divinity lay within the present world, and within each human being, so that this divine force, though hardly personal, could be discovered and harnessed. Good human living then ('virtue') consisted in getting in touch with, and living according to, this inner divine 'rationality'. What would a Jew, or a Christian, say to either of those? We are about to find out.

But the request for Paul to speak at the Areopagus, the highest court in the city, set on a rock from which one could look down on the famous market-place and across to the still more famous Acropolis with its spectacular temples, was not as friendly and innocuous as it sounds. It wasn't a matter of, 'Well, here's an interesting fellow; let's see what he has to say.' It contained a double veiled threat. 'This man', they said, 'seems to be a preacher of foreign divinities.' Well, yes, in a sense, though that was based on their misunderstanding of the fundamental content of Paul's **message**, which was Jesus and the **resurrection**. Resurrection, which in Greek is *anastasis*, seems to have sounded to them like another god, or rather, since the word is feminine, a goddess: Jesus and his female consort! Who on earth are they? 'What is this word-scatterer trying to say?' (The term 'word-scatterer' is full of contempt: this man who scatters words all over the place like a jackdaw picking up interesting things and dropping half of them on the way back to his nest.)

In particular, the charge of 'preaching foreign divinities' was the charge, famously and classically, on which Socrates, the greatest philosopher of all time, had been tried and condemned. Athens may have been interested in new ideas, but divinities from elsewhere could easily get you into trouble. Serious trouble. Especially if someone proclaiming them was starting a secret society with mysteries only open to the initiates. '*Are we permitted* to know', they asked with veiled and sarcastic threat, 'what this new teaching is all about?' Are you allowed to tell us these secret doctrines, or are they only for those you will collect into a dangerous little gang? In other words, you'd better get your philosophy sorted out, or we have other questions we may want to ask as well. Are you a danger to our state? Paul is thus given the chance of a lifetime, but also a multi-layered challenge which will stretch his theological and rhetorical skills in quite a new way.

ACTS 17.22–34

Paul Among the Philosophers (I)

[22]So Paul stood up in the midst of the Areopagus.

'Men of Athens,' he said, 'I see that you are in every way an extremely religious people. [23]For as I was going along and looking at your objects of worship, I saw an altar with the inscription, TO AN UNKNOWN GOD. Well: I'm here to tell you about what it is that you are worshipping in ignorance. [24]The God who made the world and everything in it, the one who is Lord of heaven and earth, doesn't live in temples made by human hands. [25]Nor is he looked after by human hands, as though he needed something, since he himself gives life and breath to everyone. [26]He made from one stock every race of humans to live on the whole face of the earth, allotting them their properly ordained times and the boundaries for their dwellings. [27]The aim was that they would search for God, and perhaps reach out for him and find him. Indeed, he is actually not far from each one of us, [28]for in him we live and move and exist; as also some of your own poets have put it, "For we are his offspring".

[29]'Well, then, if we really are God's offspring, we ought not to suppose that the divinity is like gold or silver or stone, formed by human skill and ingenuity. [30]That was just ignorance; but the time for it has passed, and God has drawn a veil over it. Now, instead, he commands the whole human race, everywhere, to repent, [31]because he has established a day on which he intends to call the world to account with full and proper justice by a man whom he has appointed. God has given all people his pledge of this by raising this man from the dead.'

[32]When they heard about the resurrection of the dead, some of them ridiculed Paul. But others said, 'We will give you another hearing about this.' [33]So Paul went out from their presence. [34]But some people joined him and believed, including Dionysius, a member of the court of the Areopagus, and a woman named Damaris, and others with them.

One of the signs of being really good at chess is that you can play more than one opponent at the same time. Sometimes grand masters will put on a display where they play several different people all at once, walking from one chessboard to the next and making the next move, leaving a string of opponents, with only one game each to concentrate on, baffled and eventually defeated.

Something like that is the effect Luke intends to create with this summary of what Paul said on the Areopagus. We're going to take two bites at this cherry, because it's so important, so unique, and so dense that it's better to give ourselves the space to mull it over properly, not splitting it in two in the process but reading the whole thing twice over.

I assume, by the way, that Acts 17.22–31 is a summary of what Paul said on that day. I make this assumption for two reasons. First, there is a tradition in Greek history-writing, which Luke certainly knows and is certainly imitating, that even if you don't have a full record of what was said on a particular occasion you ought to make up something that more or less summarizes what would have been said. Second, this is the Paul who, when preaching to friends, went on and on past midnight so that someone fell out of a window asleep (20.7–12). Can we really believe that when he was given his big chance in the highest forum in the Greek world he spoke for only *two minutes* – which is roughly how long, even going slowly, it takes to read verses 22–31 aloud in the Greek?

But even if Luke has telescoped things together, we can still see what Paul is up to. It's a highly skilled performance, giving a vivid example of what Paul meant when he said, writing later to Corinth, that it was his aim to 'take every thought captive to obey the **Messiah**' (2 Corinthians 10.5). He is not just content to press the buttons of the local culture, to give a nod to an inscription here and a poet there, to show (as it were) that what he has to say hooks in nicely to their way of thinking, so that his **message** isn't really so very different from what they know already. Nothing of the kind. The grain of truth in the suggestion, though, comes right at the beginning, when Paul talks about the famous altar with the inscription, 'to an unknown god'. What might this be all about?

86

One of the other philosophical options available to a serious first-century pagan, discussed by Cicero in a book written about a century before Paul's day, is what became known as the Academic, or the view taken (at one time at least) by the 'Academy' founded by Plato himself. According to the Academic point of view, there is simply not enough evidence for us to be able to tell whether the gods exist or not, and, if they do, what if anything they want from us. This can breed a shoulder-shrugging couldn't-care-less attitude; or it might produce – and Paul gives it the benefit of the doubt here – a kind of humility, an openness, a readiness for something new. There is all the difference in the world between someone who says, 'I know we'll never know much about the gods, and actually I'm quite happy about that. I'm just going to offer a lamb on this altar once a year in case, and I hope that does whatever needs doing because I'd rather live my own life my own way', and someone who says, 'I can't help believing that there must be, somewhere, some divine being who is actually more than we have realized, and more important than we have usually supposed. So I'm keeping the windows of my heart open, and I'm hoping that one day I'll find out.' The first we might call 'closed agnosticism': we don't know, we can't know, and I like it like that. The second we might call 'open agnosticism' or even 'humble agnosticism': we don't seem to know at present, but that means it's quite possible, perhaps even likely, that there is something more that we could know in principle if only we could discover how; and I would love to know if we could. Actually, you could call the first inconsistent agnosticism, since it professes absolute certainty that we can't know anything, which is paradoxical to say the least. In that case the second could be consistent agnosticism, being agnostic about agnosticism itself.

And it is the second that Paul assumes was intended by whoever put up the altar 'to an unknown god'. In fact, he begins and ends the address with the question of ignorance and what God is doing about it. Having begun with this peculiar altar, he ends with a remarkable statement, that God has been well aware that people have been ignorant, but that this was for a period of time only, and the period has now run out (verse 30).

Here we see, creeping up upon the Athenian listeners, an idea which must have been very strange to them: that history is moving in a forwards direction, with a divinely ordained goal in view, and that it matters to discern where we are within that particular plan. This is, of course, a deeply Jewish view, and it prepares the way for the decisive announcement of what God has done in Jesus and what he has thereby promised to do. But the theme of ignorance, at the start and finish of the address, is Paul's way both of starting at a point within the Athenians' own complex and many-sided systems of worship and (having found there an open window which might just let in some light) declaring that the Academics had a point, but that the time for that point has now passed. Simultaneously, of course, he is declaring, over against the sharp hint in verse 19, that his hearers are indeed permitted to know what it is he is saying. He has nothing to hide, but rather something to reveal.

But reading further we quickly discover that Paul was not simply constructing a would-be theology out of bits and pieces of the local culture, in order, as the phrase goes, to discover what God might be doing in this place and do it with him. According to Paul, the main thing that God was doing in Athens was shaking his head in sorrow and warning of imminent judgment: because Athens was full of temples, and the local people were constantly bringing **sacrifices** and offerings to gods and goddesses of every possible kind. And the God who made the whole world, Paul declares, does not live in houses made by human hands – with a wave of the arm, we may imagine, towards the Parthenon, standing majestically in the background as it still does, one of the wonders of the architectural world and one of the most beautiful buildings ever built. Nice job, says Paul in effect, but it misses the point: *c'est magnifique, mais ce n'est pas le Dieu.* And as for bringing animal sacrifices to the true God: well, this is the wrong way round! It is *he* who gives everything to *us*, not the other way about. At this point Paul is close to the short, breathless statement in 14.15–18.

And, in particular, the one thing we should be clear about is this: whatever God may be like, we can be sure that all these idols – gold, silver, stone or whatever – are similarly missing the point (17.29). They too are merely a sign of ignorance, of humans blundering about: sensing a presence, a divinity, but not really knowing what to do about it or why.

So far, so Jewish. All this is very typical of the anti-pagan stance taken by many Jewish apologists at the time and since. And it conforms closely, as Paul reminds the Thessalonians, to what he said in his initial preaching to them (1 Thessalonians 1). It is the message about the creator God, which is the foundation of all **good news**, all **gospel**. Without a creator God, even such good news as you might have (there is hope for bliss yet to come) is purchased at the cost of very bad news (this bliss will not involve the rescue of the present beautiful creation). With a creator God, you know that even though things seem to have gone very badly wrong in certain respects you are not simply in the hands, or at the disposal, of a bunch of incompetent, mutually squabbling, or actually malevolent deities. People sometimes grumble that Paul doesn't seem to have put much 'gospel' into this speech. But actually the whole thing is good news, from start to finish. The specific 'good news' of Jesus Christ grows directly out of this doctrine of creation. But to see this more clearly we need another section.

ACTS 17.22–34

Paul Among the Philosophers (II)

[22]So Paul stood up in the midst of the Areopagus.

'Men of Athens,' he said, 'I see that you are in every way an extremely religious people. [23]For as I was going along and looking at your objects of worship, I saw an altar with the inscription, TO AN UNKNOWN GOD. Well: I'm here to tell you about what it is that you are worshipping in ignorance. [24]The God who made the world and everything in it, the one who is Lord of heaven and earth, doesn't live in temples made by human hands. [25]Nor does he need to be looked after by human hands, as though he needed something, since he himself gives life and breath to everyone. [26]He made from one stock every race of humans to live on the whole face of the earth, allotting them their properly ordained times and boundaries for their dwellings. [27]The aim was that they would search for God, and perhaps reach out for him and find him. Indeed, he is actually not far from each one of us, ²⁸for in him we live and move and exist; as also some of your own poets have put it, "For we are his offspring".

²⁹'Well, then, if we really are God's offspring, we ought not to suppose that the divinity is like gold or silver or stone, formed by human skill and ingenuity. ³⁰That was just ignorance; but the time for it has passed, and God has drawn a veil over it. But now he commands the whole human race, everywhere, to repent, ³¹because he has established a day on which he intends to call the world to account with full and proper justice by a man whom he has appointed. God has given all people his pledge of this by raising this man from the dead.'

³²When they heard about the resurrection of the dead, some of them ridiculed Paul. But others said, 'We will give you another hearing about this.' ³³So Paul went out from their presence. ³⁴But some people joined him and believed, including Dionysius, a member of the court of the Areopagus, and a woman named Damaris, and others with them.

So we continue with our chess game, with Paul playing the role of grand master and taking on all the players of Athens at once. We have seen how he agrees with the Academy that it is indeed impossible, granted what was available to them, to know very much about the true God. Ah but, he says, God himself has been aware of this difficulty, and has now brought this 'time of ignorance' to an end. We have seen that, in typically Jewish style, and building on the critique of idols and temples throughout Jewish scripture and tradition, he rejects utterly the whole idea of temples, **sacrifices** and statues of the gods. Instead, he tells the **good news** of a creator God who made the world and everything in it.

Now we shall see how, in dealing with both the Epicureans and the Stoics, he shows how this God not only *can* be known, in a way which Greek philosophy never bargained for, but actually *wants* to be known. And he brings the address to a close with a flourish by telling the (again, very Jewish) story of the future hope: God is going to hold a great assize, and put the whole world right!

The Epicureans, we recall, believed that the gods, if they existed, were very far away, and had more or less nothing to do with human beings. As a result, they were supremely happy; and if we want to approximate to them as best we can we will learn to moderate our desires, to do nothing that would feed our natural hopes or fears, to live as quietly as possible with just the right amount of everything. The ideal life is independent, untroubled, unworried about larger questions, including that of one's own destiny.

An Epicurean would therefore have agreed substantially with Paul's rather scathing comments about normal pagan worship, but for more or less the opposite reason to the one Paul gives. For the Epicurean, the gods were far away and so didn't want anything from us; for Paul, God is very close to us, the giver of everything to us, the passionate seeker who wants us to seek him in return – and therefore doesn't want animal sacrifices from us. Paul agrees with the Epicurean that God and the world are not the same thing. But he confronts the Epicurean head on when he says that God is not far from any one of us, and longs for a relationship of love with all his human creatures. The Epicurean would be fascinated, startled, irritated perhaps, but teased enough to want to hear more.

The Stoic, by contrast, would be happy to hear that there is indeed a divine **life** which is in all human beings, though Paul has identified it with life and breath rather than the cold principle of the *logos*, 'rationality'. And the Stoic could accept, in his own sense, the quote from the Athenian poet Aratus in verse 28, 'for we are also his offspring'. Aratus pretty certainly meant this in a Stoic sense; Paul is treading the fine line here between demonstrating his familiarity with their own culture, inviting Stoics to come on board with what he's saying, and offering something quite new and revolutionary. For Paul, as a Jew, the idea of humans as 'children of God' has to do with our being made in God's image (he does not here have in mind the specifically Christian notion of believers as God's adopted sons and daughters, as in Galatians 4.4–7). To the Stoic pantheist, in other words, Paul declares that God and the world are not the same thing, but that the impulse which pushes you to suppose that they are is the true impulse which ought to lead you to reach out and grope for the real God who is indeed not far off. The Stoic, like the Epicurean, is thus challenged, encouraged, teased and perhaps drawn to consider the matter more closely.

But the really stunning moment of the address comes, of course, at the end. Indeed, the whole build-up, the careful discussion of who God really is and his relation to the world, the standard Jewish critique of idolatry and temples coupled with the creative use of local colour – all this is to ensure that, when Paul finally gets to explain his supposed 'foreign divinities' of Jesus and **resurrection**, there will at least be a small chance that some will understand what he is saying. We notice again that as the speech turns the corner into the home straight Paul insists that he and his hearers are living at a new moment in the history of the world, a moment at which the 'times of ignorance', the times when people could hardly be expected to know who God was, were being brought to an end. Now something new had happened! Now there was something to say, particular news about particular events and a particular man, which provided just the sort of new evidence that the genuinely open-minded agnostic should be prepared to take into account, that the Epicurean and Stoic should see as forming both a confirmation of the correct elements in their worldviews and a challenge to the misleading elements, and that the ordinary pagan, trundling off to yet another temple with yet another sacrifice, should see as good news indeed. This God, declares Paul, has set a time when he is going to do what the Jewish tradition always said he would do, indeed what he must do if he is indeed the good and wise creator: he will set the world right, will call it to account, will in other words *judge* it in the full, Hebraic, biblical sense.

And the creator God will do this through a particular man whom he has appointed for the task, in other words, Jesus himself. Whether it is significant that Paul does not mention the name of Jesus throughout the speech it is hard to say, but he has been talking about him in the market-place and it's clear who he means. How do we know that Jesus is the coming judge? Because, says Paul, God has raised him from the dead.

It's important to note that, there in the Areopagus, this wasn't just a ludicrous notion which every sensible person knew was out of the question; it went directly against the founding charter of the Areopagus itself. In a fifth-century BC play by the Athenian dramatist Aeschylus, which would have been well known in Paul's day, the god Apollo inaugurates the court of the Areopagus. And one of the things he says, solemnly and as it were bindingly, is that 'when a man dies, and his blood is spilled on the ground, *there is no resurrection*'. Resurrection is flatly ruled out, according to the ground rules of the Areopagus. Paul firmly puts it back in. This is the fulcrum around which the world turns.

And it is resurrection which explains why Jesus is the coming judge. It isn't anything so trivial as that the resurrection demonstrates Jesus' divinity, or even his human superiority, and thus qualifies him for this particularly tricky task. Rather, it is that with the resurrection of Jesus God's new world has begun; in other words, his being raised from the dead is the start, the paradigm case, the foundation, the beginning, of that great setting-right which God will do for the whole cosmos at the end. The risen body of Jesus is the one bit of the physical universe that has already been 'set right'. Jesus is therefore the one through whom everything else will be 'set right'.

The double challenge, then, is: first, repent. Turn back from your ways, particularly from your idolatry, your supposing that the gods can be made of gold or silver, or that they live in man-made houses, or that they want or need animal sacrifices! Turn away from these things, give them up, shake yourself free of them. And, second, turn to the living God (see 1 Thessalonians 1.9), grope for him and find him (Acts 17.27). You will only do that if you abandon the parodies, the idols that get in the way and distract you from the true God. But it can be done. And it can be done because the living God is at work, changing the times and seasons so that now the day of ignorance is over and the time of revealing the truth has arrived. Recognize where you are in God's timetable, with the landmark of Jesus' resurrection to guide you. Think hard about the unknown God, and let new light from the true God flood through this open window and transform you. Leave behind the distant signposts of philosophies, poets and the religious rubbish that humans manufacture. There is a living God, and he is now calling everyone, everywhere.

Paul has not only answered their question, to explain about Jesus and the resurrection. He has shown the Epicureans and Stoics that he isn't just someone who scatters words around to no good purpose. And, in case anyone should still imagine he might be subversive, he is – but in the way that a person is subversive who, seeing the band struggling to play a difficult piece of music, and making various mistakes, comes along and shows how to play the whole thing perfectly. It may be galling, but they can't grumble. The tune makes sense. The harmony works. The question of whether they will now want to play it themselves remains open. Luke indicates at the end that some were prepared to try.

ACTS 18.1–11

A Year in Corinth

¹After this, Paul left Athens and went to Corinth. ²There he found a Jew named Aquila, who hailed from Pontus, and had recently arrived from Italy with Priscilla his wife, due to Claudius' edict banishing all Jews from Rome. Paul paid them a visit ³and, because they were in the same business, he stayed with them and worked. They were, by trade, tent-makers.

⁴Paul argued every sabbath in the synagogue, and persuaded both Jews and Greeks. ⁵When Silas and Timothy arrived from Macedonia, Paul was putting great energy into the task of bearing forthright witness to the Jews that the Messiah really was Jesus. ⁶When they opposed him, and blasphemed, he shook out his clothes.

'Your blood be on your own heads!' he said. 'I am innocent. From now on I shall go to the Gentiles.'

⁷He moved on from the synagogue, and went in to the house of a man named Titius Justus, a godfearer who lived opposite the synagogue. ⁸But Crispus, the ruler of the synagogue, believed in the Lord, with all his household, and many of the Corinthians heard about it, came to faith, and were baptized.

⁹The Lord spoke to Paul by night in a vision.

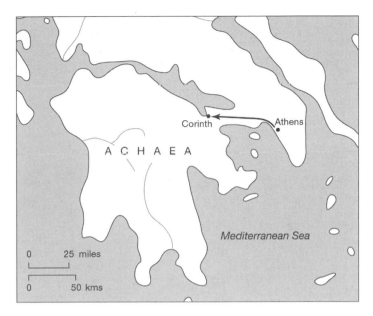

Acts 18.1

'Don't be afraid,' he said. 'Speak on, and don't be silent, [10]because I am with you, and nobody will be able to lay a finger on you to harm you. There are many of my people in this city.'

[11]He stayed there a year and six months, teaching the word of God among them.

This morning, knowing I was going to be thinking about Corinth, I helped myself to a big bowl of Greek yoghurt and honey for breakfast. It still takes me straight back to the little streetside cafe where, in the early 1990s, I first tasted that simple, but wonderful, Greek dish. It was my first visit to the famous city to which Paul wrote more than to anywhere else.

Corinth was known in the ancient world, of course, for delicacies of every kind, and several of them considerably less innocent than yoghurt and honey. With seaports notorious in the ancient world, as in the modern, for every kind of immorality, Corinth sat on the isthmus that bears its name

95

with not one but two seaports, and a clever system by which ships could be hauled across from one gulf to the other. (The canal which now enables ships to sail right through was dug much later, though Nero made a vain attempt at such a project not long after Paul's time there.) Corinth had been destroyed a couple of hundred years earlier, and then refounded in 44 BC as a Roman colony and the capital of the province of Achaea. Like Philippi, perhaps even more so, Corinth was very proud of its Roman status. More Roman than Rome itself, some people commented.

In Corinth, Paul was back to the normal procedure: debate in the synagogue, and then, if they rejected the **message**, turning to **Gentiles**. But here it was with a difference. In the Galatian cities on his first journey, and then in Philippi, Thessalonica and even Beroea, his visits were cut short by angry reaction, often initiated by 'zealous' Jews who resented both his message and its simultaneous claim to be both the fulfilment of the ancient scriptures and freely available to all without distinction, Jew and Gentile alike. But in Corinth he stayed longer than a few days, or even a few weeks. He stayed for a year and a half – the longest time he had been in any one place for quite some while, probably since the time back in Syrian Antioch in 11.26.

There are three reasons for this, and the present passage indicates two of them. The first is that he met a Jewish couple who ran a business in the same line of work that Paul himself practised, namely, tent-making. This last piece of information is new to us in Acts. The impression Luke might have given is that Paul hadn't been staying anywhere long enough to set up shop, to sort out his tools and acquire raw materials, and to offer his services for trade. In fact, as we know from the Thessalonian letters in particular, he certainly worked there (night and day, he says), partly so as not to be a burden on the church and partly to set them an example of how Christians should behave (1 Thessalonians 2.9; 3.11; 2 Thessalonians 3.7–13). He emphasizes this point again in writing to Corinth, later on (1 Corinthians 9). Some may be surprised to think of Paul as a manual worker, but he wouldn't have seen anything strange in it. It was commonplace among Jewish teachers for

rabbis to have a trade by which to support themselves and their families. Paul had no pretensions on such a matter.

'Tent-making' is a little tight as a description of what he, Priscilla and Aquila actually did. The word in question probably covered all kinds of other leather and similar goods, and the 'tents' in question would be used, not just as mostly in today's Western world for tourist and recreational purposes, but for a wide variety of military, industrial and other uses. It looks as though Aquila and Priscilla had set up a business in Corinth, in which Paul was, in effect, taken on as a partner, or even as a hired worker.

Aquila and Priscilla seem, in fact, to have become close friends of Paul. He refers to them in his first letter to Corinth (16.19) as well as in Romans 16.3; by the time of the latter, they are back in Rome, having spent some time in Ephesus in between (Acts 18.26). They are almost as widely travelled as Paul himself.

The reason Luke gives for their being in Corinth, rather than Rome where they had settled and to which they were obviously happy to return, is that Claudius, the emperor at the time, had expelled all Jews from Rome. This interesting piece of information tallies reasonably closely with two parallel reports in later pagan historians. The exact date of this expulsion is unclear. We may well be right in assuming that 'all Jews' actually meant 'most Jews', but it is still a fact of some importance, for two reasons in particular.

First, the Roman historian Suetonius explains that Claudius expelled the Jews because they were rioting, and he gives an explanation for the riots: *impulsore Chresto*. That cryptic Latin phrase could mean 'at the instigation of Chrestus'; and 'Chrestus', whose middle vowel would be pronounced 'ee' to rhyme with 'cream', would sound very similar to the word 'Christus', whose 'i' would be similarly long, as in the first vowel of the name 'Ian'. Was Suetonius, perhaps, aware of a dim or second-hand report that some people in the Jewish community had been squabbling, and then rioting, because a message about a **Messiah**, a *Christus*, had arrived in Rome and caused the same kind of uproar that it had done in Antioch, Thessalonica and other places? This is typical of the kind of question ancient historians have to deal in all the time. It may just be coincidence, but it may just be a telltale hint.

The second reason that Claudius's edict is important is that, like other similar imperial edicts, it was rescinded when Claudius died and his successor, Nero, came to the throne (AD 54). That's why Priscilla and Aquila were able to return to Rome, being there by the time Paul writes his letter. Perhaps it is from them that he has heard of the difficulties caused for the Gentile Christians in Rome, who, having lived for some years as a (more or less) Gentiles-only church, were now having to come to terms with a large number both of believing and of unbelieving Jews in the city once more. And that, in turn, helps us understand why Paul wrote Romans; but that again is another story.

Coming rapidly back to Corinth, I said there were two reasons why Paul stayed so long – apart from the fact that, for whatever reason, he wasn't thrown out; maybe the city was sufficiently large and cosmopolitan to cope more easily than some other places with the toing and froing between Paul and the synagogue community; and maybe, as we shall see, a larger number of the leading Jews in Corinth believed the **gospel** than had been the case elsewhere. The second main reason is the remarkable vision he had one night (verses 9–10). Whereas the last vision he had had was of someone telling him to go somewhere he hadn't expected (16.9), this one was telling him to stay put. And the Lord, speaking to him personally and not through an angel or a figure like a 'man from Macedon', gave him an interesting reason: There are many of my people in this city. In other words, evangelism is only just beginning here. Settle down and get on with it. I am at work here, and you must trust me and stick it out.

Presumably Paul needed that encouragement. Visions, both in the New Testament and in much later experience, are not normally granted just for the sake of it. Perhaps, having been opposed and reviled in the synagogue, he had expected to be run out of town, or at least to be sufficient of an embarrassment to the new church that it would be better for him to leave. He may even have had a desire to move on, since travelling from place to place gets into the blood and he may well have wanted, not only to return to Antioch and Jerusalem, but also to get back on the road that would eventually take him to Rome. But no: he must stay put. One of the many lessons Acts teaches quietly, as it goes along, is that you tend to get the guidance you need when you need it, not before, and not in too much detail. Enough to know that the Lord Jesus has many people in this city, and that he wants you, Paul, to stay here and work with them.

The details of his accustomed torrid time in the synagogue are interesting for two things in particular. First, he makes a kind of formal protest against the synagogue, declaring as he does to the Ephesian elders in 20.26 that he is innocent of their blood – which sounds alarming, as indeed in a sense it is. Paul takes his office of apostleship extremely seriously. He really does believe that from place to place he is going round giving the Jewish communities their main chance to respond to the news about their own Messiah. If they reject it, he will turn, as he usually does, to the Gentiles. But this leads to the second point of considerable interest: because the synagogue ruler, a man named Crispus, becomes a believer, as do many others. Paul himself baptizes Crispus, as we discover in 1 Corinthians 1.14. Perhaps this high-profile convert is part at least of the reason why there is less immediate, and less violent, trouble than there might otherwise have been.

In any case, Paul could hardly be accused of being shy in his next move. Having left the synagogue, he begins to teach in the house of Titius Justus, a godfearer who had presumably heard the gospel in the synagogue and, like many in this category, had responded in **faith**. And Titius Justus' house, we learn, was right across from the synagogue itself. The slang but in this case appropriate phrase 'in your face' comes readily to mind. The gospel is not something to be hidden.

ACTS 18.12–17

Christianity Declared Legal in Achaea

[12]When Gallio was proconsul of Achaea, the Jews made a concerted attack on Paul, and led him to the official tribunal.

¹³'This man', they said, 'is teaching people to worship God in illegal ways.'

¹⁴Paul was getting ready to speak when Gallio intervened.

'Look here, you Jews,' he said to them. 'If this was a matter of serious wrongdoing or some wicked villainy, I would receive your plea in the proper way. ¹⁵But if this is a dispute about words, names and laws within your own customs, you can sort it out among yourselves. I don't intend to be a judge in such matters.'

¹⁶Then he dismissed them from the tribunal. ¹⁷But the crowd seized Sosthenes, the ruler of the synagogue, and beat him right there in front of the tribunal. Gallio, however, totally ignored this.

Though I have walked with great pleasure in the hills of the north of England, both the Lake District in the west and the Cheviot hills in the east, I have only once walked in the almost equally famous Peak District of Derbyshire, in the middle of the country. (Southerners think the Peak District is in the north, but it is in fact more or less equidistant from the Isle of Wight on the south coast and Berwick on Tweed on the Scottish border. Maps are important for understanding Acts, so we might as well clear up some local issues while we're about it.) I had a day all to myself and set off with map and compass. The cloud was high, but sufficiently thick to make it unclear where exactly the sun was. And it wasn't long before I found myself, on a high plateau, more or less entirely lost.

There were no particular paths in the area I was traversing. Though the ground rose and fell this way and that, the absence of major landmarks made it actually quite difficult to tell whether I was higher or lower than the hillocks I was looking at within a large area of a few square miles. I could tell from the light and the compass the general direction I ought to be heading in, but it wasn't at all clear just where I actually was. It's not that helpful to know which way is north if you don't know where on the map you happen to be standing.

Just as I imagined that maybe I was starting to go round in circles, with all the terrain around me looking the same, I spotted something that looked like a small cairn, a good mile or so away. I made for it with relief. When I got to it I was able to identify it exactly on the map; and from there I could at last figure out where I was going. From being almost totally lost I suddenly knew exactly where I was.

That is the sense that historians have had when Gallio appears on the scene in Acts 18.12. Figuring out how to date Paul's life and journeys has been a notorious puzzle for many generations of scholars. There were no fixed points, no landmarks, nothing really you could latch on to and say, 'Here at least we are on solid ground.' Then the archaeologists turned up an inscription in Delphi, a few miles north-west of Corinth, and quite suddenly we knew exactly where we were. Gallio, who was the younger brother of the famous philosopher Seneca (who was himself tutor to the Emperor Nero) was proconsul of Achaea in the second half of 51 and on into early 52, before leaving through ill health. Scholars are now more or less agreed that Paul must have appeared before him some time in late 51. Since Paul seems to have left Corinth shortly after being acquitted, his 18 months in the city will therefore date from late 49 or early 50 to the middle or end of 51. From being just another odd reference in Acts, the reference to Gallio has become the peg on which a good deal of the rest of Pauline chronology can hang.

But the Gallio incident is a landmark for another reason as well. The question dangling over the young church at several points in the narrative, and perhaps nowhere more strikingly so far than in the charges hurled at Paul and Silas in Philippi (16.20–21) and Thessalonica (17.7), is this: does being a Christian mean you are acting illegally according to Roman law and custom? Ought (in other words) the Roman state to be doing its best, for its own reasons, quite irrespective of theological disputes with the still unbelieving synagogue community, to be doing its best to stamp out the new movement?

Or was the community of Jesus' followers rather to be seen simply as a variant of Judaism, and therefore to be permitted? This latter possibility hooks in to a tricky set of questions which historians still puzzle over. It used to be said that the Romans had given the Jews the official status of a 'permitted religion', but this whole concept now turns out to be more complex than we used to think. Certainly, since at least the time of Julius Caesar, Jews had been allowed to practise their own religion and were not forced to worship the Roman gods. The Romans were, at their best, pragmatic rather than dogmatic, and had realized that (from their point of view) the Jews were remarkably stubborn in matters of religion and would resist tooth and nail any attempts to force them either to quit their own religion or to worship Roman gods as well. This came into a new focus because of the imperial cult which was rapidly introduced around the Roman Empire. Corinth itself had a large temple to the imperial family, which you can still see, on a plinth at the west end of the Forum, deliberately built up so that it was higher than all the other temples in the town (and there were several). Would the Jews be required to worship the emperor and his family, as everyone else was? No, came the answer; a deal was struck, and they agreed to pray *for* the emperor but not to pray *to* him.

So the question came back as a matter of urgency. The Christians claimed that they were the fulfilment of what Israel's God had always promised. They naturally saw themselves, therefore, as sharing the status of the 'parent' body (however formal or informal that status actually was, or was interpreted as being). Many in the Jewish communities, however, being as we have seen 'righteously indignant' at such claims, and intending to repudiate them fiercely as the young Saul of Tarsus himself had done, wanted to see the Christian movement as a nonsensical heresy, a way of life which had cast off Judaism entirely.

We can see why. The Christians didn't insist on **circumcision** for non-Jewish converts; they did insist on believing Jews and **Gentiles** sharing table-**fellowship**; and they had expressed, early on, a strong repudiation of the **Temple** in Jerusalem. This situation had many potentially explosive elements, one being the question: if the Christians were getting into trouble for whatever reason (say, for being heard to suggest that there was 'another king'), might this rebound on the Jewish communities as well? Might non-Christian Jews be at risk, in other words, through 'guilt by association', if the Roman authorities came to see the Christians as simply a particularly troublesome variety of Judaism? And might not this sense have been increased if

Claudius had already expelled Jews from Rome because of riots over someone who sounds suspiciously like 'Christus'?

At times of cultural, political and religious tension, logical precision isn't nearly as important as moods and feelings. And feelings in Corinth were running high among those who had stayed in the synagogue community, resisting the **message** of Paul and the example of their synagogue ruler Crispus, who had believed in Jesus. So their charge against Paul, brought at the tribunal platform which you can still see in Corinth, is that he is inciting people to worship God in illegal ways.

Illegal, comes the question, for whom? Gallio, who has presumably taken the trouble to inform himself both about the relevant laws and about what the new 'religion' is up to, dismisses the charge. *It is an internal matter within Judaism*, not something that Roman law need bother its head, or its lawyers, about.

Paul hadn't brought the case; he was the defendant. But all the same it was a major victory for him and his friends. Not only was he vindicated (another example of Luke telling the story of Paul on trial); the case set a new benchmark which the Christians could hardly have dared to hope for. In Achaea at least (central and southern Greece) Christianity could now presume to share such permitted status as the Jews enjoyed. How this situation changed so that by about AD 110, when Pliny was governor of Bithynia, his correspondence with the Emperor Trajan could assume that professing Christianity was a serious offence, is difficult to say. But Gallio's ruling provided a very welcome breathing space for the church, at least in southern Greece. Sometimes, as Luke no doubt wants us to remark once more, even pagan officials do things which genuinely and thoroughly advance the cause of the **kingdom of God**.

Why the crowd at the trial proceeded to beat up the new synagogue ruler, Sosthenes, is not at all clear. Quite possibly a crowd had gathered who were not particularly in favour of either the Jewish community or the Christians, and who were just annoyed at the whole fuss. Gallio pays no attention to the violence. Luke doesn't want us to imagine that Gallio, or any officials, have suddenly become saints, able to do no wrong and to administer an absolute justice. They can bring a measure of good judgment into play, but the world still waits for the true judgment which will sort everything out once and for all.

ACTS 18.18–28

Apollos in Ephesus and Corinth

[18]Paul stayed on for several more days with the Christians, and then said his farewells and sailed away to Syria, taking Priscilla and Aquila with him. In Cenchreae he had his hair cut off, since he was under a vow. [19]When they arrived at Ephesus he left them there, while he himself went into the synagogue and disputed with the Jews. [20]When they asked him to stay with them for a longer time, he refused, [21]and took his leave.

'I will come back to you again,' he said, 'if that's God's will.'

Then he left Ephesus, [22]and went to Caesarea. Then he went up to Jerusalem, greeted the church, and went back to Antioch. [23]When he had spent some time there, he went off again and travelled from one place to another throughout the region of Galatia and Phrygia, encouraging all the disciples.

[24]Now there arrived in Ephesus a Jew named Apollos, who came from Alexandria. He was an eloquent man, and powerful when it came to expounding scripture. [25]He had received instruction in the Way of the Lord. He was an enthusiastic speaker, and taught the things about Jesus accurately, even though he only knew the baptism of John. [26]He began to speak boldly in the synagogue. When Priscilla and Aquila heard him, they took him to one side and expounded the Way of God to him more accurately.

[27]He wanted to go across to Achaea. The Christians in Ephesus, by way of encouragement, wrote letters to the church there to welcome him. On his arrival, his work made a considerable impact, through God's grace, on the believers, [28]since he openly and powerfully refuted the Jews by demonstrating from the scriptures that the Messiah really was Jesus.

These days people will do anything for sponsorship. Recently a Christian leader made well over a million pounds (roughly US$2 million) by running in the London Marathon. I once had a colleague who made a lot of money for his church by

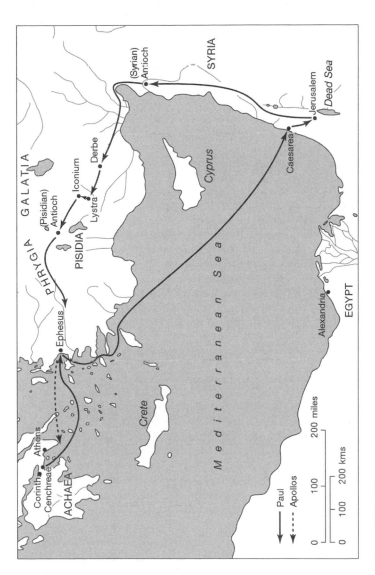

Acts 18.18–28

losing weight during Lent (he put most of it back on quite quickly afterwards, with Easter eggs and so on). Another colleague ran across burning coals in his bare feet; it's one thing to roll your sleeves up and get your hands dirty, but quite another to roll your socks down and get your feet scorched. And, coming closer to this passage, I have witnessed people having their hair cut off, or indeed their beard and moustache cut off, all for the sake of charity.

Was it for something like this that Paul had his hair cut at Cenchreae? Not for charity, of course; I don't think anyone thought of raising money by doing stunts like that until very modern times. But for some more serious purpose, perhaps? Verse 18 often startles people whose impression of Paul is that he sat loose to all rules and regulations, and especially to religious 'rituals'. But there would be nothing in such an act which would imply that Paul was denying the fact, and the sovereignty, of God's grace. It may be that, as we see again in 21.23–24, he was simply following through on what he says in 1 Corinthians 9.20–22: 'To the Jews I became as a Jew, in order to win Jews; to those under the **law** I became as one under the law (though I myself am not under the law) so that I might win those under the law . . . I have become all things to all people, so that I might by any means save some.' Paul would know, from his own experience as a zealous fighter for the glory of God and the law, that anyone with the reputation he himself now had might well be a marked man on arrival in Jerusalem, and if he could be seen on arrival to be visibly and obviously devout according to Jewish tradition, so much the better.

It is possible, though, that there is another explanation. (As to why Luke doesn't explain it more fully himself, it is quite possible, as often in ancient history, that there is an explanation which would be obvious to people at the time, relating to something taken for granted in their world, but which has long since ceased to be obvious to us.) Sometimes, in Paul's world, people would make special promises as a sign and reminder to themselves of solemn prayers and undertakings they had given to God. Perhaps, when the Lord told Paul to remain in Corinth for longer than he had been expecting to do, he decided to mark the moment by not having his hair cut again until he left the area. Cenchreae, where he had it cut, is the eastern port of Corinth. (It is the place in whose church there was a deacon called Phoebe, to whom Paul would later entrust his letter to Rome.) In other words, Paul was finally about to leave Corinthian soil; so, if he had been growing his hair as a sign of his trust in God to keep him safe through a long time in Corinth, now would be the appropriate time to have it cut.

Paul's subsequent travels are hurried through at this point by Luke: ship to Caesarea, up to Jerusalem, back to Antioch, then off again on what is sometimes seen as Paul's 'third missionary journey', going back once more through Galatia and Phrygia, in other words, through central Turkey. He will arrive at Ephesus in due course (19.1), which says something about the route he took to get there, since Ephesus is more or less due west of Iconium and Pisidian Antioch, and the natural way would be to come down into the Lycus valley and along past Laodicea to the coast. But, to prepare us for his arrival and the strange things that happened next, Luke introduces us to another missionary who looms large in one of Paul's letters but who, apart from this passage and the briefest of mentions elsewhere (Titus 3.13), we never meet again: Apollos.

Apollos is one of those fascinating characters in early Christianity who we wish we could get to know better. Paul clearly has a great respect for him, even though, as 1 Corinthians makes clear, his ministry in Corinth, subsequent to Paul's, caused some in the church to declare that they preferred him, resulting in some unpleasant factionalism which Paul had to address head on. 'I planted', he says, 'and Apollos watered, but it was God who gave the growth' (1 Corinthians 3.6). Luke makes a similar point in Acts 18.27 when he insists that the considerable impact Apollos had on arrival in Corinth was 'by God's grace', just as Paul stresses the same thing in a similar context in 1 Corinthians 15.10.

But what was it that Apollos did not know, and so did not teach accurately, when he first arrived in Ephesus? How could such an evidently highly educated and intelligent man, who knew his Bible, knew about **John**'s **baptism**, and knew the facts about Jesus and taught them accurately – how could he be missing out on something vital, something which Aquila and Priscilla knew and he didn't? It is true that Luke may well have included this little snippet in order to introduce the next story about Paul discovering some **disciples** of John the Baptist in Ephesus, and he wants to tell that story, in turn, because it introduces his next major set piece, which is about Paul's over-all impact in Ephesus and what happened as a result. And it is also true that Luke is not averse to making the point, this way and that, that women played an important role in the life of the early church, so that to have Priscilla helping her husband Aquila to teach a learned scholar from the great university city of Alexandria something he didn't already know is a pleasing and telling point. But this still hasn't got us right into the centre of things.

The heart of the matter seems to be something about Christian baptism in the name of Jesus, and about baptism in the **holy spirit**. It may well be that Apollos does indeed already possess the spirit, though verse 25, sometimes cited to prove this because literally it reads 'burning in spirit', can't be pressed into service to make that point. But, though he knows a lot about Jesus, and presumably already regards him as the **Messiah**, he only knows John's baptism. In other words, by whatever (to us) strange chain of circumstances, he has followed the story well into the ministry of Jesus, and perhaps also into his death and **resurrection** – the story which, we recall, is carefully anchored, even at the start of Acts, with reference to John the Baptist (1.5, 22). But nobody has told him that from the **day of Pentecost** onwards the church had welcomed people into its full **fellowship** through baptism in the name of Jesus (or, as it quickly developed, in the name of the Trinity, as in Matthew 28.19). And perhaps – just perhaps – he may after all be in the same situation as the 12 people in the next story, who haven't realized that God has been pouring his spirit upon the fol-lowers of Jesus, and that this is open to everyone who believes. Perhaps.

Luke offers us no set pattern for the way in which people come, step by step, into full membership of the Christian family and full participation in all the possibilities that are thereby open to them. Sometimes it happens this way, sometimes that. Just as humans grow to maturity at different paces, and some make great strides in one area while others have to catch up later, so it seems to be in the church. What matters is that we are open, ready to learn even from unlikely sources, and prepared for whatever God has to reveal to us through the scriptures, the apostolic teaching, and the ongoing and always unpredictable common life of the believing family.

ACTS 19.1–10

Paul in Ephesus

¹While Apollos was in Corinth, Paul travelled through the interior regions and arrived at Ephesus. There he found some disciples, ²and said to them, 'Did you receive the holy spirit when you believed?'

'We had not heard', they replied, 'that there *was* a "holy spirit".'

³'Well then,' said Paul, 'into what were you baptized?'

'Into John's baptism,' they replied.

⁴'John baptized with a baptism of repentance for the people,' said Paul, 'speaking about the one who was to come after him, and saying that that person would be the one that people should believe in – and that means Jesus.'

⁵When they heard this, they were baptized in the name of Jesus. ⁶Paul then laid his hands on them, and the holy spirit came upon them, and they spoke in tongues and prophesied. ⁷There were about twelve men in all.

⁸Paul went into the synagogue and spoke boldly there for three months, arguing and persuading them about the kingdom of God. ⁹But when some of them were hard-hearted, and wouldn't believe, and made wicked allegations about the Way in front of everybody else, Paul left them. He took the disciples with him, and argued every day in the lecture-hall of Tyrannus. ¹⁰He did this for two years, so that all the inhabitants of Asia, Jews and Greeks alike, heard the word of the Lord.

The response of the **disciples** Paul met at Ephesus has passed into common parlance, at least among theologians. Not long ago I was helping to organize a conference, and was inviting distinguished speakers from various parts of the world to attend

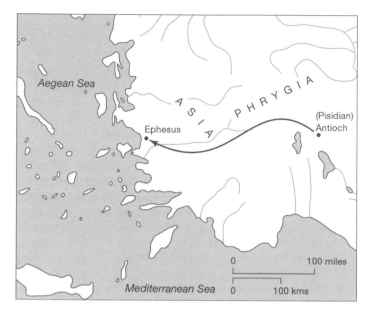

Acts 19.1–10

and read papers. When I had obtained preliminary acceptances from my key speakers, they were all supposed to send in a form to the main organizers with their personal details. Some while after this should have been done, I contacted one of the main participants, an internationally known teacher and writer, to ask why his form had not appeared on time.

'I'm sorry,' he said. 'Like the disciples of John at Ephesus, I hadn't even heard that there *was* a form to be filled out.'

The point being, of course, that it is very odd – picking up what we said about Apollos, earlier – to suppose that people who could be referred to as 'disciples' (verse 1) might not be in some quite full sense 'Christians'; just as it was quite odd that such a senior and respected scholar didn't know which forms he was supposed to fill out. (Actually, that's not so odd, since scholars are notoriously bad at that kind of thing, their minds being taken up with more important issues.)

But was it so odd? We tend to have, perhaps, too mono-chrome a view of early Christianity and what went on. Anyone with detailed experience of the life of any local church over a number of years will know that, however well people are taught, and however much careful and wise pastoral work has gone on, some people never quite seem to get the point, other people persist in holding to strange or bizarre opinions or practices, and things still happen which from a strictly purist point of view would be regarded as, to say the least, 'irregular'. I once knew a church where, despite the protesta-tions and careful teaching of successive rectors and curates, an old lady kept bringing her cat to church, and breaking her communion wafer in half to feed the other half to the cat. When challenged, she always explained that the cat *was the reincarnation of her late husband*. By comparison (and when you start telling stories like that in clerical company, everybody has more to contribute) the disciples of John at Ephesus look quite mild.

After all, they were disciples, presumably meaning at least that they intended to be part of the **kingdom-of-God** move-ment which **John the Baptist** had launched, and they had been **baptized**. Paul's question, 'Into what were you baptized?', indicates that he assumes that if they are 'disciples' they must have been baptized. They were together as a group, presumably meeting for worship, or perhaps – Luke doesn't say – worship-ping with the synagogue, which might be how Paul met them, and then getting together regularly as a sub-group who believed that John the Baptist had been a true prophet and that the kingdom was indeed on the way, perhaps even that Jesus had been a further teacher of the same thing. One strik-ing fact shows that this is a plausible way to understand what was going on. Luke describes Paul's early ministry in Ephesus in terms precisely of his 'speaking about the kingdom of God' (verse 8), which apart from this reference, and Paul's own summary of his Ephesus ministry in 20.25, only occurs else-where in Acts at the very beginning (1.3), the very end (28.23, 31), and once in connection with Philip's ministry (8.12).

This time, unlike the uncertainty over what it was that Apollos was still lacking, Luke makes it quite clear. They have not only not received the **holy spirit**; they haven't heard either that there is a holy spirit, now freely available for all who trust in Jesus, or that Jesus was not just a follower or successor of John but the decisive person to whom John had been pointing. They therefore needed full Christian baptism and, with it, the holy spirit. Once more, Luke does *not* say that **tongues** always accompanies such baptism, or that baptism 'in the name of Jesus' should be played off against trinitarian baptism (as I have heard some people argue on the basis of this passage), or indeed that there is anything about this passage which should be taken as normative for subsequent church life. In fact, to look at the passage in that way may well be to misunderstand it from the start. The main thing Luke is doing in this little story is to introduce Paul's work in Ephesus, and to show that, from the very beginning, he was concerned with the spirit's powerful work both in the lives of individuals and out into the wider community. He may also – this is just a possibility, but worth thinking about – be concerned to make it quite clear that, though Paul did indeed have to sort out a muddle with some 'disciples of John' when he came to Ephesus, this did *not* include Apollos, who had received his further instruction, not from Paul, but from Priscilla and Aquila. The stress in verse 1 on the fact that Paul arrived in Ephesus 'while Apollos was in Corinth' – which is otherwise a strange way to open a long section about Paul's ministry in a particular place – may well indicate both that some people had been suggesting that Apollos owed his full instruction to Paul and that Luke was keen to explain that, while he had indeed received further instruction, this wasn't from Paul but from two of his friends.

The opening summary of Paul's time in Ephesus then proceeds (verses 8–10) according to the pattern with which we have become familiar. Paul stays in the synagogue as long as he can. By now in his public career he is at the height of his power, and he is able to speak boldly and persuasively, presumably along the lines we have already seen several times, and with the advantage of considerable stable ministry in Corinth as well as innumerable debates in public and private. But when, one more time, the local Jewish community begins to reject what he was saying, he goes, again, to a **Gentile** location, as he did in Corinth, and continues to teach from there. Luke doesn't say that all the Jews rejected Paul's **message**, only that some were doing so angrily, and were making wicked allegations about the Christian **faith** (which he here calls 'the Way'). We may catch an echo of the kind of charges that people were making against Paul when, in some of his letters, he adopts the writing style which allows him to engage with imaginary opponents. At one point, for instance, he says that if you follow a certain line of thought, you might as well say 'Well, let's do evil, then, so that good may come of it!' – adding, with a snort, 'and that's what some people blasphemously charge me with saying!' (Romans 3.8).

But Luke's overall point is clear. Paul had spent a day or two in each of the Galatian churches. He had stayed a few days in Philippi, a few weeks in Thessalonica, a day or two in Beroea, a few days in Athens. Then he had spent 18 months in Corinth; and now, as a kind of climax to his work, he was in one of the major centres of the Mediterranean world, Ephesus itself, a great city at the hub of the trade routes of the world, full of culture and money and temples and politics and soldiers and merchants and slaves.

And power. Everything we know about Ephesus indicates that it was a place where not only social and civic power, but also religious and spiritual power, were concentrated. Perhaps that, too, is why Luke has begun his account of Paul's work there with a story about a fresh outpouring of the spirit. There must be nothing second-hand about the spirit's power when you are faced with the powers of the world.

ACTS 19.11–22

The Power of God and the Powers at Ephesus

[11]God performed unusual works of power through Paul's hands. [12]People used to take handkerchiefs or towels that had touched his skin and put them on the sick, and then their diseases would leave them and evil spirits would depart.

[13]There were some travelling Jewish exorcists who tried to use the name of Jesus on people with evil spirits.

'I command you', they used to say, 'in the name of Jesus, the one Paul proclaims!'

[14]There were seven of them who used to do this. They were the sons of Sceva, a Jewish high priest. [15]But on one occasion the evil spirit answered them back.

'I know Jesus', it shouted, 'and I am well acquainted with Paul; but who are you?'

[16]The man who had the evil spirit pounced on them and, since he was much too strong for them, overpowered all of them, so that they fled out of the house naked and battered. [17]This became common knowledge among both Jews and Greeks living in Ephesus. Fear came on all of them, and they praised the name of the Lord Jesus.

[18]Many people who became believers came forward to make public confession, revealing what they had been up to. [19]Some who had been practising magic brought their books and burnt them in front of everyone; someone calculated how much they were all worth, and it came to fifty thousand silver pieces. [20]So the word grew and was strong, in accordance with the Lord's power.

[21]Once all this had been finished, Paul decided in his spirit to go back through Macedonia and Achaea and, from there, on to Jerusalem.

'After I've been there', he said, 'I'll have to go and see Rome.'

[22]He sent two of his helpers, Timothy and Erastus, on ahead to Macedonia, while he himself spent a little more time in Asia.

When I was growing up, one of the leading politicians in the British Labour Party was a man named George Brown. He was extremely able, very shrewd. Some thought at one point he might have been a challenger for the job of party leader, and perhaps even Prime Minister. He became, in fact, deputy leader, and that was the peak of his career. He went his own way, though, and in later life was quite an outspoken critic of his own party. The impact of his views was somewhat lessened by his increasingly eccentric behaviour.

But I recall George Brown here because of something he once said about power. When he was a young man, he said, he knew that things had to be changed. British society was in a mess; someone needed to get to the levers of power and make things happen, make things different. So he went into politics. But in local politics, even once he'd been elected to council office, he discovered that neither he nor the council had any real power. Things were decided elsewhere. So he decided to run for Parliament. But, he said, when he got into Parliament, he found that members of Parliament didn't have any real power. They could talk, and they could vote, but nothing much seemed to change, and the real decisions still seemed to happen somewhere else. So he pushed his way to the front and got into the Cabinet. To his amazement, it was the same there. And even when he got within one place of the top of the tree, to be Deputy Prime Minister under Harold Wilson, he looked around and still couldn't see where the real power lay. Everyone just seemed to be doing the next thing that came to hand. Things happened but it wasn't obvious why. Where was the power?

(In case anyone reading this is unfamiliar with the way British society works, let me just say: the answer isn't 'with the Queen or the royal family'. That's not how a constitutional monarchy works. I know we haven't got a constitution, so the idea of a 'constitutional monarchy' may be peculiar; but that doesn't answer the question, either.)

The question of power – how to get things done – is at the heart of a great many of today's debates as well. There are the regular alternatives. At one end of the scale you have societies where the rulers simply decree what's going to happen and if people kick up a fuss they send in the tanks or the bulldozers. Simple. And costly. At the other end, you have societies where there is so much discussion, so much referendum-voting, so much lobbying in newspapers and the media, that people drown in a sea of words and paper, and the real things that perhaps ought to happen are lost in the fog of multiple compromises.

And in the middle many people are uncomfortably aware that the question of *political* power – how to order, steer, or change the way a society functions – is only one aspect of a much larger and more nebulous question: how to transform people's lives. Perhaps the two dimensions are more closely connected than we sometimes imagine. It isn't just a matter of transforming individuals, one by one, so that society gradually transforms with them. Sometimes you can't wait for that.

If William Wilberforce and his friends had waited until enough people had been transformed so that they could see how evil slavery was, he would have been dead half a century before the urgent and crying reforms were accomplished. But it can't be just a matter of transforming social institutions and public life, otherwise you have a mere outer shell of how things should be, with the people inside the shell grumbling and unwilling: a kind of corporate hypocrisy.

It is perhaps no accident that, in the great scene at Ephesus, which Luke has carefully designed as the climax of Paul's public ministry, the question of power is front and centre. It is striking that in the summary statement in verse 20, corresponding to many similar summary statements earlier in the book such as 6.7 and 12.24, for the first time we have a mention of power – and not just a mention, either, but a strong and emphatic statement: the **word** of God grew *and was strong* in accordance with the *power* of the Lord.

Some of the regular translations don't quite bring out this emphasis, with the result that we miss the striking parallel with such passages as Ephesians 1.19 ('that you may know the surpassing greatness of his energy upon us who believe, according to the working of the *strength* of his *power*'); 3.16 ('may God grant you, according to the riches of his glory, that you may be *strengthened* with all energy through his **spirit**'); 3.20 ('to him who has the capability to do far more abundantly than all we can ask or think, according to the energy that is working in us'); 6.10 ('be energetic in the Lord, and in the *strength* of his *power*'); or Colossians 1.11 ('may you be given energy, according to the *strength* of his glory'). I have translated the same words in the same way throughout that list. It is fascinating that we find such a concentration on this theme in these letters, written to churches in this area (Colossians is inland from Ephesus), and that Luke has drawn attention to the same theme as the major subtext of Paul's ministry in this place. Of course, other similar passages ask to be included as well, not least in letters Paul wrote from Ephesus during this period; for instance, 1 Corinthians 1.18, 24–25; 2.4–5; 4.20 ('God's **kingdom** doesn't depend on talk, but on power'); and 2 Corinthians 4.7; 6.7; 10.4; and 12.9 ('I will gladly boast of my weaknesses, so that the power of the **Messiah** may rest upon me'). Yes, Paul had to learn the lesson of that latter verse, and it may well be that it was in Ephesus, during this period, that he learnt it . . .

Because it really does appear that something happened to him at this time which has left no trace in Luke's work. When C. S. Lewis wrote the preface to his autobiography, *Surprised by Joy*, he warned his readers that one entire episode had been omitted. Later biographers have guessed, probably rightly, that he was referring to the odd relationship he had with the mother of his friend who had been killed in the war; and we can see why, with family still around, it was impossible for Lewis to write about it at that time. Luke, in being (like all historians, including modern critics!) highly and necessarily selective, has chosen to miss out entirely the episode in Ephesus which, according to 2 Corinthians 1.8–9, left Paul feeling as though he had been crushed to the point of despair. That is no doubt why the tone of voice he adopts when he writes about power in 2 Corinthians is different from what we find when he writes about it in 1 Corinthians. Something has happened in between. He still believes most emphatically in the power of God, at work through his ministry. But he has discovered that this power is most splendidly displayed in and through his own utter weakness. My own best guess is that he suffered a period of persecution and imprisonment in Ephesus, during this two-year visit, and that at some point he really did think he was facing imminent death. Maybe it had something to do with the riot we read about later on in the present chapter, or maybe it didn't. God moves (and historians write) in a mysterious way. That's why, though Paul says musingly that it will soon be time for him to go to Rome (verse 21), he has no idea of the complicated route he will have to take to get there.

But the point is of course that Ephesus was, as we said, a centre of power: magic power, political power, religious power. And Paul's ministry demonstrated that the power of the name of the Lord Jesus was stronger than all of them. It was strong to heal, in ways that hadn't happened before (and, Luke implies, hadn't happened since, either), with handkerchiefs and towels that had touched Paul's skin somehow bearing healing power to the sick. In particular, Luke tells this splendid little tale of the exorcists who thought they could just add the name of Jesus to their repertoire of magic charms, only to discover that the **demon** they were addressing on this occasion respected Jesus (and Paul as well, as it turned out) but had no respect for them. Here is a vital principle, which Luke has emphasized already in chapters 8 and 13: the **gospel** does indeed provide power, *but it is not 'magic'*. Magic attempts (having mentioned C. S. Lewis, I should acknowledge that this was something I learnt from him many years ago) to gain that power without paying the price of humble submission to the God whose power it is. But to reject the power, as some (alas) do, because you are afraid of magic, is to throw out the teapot with the old teabags. The seven sons of Sceva, incidentally, are as much of a puzzle as the disciples of John at Ephesus. There never was an official Jewish **high priest** called 'Sceva', and it's possible that these were Jews who, living in pagan territory for a long time, had developed a kind of mixed economy of Jewish and pagan religion, ritual and magic.

The most striking example of God's power at work in the region is, of course, the burning of the costly magic books, and the confession and renunciation by those who had been prac-tising magic – again, something Luke is glad to emphasize, in line with the earlier stories of individual magicians. But the mention of the money in verse 19 ought to run up, for us, a little warning flag. As we found in Philippi, when the gospel begins to have a financial impact, trouble will be just around the corner.

ACTS 19.23–41

'Great Is Ephesian Artemis!'

[23]Around that time there was a major disturbance because of the Way. [24]There was a silversmith called Demetrius who made silver statues of Artemis, which brought the workmen a tidy income. [25]He got them all together, along with other workers in the same business.

'Gentlemen,' he began. 'You know that the reason we are doing rather well for ourselves is quite simply this business of ours. [26]And now you see, and hear, that this fellow Paul is going around not only Ephesus but pretty well the whole of Asia, persuading the masses to change their way of life, telling them that gods made with hands are not gods after all! [27]This not only threatens to bring our proper business into disrepute, but it looks as if it might make people disregard the temple of the great goddess Artemis. Then she – and, after all, the whole of Asia, indeed the whole world, worships her! – she might lose her great majesty.'

[28]When they heard this, they were filled with rage.

'Great is Ephesian Artemis!' they shouted. 'Great is Ephesian Artemis!'

[29]The whole city was filled with the uproar, and everyone rushed together into the theatre, dragging along with them the Macedonians Gaius and Aristarchus, two of Paul's companions. [30]Paul wanted to go in to speak to the people, but his followers wouldn't let him. [31]Indeed, some of the local magistrates, who were friendly towards him, sent him a message urging him not to take the risk of going into the theatre. [32]Meanwhile, some people were shouting one thing, some another. In fact, the whole assembly was thoroughly confused, and most of them had no idea why they had come there in the first place. [33]The Jews pushed Alexander forward, and some of the crowd informed him what was going on. He motioned with his hand, and was going to make a statement to the people to explain things. [34]But when they realized he was a Jew, they all shouted together, for about two hours,

'Great is Ephesian Artemis!'

[35]The town clerk quietened the crowd.

'Men of Ephesus,' he said, 'is there anyone who doesn't know that our city of Ephesus is the place which has the honour of being the home of Artemis the Great, and of the statue that fell from heaven? [36]Nobody can deny it! So you should be quiet, and not do anything rash. [37]You've brought these men here, but they haven't stolen from the temple, or blasphemed our goddess. [38]If Demetrius and his colleagues have a charge they want to bring against anyone, the courts are open and we have magistrates. Let them present the case against one another. [39]But if you are wanting to know anything beyond that, it must be sorted out in the authorized assembly. [40]Let me remind you that we ourselves are risking legal proceedings because of this riot today, since there is no reason we could give which would enable us to present a satisfactory explanation for this uproar.'

[41]With these words, he dismissed the assembly.

We ought to know the scene by now. We see it often enough on our television screens. A huge gathering, assembled in the street and the public square. Faces are flushed with excitement and anger. Being reminded of some great hero or leader has whipped them up into excitement, and they are eager to show what's what. The chanting gets louder and louder, rhythmic and strong, summoning up the energy of blood, tribal identity and local pride. It's designed to give energy to those who are going out to fight their battles, and to strike terror into their enemies. It often works.

And that's just a football match.

People say that sport – and, in the UK, football particularly – has become a religion, or if anything something more powerful. That is said, of course, in a world where 'religion' has been officially toned down, smoothed over, patted into place so that nothing too disturbing or powerful will burst out. After all, when we look at other crowds on our television screens, with chants that have nothing to do with Manchester United or Arsenal, and everything to do with the victory of one religion and way of life and the violent overthrow of the infidel, then we in the West know we want nothing to do with anything like that.

But if we want to understand what it was like in the great amphitheatre at Ephesus that day, we need to think about crowds like that, with their threatening, rhythmic chanting, their fists raised in unison, their collective anger growing to much more than the sum of its parts, and their readiness to do anything at all, including murder, to satisfy the lust that has been aroused. I once went, with a party of tourists and pilgrims, to Ephesus. We had planned that I would give a talk on Paul right there, in the ancient theatre. I was looking forward to it, imagining myself (with some amusement) holding forth to the rank upon rank of seats in the huge open-air auditorium. Of course, when we got there our quite substantial party made about as much impact on the theatre as a bucket of water poured into the Mississippi. The theatre in Ephesus holds around 25,000. I stood there, eyes half shut, imagining, instead of my 50 or so middle-aged English folk with sunhats and cameras, the whole place full of angry faces and threatening gestures, and two hours of chanting, louder and louder, 'Great is Ephesian Artemis! Great is Ephesian Artemis!'

Artemis was indeed great. She (Artemis is her Greek name; her Roman name is Diana) was the most powerful divinity in the place, and had been for a long time. In the distant past a meteorite had smashed into the surface of the earth somewhere near Ephesus, and the local people had regarded it as a gift from **heaven**, a statue (though presumably not very lifelike) of the goddess herself. That's what the town clerk is referring to in verse 35. The temple of Artemis was massive, and her cult – run entirely by female officials – was the religious centre of the whole area. Images of Artemis, large and small, dominated the city. Archaeologists have found dozens of them, with the distinctive mother-goddess feature of multiple breasts. What was once manufactured as an object of religious devotion is still today manufactured for sale in the area, only as a tourist souvenir.

And, as in Philippi and elsewhere, the **message** of Jesus the **Messiah**, as the sharp leading edge of the major Jewish critique of idolatry, was having its impact on business. Imagine someone setting up shop in the heart of the financial district of one of our great cities – London, Frankfurt, New York, Tokyo – and using the basis of a powerful ministry of healing to declare, over and over again, that the money markets and the stock markets were simply a way of worshipping the god Mammon, that this was destroying the lives and the livelihoods of millions in other parts of the world, and that the whole system was rotten and anyone who saw the light ought to reject it outright. You might get more than just a sharp word now and then, especially if the idea seemed to be catching on (remember all those magic books on the bonfire in verse 19). No wonder Demetrius and his friends were alarmed.

This rushing together of the economic, religious and cultural impact of the **gospel** is one of the major issues that Christians are having to grapple with once more in our time. Many of us in the West have lived quite comfortably with all these things in separate compartments, and everything clinically wrapped so that nothing can leak from one compartment to another. We are inclined to look at the riot in Ephesus, shudder, and thank God that we don't do things like that any more. But, as I mentioned William Wilberforce in an earlier passage, so we should think again about the way in which wickedness gets a grip on a society, somewhere down below its polite exterior, and about the way in which, sooner or later, someone needs to take their courage in one hand and their Bible in the other, throw to the winds any caution about their own prospects, and say what needs to be said. And we shouldn't miss, either, the way in which, once again, the gospel functions as a critique of all temples, whether the Parthenon in Athens, the temple of Artemis in Ephesus, or even, as in chapter 7, the **Temple** in Jerusalem itself. Is that, too, a theme which Luke is gently rubbing in? Is he pointing out that, even if Paul did implicitly undermine the great pagan temples, this was only following through on the early Christians' negative attitude towards even the great Temple in Jerusalem?

But there is also a wisdom about how to do it. Paul, of course, was eager to get into the theatre and grab the opportunity to address his largest crowd yet. This could be like the Areopagus, only more so! Imagine if all of them came to **faith** in the Lord Jesus just like that! Not only his friends, but some of the local officials who were friendly to him as well (verse 31), knew this would be a big mistake, partly, no doubt, because they knew, as Luke goes on to say, that most of the people who were chanting so enthusiastically were just letting off steam, having a good day out, and had little or no idea of what all the fuss was about in the first place.

If Luke had ever wanted to give his readers the impression that Paul was the sort of person who any town, any society, any culture would be glad to have arrive on their doorstep, since he would bring peace and stability and help everyone to get on with having a quiet life, he had long since abandoned the attempt. But he does still want to insist, and this scene is yet one more example of it, that even when great riots like this had taken place, eventually the local magistrates made the point that it wasn't actually Paul's fault, that they shouldn't have rioted like that, and that if anything it was everyone else's fault and they should take care not to do it again (verses 36–40). Ephesus, as a major city of the Roman Empire, was under the eagle eye of senior Roman officials, and disturbances of public order would not be looked on kindly. What's more, Ephesus had recently become a major centre of the new and rapidly spreading imperial cult, the worship of Rome and the emperor himself. Artemis had been joined by a much more recent divinity, with a massive claim to religious as well as political and military power.

So, as with the public apology in Philippi and Gallio's verdict in Corinth, the town clerk in Ephesus gives his verdict: Demetrius and his friends are welcome to bring charges against Paul and his companions if they have done something wrong, but there is no sign that they have done. Pagans often accused Jews of blaspheming the local gods and goddesses or robbing their temples, but nobody is suggesting Paul did either of those. He is innocent until proved guilty. And, with that, Luke rounds off the story of Paul's most sustained piece of missionary and pastoral work, and moves the story on to the point where, before too long, Paul will face one trial after another and, by the skin of his teeth, receive substantially the same verdict.

There are all kinds of lessons here for the church in later days. Have we learnt the lesson of being so definite in our witness to the powerful name of Jesus that people will indeed find their vested interests radically challenged, while being so innocent in our actual behaviour that there will be nothing to accuse us of? There is a fine line to be trodden between a quiet, ineffective 'preaching' of a 'gospel' which will make no impact on real life, on the one hand, and a noisy, obstreperous, personally and socially offensive proclamation on the other.

ACTS 20.1–12

Round the Coast and Out of the Window

¹After the hue and cry had died down, Paul sent for the disciples. He encouraged them, said his farewells, and set off to go to Macedonia. ²He went through those regions, encouraging them with many words and, arriving in Greece, ³stayed there three months. He was intending to set sail for Syria, but the Jews made a plot against him, and he decided to return instead through Macedonia.

⁴He was accompanied on this trip by Sopater, son of Pyrrhus of Beroea; by Aristarchus and Secundus from Thessalonica; by Gaius from Derbe; and Timothy, and Tychicus and Trophimus from Asia. ⁵They went on ahead and waited for us at Troas, ⁶while we got on board ship at Philippi, after the days of Unleavened Bread, and joined them in Troas five days later. We stayed there for a week.

⁷On the first day of the week we gathered to break bread. Paul was intending to leave the following morning. He was engaged in discussion with them, and he went on talking up to midnight. ⁸There were several lamps burning in the upper room where we were gathered. ⁹A young man named Eutychus was sitting by the window, and was overcome with a deep sleep as Paul went on and on. Once sleep had got the better of him, he fell down out of the third-storey window, and was picked up dead.

¹⁰Paul went down, stooped over him and picked him up. 'Don't be alarmed,' he said. 'There is life still in him.'

¹¹He went back upstairs, broke bread and ate with them, and continued speaking until dawn. Then he left. ¹²They took up the young man alive and were very much comforted.

The greatest epic of modern times is based on a journey. Millions who have seen the movies of J. R. R. Tolkien's *The Lord of the Rings*, not to mention the millions who have read the books, sometimes over and over, are often so taken up with the power and fascination of the story that they do not step back and reflect on what Tolkien was doing. He was standing in a long, ancient and noble tradition, telling the story of the world, and of the central human dramas, in the form of a travel narrative, getting Frodo and his companions to Mount Doom

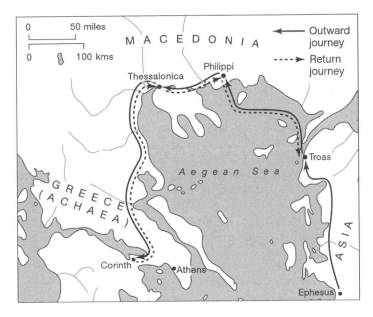

Acts 20.1–12

in order to do what needs to be done, but what only they can do. Many of us lead sedentary lives, seldom moving from home for more than a brief holiday. Few people, even today, spend most or all of their lives on the move. We nevertheless feel the power and the pull of a story which enables us to reflect, at a deep, structural level, on the journey through time which we are all making. The 'journey' of our lives has many twists and turns. We carry memories of, as we say, 'where we've been' in the sense of 'what has happened to us'. We carry hopes and fears for 'where we might go next' in the sense of 'what may yet happen to us'. Even if we live in the same street, or the same house, all our life long, we are on a journey whether we like it or not, and we greatly value stories that help us to see things like that.

The journey is of course the other great theme, alongside the continual trial-and-vindication, that Luke is tapping into as he tells his story, particularly his story of Paul. We are now coming to another 'we' passage, where the author (or his source) seems to be particularly keen on telling us in considerable detail where they all went, which islands they put in at and which ones they sailed past, and so on. It's worth pondering what Luke is doing, and what, at quite a deep level, he is accomplishing.

Two of the great epics of the ancient world were travel narratives. The *Odyssey*, Homer's marvellous story of Odysseus returning home to Ithaca (off the north-west coast of Greece) after the Trojan war, contains, inevitably, many passages in which the hero and his companions are sailing from island to island, meeting various adventures, getting into and out of remarkable scrapes, and ending up with Odysseus, battered and scarcely recognizable, coming home at last. Luke's story has some things in common with that, though of course also, in other respects, it is radically different; would people have found some faint stabs of recognition? What might they have thought of Paul as a new, subversive type of hero? And of course, just a generation or so before the time of Paul, Virgil, the greatest ever Roman poet, had written a new epic, taking his hero, Aeneas, from Troas (ancient Troy), where Luke has now brought Paul, all the way to Rome. Would some have made that connection? If so, what might they have thought of it?

The Pentateuch, the first five books of the Old Testament, contains at its heart a very different travel narrative: the journey of the children of Israel out of Egypt and home to their promised land. Of course, it could hardly be more different in terrain: the dry, dusty desert over against the stormy Mediterranean Sea. But, like Acts, the Pentateuch ends just before we want it to. If it was all we had, we would want to ask, 'But what happened? Did they get into the land?', just as, at the end of Acts, we rightly want to ask, 'But what happened at the final trial? What did Paul say to Nero, and Nero to Paul?' And the idea of a journey which, through many twists and turns, gets God's people to their final destination, the place they have been promised, has strong echoes in Luke's story, which sets out a programme at the start ('You will be my witnesses in

Jerusalem, Judaea, Samaria and to the ends of the earth', 1.8) and by the end gives every appearance of having accomplished the task. Since all roads in the ancient world led to (and therefore also from) Rome, once the **gospel** has got there it will, in principle, get everywhere else as well.

Did Luke's Jewish readers make this sort of connection? Would they have realized that the story of the gospel and its progress could not only be a wonderful picture for the story of every Christian, journeying through life like Bunyan's Pilgrim, but might also be a way, a deep-level God-given way, of enabling us to understand the profound mysteries of life and death, of slavery and freedom, of the way in which we are called to take each day step by step as a kind of pilgrimage through time, if not through space?

Certainly Paul himself was thoroughly familiar with the **Exodus** story, and he made it a major theme in many of his writings, not least the ones he wrote in the time covered by this brief account. Two of his most powerful letters emerge from this period: he was writing 2 Corinthians, it seems, while on the way round northern Greece (verses 1, 2) before ending up in Corinth, where, during his time in Ephesus, there had been all kinds of trouble, and strong opposition to him personally. Then, while at Corinth, perhaps while waiting for the ship for Syria which he eventually decided not to take (verse 3), he wrote his masterpiece: the letter to Rome, announcing and explaining how the gospel message of Jesus as Lord was undergirding and informing all his plans, all his work for the mission and unity of the church.

And he asked them, tellingly, to pray for the success of his special work, to which Luke, perhaps tactfully, draws no attention at this point (though he does later, in 24.17): the collection of money from the Greek churches, to give to the poor Christians in Jerusalem, as a sign of something Paul was constantly emphasizing, that Greek and Jew in Christ form a single family (Romans 15.25–33). Perhaps part of the reason for the enlarged company, representative of so many churches (Acts 20.4), is that Paul wanted to have both the safety of a larger group of travelling companions when carrying a substantial amount of money and the clear accounting of several who could witness that the money had safely reached its destination.

The sudden and touching story of Eutychus – his name, a common slave's name, means 'Lucky', and on this occasion he was – both lightens the mood and gives us a telling insight into the life of the early church. There is always plenty to talk about, questions to address, biblical passages to puzzle over, and everything we know of Paul makes it extremely likely that, given half a chance, he would go on to midnight and beyond. (It is fascinating, as one of my teaching colleagues once observed, how an idea which presents itself to your mind as a complete, small, satisfying entity can take five or ten minutes, or even half an hour, to explain even to someone very intelligent who wants to understand it. The colleague in question was a mathematician.) And, given that Eutychus may have been working all day (it was a Sunday, but of course that was an ordinary working day, and the church would meet either very early in the morning or very late at night, or both), and that there were oil lamps burning in the room, it is hardly surprising that he nodded off and fell out of the window where he was sitting. A sudden apparent tragedy to cast a gloom over everything. But no: Paul, like Elijah (1 Kings 17.21), seized him and hugged him and found him alive – whether because he had died and been brought back to life, or because he was only stunned, Luke doesn't say. Then they celebrated the meal which speaks of the dying and rising of Jesus himself (Acts 20.11). The talking continued until it was time to go.

The grand sweep of the total narrative, the great story moving across land and sea and bringing the hero (in Paul's case, the anti-hero) safely through to his destination despite it all, catches up within it these sharply described moments of death and life, of worship, **fellowship** and celebration. Somehow the church is called in every generation to keep its eyes both on the larger horizon and on the immediate, practical, homely, personal and often pressing calls on our time, prayer and attention. The slave-boy in the window and the thousand-mile journey, like the rose and the yew tree, are of equal significance.

ACTS 20.13–27

Paul the Pastor Looks Back – and Looks On

[13]We went on ahead to the ship and set off for Assos, with the intention of picking Paul up there (he had decided that he would walk to that point). [14]When we arrived at Assos, we picked him up and went on to Mitylene, [15]and from there we sailed on the next day and arrived opposite Chios. The following day we got near to Samos, and the day after that we came to Miletus. [16]Paul had decided, you see, to pass by Ephesus, so that he wouldn't have to spend more time in Asia. He was eager to get to Jerusalem, if he could, in time for the day of Pentecost.

[17]From Miletus, Paul sent to Ephesus and called for the elders of the church, [18]and they came to him.

'You know very well', he began, 'how I have behaved with you all the time, since the first day I arrived in Asia. [19]I have served the Lord with all humility, with the tears and torments that came upon me because of the plots of the Jews. [20]You know that I kept back nothing that would have been helpful to you, preaching to you and teaching you both in public and from house to house. [21]I bore witness both to Jews and Greeks about repentance towards God and faith in our Lord Jesus.

[22]'And now, look, I am going to Jerusalem, bound by the spirit. I have no idea what's going to happen to me there, [23]but only that the holy spirit testifies to me in city after city that captivity and trouble are in store for me. [24]But I don't reckon my life at any value, so long as I can finish my course, and the ministry which I have received from the Lord Jesus, to bear witness to the gospel of God's grace.

[25]'So now', he went on, 'I have gone to and fro preaching the kingdom among you, but I know that none of you will ever see my face again. [26]Therefore I bear witness to you this very day that I am innocent of everyone's blood, [27]since I did not shrink from declaring to you God's entire plan.'

'To know George', said the speaker at his funeral, 'you had to hear him preach.'

And immediately I felt a strong stab of regret. George Caird had been my teacher throughout my graduate years. I had

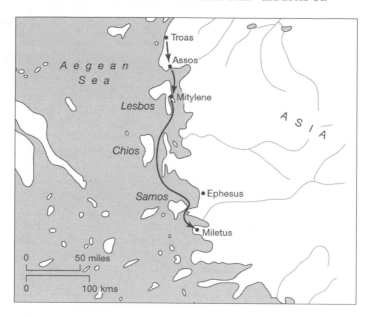

Acts 20.13–27

attended his lectures and come away spellbound. I had spent many hours with him, one to one, wrestling with texts, theology, interpretation, drafts of my dissertation, all the things that go to make up the excitement of academic life. But he was an extremely busy man, running a college, taking part in university politics, writing books, spending time with his lively family. We hardly ever met socially. And on Sundays I was normally busy elsewhere. I heard him preach only once, at a rather over-formal, stylized university occasion. I remember once reading one of his sermons where, expounding Galatians 2.20, he spoke of 'a debt of love, which only love can repay'. But I never actually heard him speak like that, with all the focused passion of his life's work laid at the feet of his Master. At one level I knew him very well; at another, hardly at all.

Getting to know Paul is a bit like that, and the present passage comes as something of a shock both to those who

think of him in terms of his letters and those who have got
to know him through his addresses in Acts 13, 14 and 17.
This address to the elders of the church in Ephesus is quite
different, both in tone and in content. It is closer to the letters,
of course, because like the letters it is not primary preaching
of the **gospel** but rather the teaching of the church which
follows from it. And it corresponds closely to things Paul does
say in the letters when he is describing, or reminding his
churches of, his own pastoral practice. We think, for instance,
of 1 Thessalonians 2.5–12, where he reminds them of how he
had never made the gospel a means of selfish gain. Rather,
he had been 'gentle as a nurse' with them, sharing not only
the gospel but his very self, working night and day so as not
to be a burden, dealing with each one of them as a father with
his children. We perhaps think, in today's Western world, that
this is a bit 'over the top', as though Paul is praising himself.
He isn't. He is showing them, in the only way he can, what
following Jesus looks like. As he says to the Philippians (and
which pastor among us would have the courage to say this
to those who knew him or her well?): 'What you have learned,
and received, *and heard and seen in me*, do; and the God of
peace will be with you' (Philippians 4.9). Perhaps our slight
hesitation about the way Paul puts it is a mask for our embarrassment at knowing that we couldn't, and wouldn't dare, say
anything like that.

So here we see Paul in a different mode, vulnerable, medita-
tive, steady in his faithful perseverance but with no hint of tri-
umphalism, of carrying all before him, sweeping through the
world in a blaze of glory. He is quiet, not combative; reflective,
not argumentative. It is as though we have finally found him,
no longer running around in a blur, but sitting still for long
enough to have his portrait painted.

And what a portrait. Luke has brought him down, island by
island, from Troas to Miletus, hurrying because he wants to be
in Jerusalem for Pentecost. They were in Philippi for Passover
(verse 6), and roughly two weeks have already elapsed since then;
he only has about another 30 days to go. So he decides not to
go into Ephesus itself (he may have suspected that it might be

easier to get in than to get out again, either because his enemies might attack again or because he was carrying a large sum of money, or both), and invites the elders of the church to meet him in Miletus, a city to the south of Ephesus which, so far as we know, Paul had not previously visited.

But he is not here to preach, but to say farewell. And not just farewell, but to reflect on his time with them, the longest period he had ever spent with a church, and to reflect with them on the pattern of his ministry and its significance. Once again, as in 1 Thessalonians, there is an element both of example ('Remember how I lived when I was with you, and carry out your own ministries in the same spirit') and of a kind of solemn declaration of innocence.

It is that latter element that strikes us as unusual. It is rare among us today, I think, for people coming to the end of a period of ministry to make a public declaration that they were not in it for their own profit, and that no guilt can be attached to them. But in the ancient world there were many reasons why one might look back on one's own public career like this. There were many wandering teachers, healers and others who were basically interested in making a living rather than the real best interests of their hearers and followers. Paul was anxious lest, after his departure, people might start to insinuate that he was really that kind of person – and, worse, that the pastors and teachers in the congregation might start to behave like that too. The speech is, in fact, about the Christ-shaped, generous love that the minister must not only speak about but also model at every level.

It is a love that, as Paul himself said, bears all things, believes all things, hopes all things, and endures all things. He had gone through a good deal in Ephesus (verse 19), but had given an enormous amount as well (verses 20–21). Verse 21 summarizes the Paul we know from Romans and Galatians and elsewhere (though '**repentance**' is not often an explicit theme): testifying to both Jews and Greeks about repentance towards God and **faith** in Jesus the **Messiah**. And, looking more broadly, and thinking back to the many late nights in lighted rooms and the many long afternoons in the lecture-hall of Tyrannus, as well as to a thousand personal conversations, bent over a text of scripture with a half-made tent on the bench beside him, he speaks of having resolutely declared to them 'God's whole plan'. The word for 'plan' indicates a settled intention of a purpose to be carried out step by step. This isn't just a matter of 'true doctrines', but of the entire divine intention, from the call of Abraham to the time of final 'restoration' (3.21), when Jesus will act as judge to sort everything out (17.31). That takes time, and application, and determination, at those points in the story where it gets complicated or awkward questions are raised; and Paul has been up for it all. Nobody will ever be able to say that he trimmed the **message** to make it easier to get it across or more palatable for his hearers. This was his commission from God, and he has been faithful to it.

This is all the more poignant in that Paul is now convinced, as a matter of deep personal vocation, that he will not be back in these parts again. He is clear that he must now go to Rome, after what he thinks (wrongly) will be a short visit to Jerusalem; and in the letter to Rome he is clear that he must then go on to Spain (Romans 15.14–29), so that he can indeed reach the ends of the earth with the gospel. It seems that he does not intend to return to the eastern Mediterranean, but to make Rome his new base for operations in the west. Significantly, Antioch, his original 'sending church', has dropped out of the picture, though whether he was hoping to pay a quick visit there after Jerusalem we cannot say. But he knows this is a final farewell, as far as the Aegean coastline is concerned. They will never see his face again (Acts 20.25).

All he knows is that it isn't going to get any easier, and in that, at least, he was absolutely correct. Those in Ephesus who had watched him through a sustained ministry knew very well that he meant it when he said what he did in verse 24, which stands as a model, challenging but also strangely beckoning, to all who work for the gospel: 'I don't reckon my life at any value, so long as I can finish my course, and the ministry which I have received from the Lord Jesus, to bear witness to the gospel of God's grace.' That witness, as much by what Paul was and did as by what he said, stands to this day.

ACTS 20.28–38

Watch Out for Yourselves, the Flock and the Wolves

[28]'Watch out for yourselves', Paul continued, 'and for the whole flock, in which the holy spirit has appointed you as guardians, to feed the church of God, which he purchased with the blood of his own Dear One. [29]I know that fierce wolves will come in after I am gone, and they won't spare the flock. [30]Yes, even from among yourselves people will arise, saying things which will distort the truth, and they will draw the disciples away after them. [31]Therefore keep watch, and remember that for three years, night and day, I didn't stop warning each of you, with tears.

[32]'So now I commit you to God, and to the word of his grace, which is able to build you up and give you the inheritance among all those whom God has sanctified. [33]I never coveted anyone's silver, or gold, or clothes. [34]You yourselves know that these very hands worked to serve my own needs and those of the people with me. [35]I showed you in all such matters that this is how we should work to help the weak, remembering the words of the Lord Jesus, as he put it, "It is more blessed to give than to receive." '

[36]When he had said this, he knelt down with them all and prayed. [37]There was great lamentation among them all, and they fell on Paul's neck and kissed him. [38]They were particularly sorry to hear the word he had spoken about never seeing his face again.

Then they brought him to the ship.

I received an email this morning from a man I have never met. He has been studying a particular subject, and has come upon an article I wrote 25 years ago. In it, I quote a line from the scholar I was discussing (Ernst Käsemann, the great Tübingen New Testament professor, as it happens), but for some reason I didn't give the reference so that he could follow up the quotation. Could I please help him?

Now in theory it might be possible. I do have boxes and boxes of old papers gathering dust in an upper room somewhere. They have followed me over the nine moves of house, five of job, and two of continent since I wrote that article.

But I have no idea which box the relevant notes are in, and I am not minded to go and start looking. And trying to work through all Käsemann's published output looking for a single and fairly typical sentence is like looking for a particular pebble on a large and shingly beach. So, sorry, but the reference is unlikely to appear for a day or two yet.

Somewhere, lost in the sands of Egypt perhaps, or in the far recesses of a forgotten Syrian monastery, there may well be an old, old piece of parchment, a fragment of a **gospel**, a collection of sayings, or just some random notes, that would answer the question that we all want to ask Luke when we read verse 35. According to him (well, according to Paul according to him), Jesus said, 'It is more blessed to give than to receive.' And we scratch our heads, and think, 'Was that in Matthew, or Mark, or Luke, or John?' And the answer is: none of the above. Was it, then, in one of the 'apocryphal' so-called gospels, like *Thomas*? Answer, again: No. Granted, Jesus says something like it in Matthew 10.8: Freely you have received, freely give. And there is a clumsier version of a saying rather like our present one in a Jewish text from about 200 years before Jesus' day: 'Don't let your hand be stretched out when it's time to receive, and closed when it's time to give' (Sirach 4.31). But Luke hasn't put in a footnote, and if there is a manuscript somewhere that gives us any more information, it might as well be in the dusty boxes in my attic for all the help it'll be.

All of which reminds us, as John says at the end of his gospel (21.25), that there were many other things which Jesus did (and presumably which he said) which are not written down here, and that if they were all written down the whole world wouldn't be able to contain the books that would be written. But, unlike some of the sayings in *Thomas* and other such books, this one rings true. It sounds like the sort of thing that might well have come in the Sermon on the Mount or a similar address. It makes sense, not only as a statement by Jesus about how his followers ought to behave, but as a statement about his own manner of life, as summarized in John 13.1 (having loved his own who were in the world, he loved them to the end) or the famous poem in Philippians 2.6–11 (he didn't regard his equality with God as something to exploit,

135

but emptied himself . . . all the way to the cross). And that, of course, is the point. For Paul, the whole essence of the gospel was found, not in a doctrine or theory, a magic formula or a secret access to a powerful Name by which he could stride through the world making things happen, but that 'by such work we must support the weak'.

The 'such work' in question was, here as before, his own determination to work with his own hands to support himself and his companions. Nobody would ever be able to say that Paul had used his biblical learning, patient study or rhetorical gifts to feather his own nest. He never cast envious eyes on fine clothing or jewellery (Acts 20.33). He was up early and, most probably, late to bed, with his settled hours of prayer and his long stretches of physical work with Aquila and Priscilla in the shop, snatching hours here and there to go and teach in the lecture-room, hurrying round to someone's house where there was sickness or sorrow, ready at the first sign of a Christian starting to wobble in understanding or behaviour to sit with them, pray with them, weep with them (verse 31) and warn them. He had given, and given, and given. Oh, he'd received as well, love and affection and support and friendship, many homes which were in effect his own when he needed them, many faces which would light up when they saw him, many voices which would cheer him up as they came into the shop. But he had lived out the **message** of the gospel as he had understood it, 'the message of God's grace' (verse 32), which isn't primarily a theory but a way of life, an image-bearing way of life. (No wonder, at the end of his speech, they wept at the thought that they wouldn't see him again.) And it is to that message, and that way of life, that he now commends them.

They are going to need it. Paul was mainly a townsman, and his imagery is normally drawn from the urban world where most of his ministry was spent. He speaks of athletic sports, of buildings with foundations (and at risk from fire), of legal documents, and of course of tents. Granted, he can talk about seeds and plants, about fields with crops in them coming to harvest, about grafting one kind of olive onto another (though some have questioned whether he really understands how to do that). But nowhere else in his writings does he talk of the sheep and the shepherd. And it is of sheep that he now thinks, sheep whose shepherd he has been, sheep that will now need feeding, leading, caring for and protecting. 'Keep watch over yourselves and the flock' (verse 28); no good using your care for the flock as displacement activity to prevent you needing to think about your own discipline, obedience and maturity. Your task is not something you have dreamed up. The **holy spirit**, who has led Paul halfway round the known world and used him in so many extraordinary ways, has made them 'overseers', guardians, *episkopoi* – a word that, within a generation of Paul, would mean something like our 'bishop', and from which indeed that English word is directly derived. Here, though, it clearly doesn't refer to a single leader, but to each of the 'elders' (verse 17). This is another footnote we wish Luke had added, but he shows no interest in sorting out the details of church office-bearers.

The task before the shepherd is a solemn one. God gave his own dear son to die a shameful, sacrificial death in order to purchase this flock (verse 28). This is perhaps the most direct, certainly the most striking, statement of the meaning of Jesus' crucifixion to be found anywhere in Acts, and it opens up vistas both of the love of God and of the responsibility of the shepherd. The shepherds are therefore to keep watch, because the wolves are prowling around, ready to come and attack. Paul no doubt has Demetrius and his friends in mind, still sore about their loss of business, and indeed the priestesses of Artemis, who may likewise have suffered a decline in attendance at their great temple. There may also be some magicians who didn't burn their books, and are eager for revenge, to show that their power is after all superior to that of this Jesus. And no doubt many more; when Paul wrote Ephesians 6.10–20, he wasn't fooling around.

More worrying still, some of the sheep, and even some of the shepherds, may turn out to be wolves in disguise (verse 30). And the attack will then take the form, not of direct contradiction or a clash of powers, but of distorting the truth. The greatest heresies do not come about by straightforward denial; most of the church will see that for what it is. They happen when an element which may even be important, but isn't central, looms so large that people can't help talking about it, fixating on it, debating different views of it as though this were the only thing that mattered. Something like that happened in the Middle Ages with the theory of purgatory (**life** after death is important, but not like that); in the twentieth century with calculations regarding the 'rapture' (the **second coming** is important, but not like that); in the twenty-first century with . . .

And when you can fill in that blank, humbly and looking at yourself hard in the mirror as you think about it, you will know something about the calling of the shepherd in today's church. 'Therefore be alert', Paul insists (verse 31). Keep watch. Stay awake. 'I commend you to God and the **word** of his grace.' God and his grace will see you through. Your part, as with the **disciples** in the garden of Gethsemane, is not to fall asleep.

ACTS 21.1–14

Disturbing Prophecies

[1]When we had left them behind and had set sail, we made a straight course to Cos, and went on the next day to Rhodes and from there to Patara. [2]There we found a ship heading for Phoenicia, and we got on board and set sail. [3]We came in sight of Cyprus, left it on our right side, sailed to Syria and arrived in Tyre, which was where the boat was going to unload its cargo. [4]We found some disciples and stayed there a week – and they told Paul, in the spirit, not to go to Jerusalem. [5]When our time there was up, we left and went on our way, with everyone, women and children included, coming with us out of the city. We knelt down on the seashore and prayed. [6]Then we said our farewells to one another. We got on the ship and they returned home.

[7]The end of our voyage from Tyre saw us arrive at Ptolemais. There we greeted the Christians, and stayed a day with them. [8]On the next day we left and went on to Caesarea, and went into the house of Philip the evangelist, one of the Seven, and stayed with him. [9]He had four unmarried daughters who prophesied.

[10]After we'd been there several days, Agabus the prophet arrived from Jerusalem. [11]He came to us, took Paul's girdle, and tied himself up with it, hand and foot.

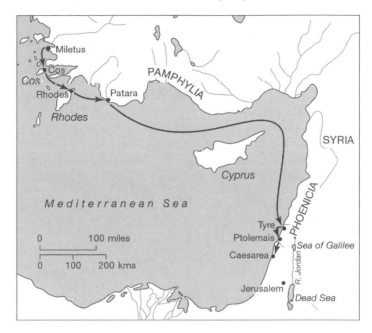

Acts 21.1–14

'This is what the holy spirit says,' he declared. 'The Judaeans in Jerusalem will tie up the man to whom this girdle belongs, just like this, and they will hand him over to the Gentiles.'

¹²When we heard that, we and the people of that place begged Paul not to go up to Jerusalem.

¹³Then Paul responded.

'What are you doing with all this weeping', he said, 'breaking my heart in pieces? I am quite prepared not only to be tied up but to die in Jerusalem for the name of the Lord Jesus.'

¹⁴When we realized we couldn't dissuade him, we gave up the attempt.

'May the Lord's will be done,' was all we said.

I was in Canada in 1983 when, on a flight over the Pacific, a Korean airliner was intercepted and shot down by Soviet jets. All on board, needless to say, were killed. There was a long argument subsequently over why the plane was where it was and why it was shot down, but my memories are not of the wrangling and recrimination. They are of the next two or three days when, in the Korean communities in Montreal and Toronto, people took to the streets to protest. And, of course, one of the main and most obvious things they did was to burn the Soviet flag.

People sometimes say that symbolic actions are a strange thing of the distant past, of other cultures and times. But the flag, whether you display it proudly on a pole or burn it in the street, says a great deal about who you are, what you are thinking, who you see as your friends and (especially) who you see as your enemies. And what you do with it can symbolize something that's just happened, and your reaction to it; or it can symbolize what you hope is going to happen.

Now I don't suppose the Koreans who burnt the Soviet flag in those days thought for a moment that their actions would somehow bring about the fall of the Soviet Union itself – though that creaky old empire did, in fact, only have a few more years to run. But often people do things which, symbolically, they see as putting down a marker, drawing a line, establishing for themselves, and anyone else who cares to know, the way things are going to be. There is a grey area, in fact, between the symbolic gesture and the attempt at downright magic, at manipulating reality as when, for instance, someone in a very different culture makes a wax model of someone they want to harm, or to kill, and then sticks a pin into it. The Old Testament prophets like Ezekiel, Jeremiah and Isaiah would have understood that kind of magic, though they would have rejected it. It is, they would say, a parody of something which, under God and in obedience to him, is a reality.

The phrase we normally give to that reality, when we see it in people like Ezekiel, is symbolic prophetic action. Ezekiel takes a brick and declares, 'This is Jerusalem.' And what happens to the brick happens to the city. Isaiah walks naked and barefoot as a sign of what is going to happen to the people as they go off into **exile**. Jeremiah smashes a pot and knows that this somehow partakes, in advance, of the reality of God's judgment that is soon to fall. And the sequence continues.

Agabus comes from Jerusalem, ties himself up with Paul's belt, and announces that the Judaeans will do this to the man whose belt it is. It isn't just a visual aid. It's what happens when, under the **spirit** who inspires prophecy, part of God's future comes forward into the present and becomes a visible, physical, albeit symbolic reality. This, actually, is how many Christians, drawing on deeply Jewish instincts, have understood the reality of the sacraments.

Paul would certainly not have dismissed Agabus and his warnings. He had depended often enough on words of prophecy, and had given some himself. And he knew already, as he said at Miletus, that he was going into a vortex of suffering, imprisonment and potential disaster. So when he arrived at Tyre, he can't have been surprised that the rapturous welcome he received was mingled with warnings from the Christian family there that he shouldn't go up to Jerusalem. Luke, reporting this, is quite happy to say that these warnings were given in the spirit, without telling us how he reconciles that with the fact that Paul is clear that it is his vocation to go. Sometimes, it seems, the spirit gives people enough information to know what is likely to await them but leaves them with the responsibility of deciding whether or not to go anyway. And Paul was settled in his mind: he had to go.

So Luke cheerfully tells us all the details, once more, about the voyage, the islands, the ports of call, the touching scene on the beach with husbands, wives and children all kneeling down and praying with Paul. It's like a celebratory procession – except that the hero, the man at the centre of it, is going to a deeply uncertain and dangerous future. As he says (verse 13), he is ready not only to be tied up but to die in Jerusalem if that is God's will, and if it will bring honour to the name of the Lord Jesus (there it is again: the Name). And eventually the whole party agrees with him, in the words of the Lord's prayer, and in the words which echo what Jesus himself said in Gethsemane: the Lord's will be done.

And it is precisely that echo which raises in our minds, if we are alert as to how Luke is telling the story, the question of whether Paul, going up to Jerusalem as Acts reaches its climax, is somehow to be seen in parallel with Jesus going up to

141

Jerusalem as Luke's own **gospel** reaches its climax. Is Acts going to be, what people have often said about the gospels, 'a passion narrative with an extended introduction'? Are we going to see the suffering of Paul set in parallel with the suffering of Jesus? Is Luke going to say, by the way he has arranged his material, that just as Jesus suffered for the **good news**, so each generation, each new wave of **kingdom**-work, will have to suffer in the same way?

There is a sense in which something like that is partly true, but the main answer is No. For Luke, as for the other New Testament writers, the suffering and death of Jesus are not principally an example of a larger truth, the sketching out of a pattern which will then simply be repeated. History isn't going round and round in circles. It reached its climax with the death and **resurrection** of the **Messiah**, and it is now going ahead in a new shape and direction. Even if Paul had died in Jerusalem; even if he had been crucified; that could never be regarded in terms of 'well, it just happened again'. The sufferings into which Jesus calls his friends to follow him are sufferings whose character, at the deepest level, has been transformed by the unique effect of his own sufferings and death. Even if, as Paul says, the **apostles** are called to 'fill up in their own flesh what is lacking in the tribulations of the Messiah' (Colossians 1.24, echoing large parts of 2 Corinthians, especially chapters 4, 6 and 11), they are doing so knowing that the enemy is already beaten and that their own pain is part of that larger victory.

But, with that in mind, there is a sense in which Luke is aware of the pattern of his gospel, and of how Acts both follows and does not follow it. At the present point, corresponding to Jesus' approach to Jerusalem in Luke 19, it might look the same. But Paul is not going to die in Jerusalem. Luke's story, in any case, isn't at bottom about Paul; it's about the gospel, with Paul as (at this stage) its primary carrier, or at least the one Luke has, for various reasons, chosen to focus on. And the equivalent of Jesus' death in Luke, when we come across into the present story, isn't either the riot in Jerusalem or Paul's supposed death, later, in Rome (which Luke of course doesn't mention). The equivalent is the suffering through which the gospel, in the person of Paul its carrier, must pass in order to get where it has to get, that is, to the ends of the earth. The equivalent of the cross in Luke is the shipwreck in Acts, when the themes of the stormy sea from the *Odyssey*, from Exodus, from Jonah and from the suffering Psalms bring Luke's narrative of trials on the one hand and sea travel on the other rushing together, and threatening Paul with the dark fate that might have prevented him standing before Caesar.

All that is, of course, six chapters ahead of us. But it's important, from time to time, to see where we are going. Paul is going up to Jerusalem. But the gospel he is carrying is going to the ends of the earth.

ACTS 21.15–26

Warding off the Inevitable

[15]After those days we made preparations to go up to Jerusalem. [16]Some of the disciples from Caesarea went with us, and took us to the house of Mnason, an elderly disciple from Cyprus. That was where we were going to be staying.

[17]When we came to Jerusalem, the brothers and sisters welcomed us gladly. [18]On the next day Paul went in with us to see James, with all the elders present. [19]He greeted them and laid out before them everything which God had done through his ministry among the Gentiles, telling it all step by step. [20]They praised God when they heard it.

'You see, brother,' they said, 'that there are many thousands of Jews who have believed. They are all of them fiercely enthusiastic for the law. [21]But what they have heard about you is that you teach all the Jews who live among the nations to abandon Moses, telling them not to circumcise their children and not to keep the customs. [22]Where does this leave us? They will certainly hear that you have come. [23]So do what we tell you: there are four men here who have taken a vow upon themselves. [24]Join in with these men. Purify yourself along with them, and pay the expenses for them as they have their heads shaved. That way everyone will know that there is no truth in the accusations against you, but rather that you too are behaving as a law-observant Jew should. [25]As for the Gentiles who have believed, we have written to them with our decision that they should

143

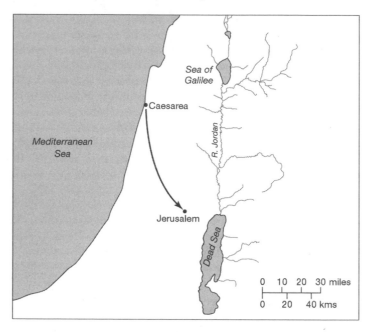

Acts 21.15–26

keep themselves from what has been sacrificed to idols, from blood, from what is strangled, and from fornication.'

²⁶So Paul took the men and, the next day, underwent the ritual of purification alongside them. He went into the Temple and made the declaration, stating when the days of purification would be completed and when the time would come for sacrifice to be offered for each of them.

One of the oldest and best-known legends in English history is the story of King Canute. (He was probably called Knut or something like that, but we'll leave him in his usual popular form for now.) According to the legend, he had his throne brought down to the sea shore and put on the sand facing the incoming tide. To demonstrate how magnificent his power was, he commanded the sea to stop, to come no further. The

144

sea, of course, took no notice, and he and his entourage had to beat a hasty retreat.

Now the clever revisionist historians have told us that actually Canute was smarter than he sounded. What he was trying to do was to show his flattering courtiers precisely that he *wasn't* as powerful as they kept telling him he was. He wanted them to have their feet on the ground, to realize that though he was indeed a king he wasn't as powerful as all that, and certainly wasn't capable of telling the ocean tides what to do and what not to do. But whatever the subtle motive, the picture remains, of the king vainly trying to stop what was going to happen anyway.

That is how it feels reading about the vain attempts of the poor Jerusalem church to stop what they could see was highly likely to happen. And, if Paul's own account of his travels and escapades (verse 19) had been anything other than the most anodyne and expurgated account, they might well have found their anxiety levels rising. Riots in Antioch, stoning in Lystra, beatings in Philippi, more riots in Thessalonica, run out of town in Beroea, court cases and anti-Jewish violence in Corinth, and then that little escapade with 25,000 chanting pagans in Ephesus: so what do we think is likely to happen now he's back in Jerusalem? A Sunday-school picnic?

Their worries were made sharper because they knew, better than he did, how the local mood had shifted. Yes, Cornelius had been **converted, baptized** and received the **holy spirit**, without being **circumcised**, because God told Peter that was All Right. Yes, when they had the big discussion, the 'Apostolic Conference', the decision had gone the same way. But since then the **gospel** had made further inroads into the Jerusalem population, and all those who had believed in Jesus were all – here comes the fateful phrase again, which we have met in one form or another several times as Paul has been out on the road – 'zealous for the **law**'. In other words, these thousands of recent converts, Paul, are taking the same line as you yourself once did, righteously indignant for God's honour, for the eternal and unbreakable law of Moses, for the sanctity of the Temple and the land, for the national dream of liberation from Rome, of Israel's vindication – of, indeed, 'restoring the kingdom to Israel' (Acts 1.6). Isn't that what Jesus had promised?

And look here, the Jerusalem leaders went on, people who think like that know only one thing about you, Paul: they know you've let the side down. 'They have all been told' (by whom? Who has been spreading these rumours? Who made them up in the first place?) 'that you teach the Jews out there in the wider world that they don't need to obey the law any more. That they don't need to circumcise their children or keep "the customs" – the things that mark out a Jew as a Jew.'

And these are the *Christians* here in Jerusalem? Paul must have thought. With friends like this, who needs enemies? *Of course I don't do that,* he will have wanted to say. *I don't know who's made this up, but it's nonsense.* There is all the difference in the world between telling **Gentile** converts that *they* don't need to be circumcised, because they don't need to become Jews in order to be full members of God's people, and drawing the further conclusion that therefore Jews should abandon their ancestral traditions and customs as well. That's something Paul has neither said nor done.

On the contrary. 'To the Jews I became a Jew.' Did he have a copy of 1 Corinthians with him so he could *show* them what he had said? Or, on second thoughts, might that be risky? Did it not also say that 'neither circumcision nor uncircumcision matters at all; what matters is keeping God's commandments' (1 Corinthians 7.19)? Yes, Paul would have mused to himself, but that was a deliberate irony to make the point: everybody knows that circumcision was itself one of the commandments. But this lot here in Jerusalem seem to suffer from irony deficiency. No point in even trying to explain. As far as they are concerned, it's all or nothing. Either you say that circumcision matters, in which case every Christian has to be circumcised. Or you say it doesn't, in which case no Christian – including Jewish Christians – should be circumcised. And it's blindingly obvious, Paul, that that's where you stand.

Speaking for a moment as a church leader, I take great comfort in Paul's uncomfortable position. It's where we often find ourselves. Zealots to left of us, zealots to right of us, zealots in front of us, volley and thunder their absolute and undoubted truths, while those of us who have to find a way through with real people who are struggling to live real lives in loyalty to the real Jesus know, but realize we simply cannot explain to such people, that things are more complicated than that. Not because we have made them complicated, or because the gospel itself isn't clear, or because we are fatally compromised, but because real life in God's world *is* complicated and the gospel must not only address that real life from a distance but must get down on its hands and knees alongside it and embrace it right there with the love of God.

And so Paul, ready for a symbolic act where explanation was obviously going to fail, agrees to go along with a potentially clever plan. 'What, Paul, our friend, disloyal to the law of Moses? Of course not! Look, there he is: purifying himself, paying the expenses of these four men who are under a vow along with him! They're doing exactly what Moses commanded! Now how can you accuse him of disloyalty?' And maybe, just maybe, it might have worked, for the moment at least. Numbers 6 did indeed prescribe a way of purification by which people, for a fixed period, could live a life of extra asceticism, extra devotion, extra care to avoid all manner of pollution, even down to avoiding the funerals of close family members because coming into contact with a dead body meant 'corpse impurity'. No wine, no strong drink, not even raw grapes, not even the *skins* of raw grapes; no more haircuts; no funerals; nothing to stop the life of purity expressing itself fully and completely.

And Paul, as we saw in the slightly puzzling passage in Acts 18.18, was up for it. This kind of thing had continued, in fact, to be part of his own prayer life, his own pattern of devotion, from time to time. No doubt he would have said that he was doing it for the Lord Jesus, but it was essentially the same: not (of course) a legalistic ritual designed to twist God's arm for special favours, but a glad response of total devotion to the one who had given himself totally for him, a way of 'pressing on to make it my own, because **Messiah** Jesus has made me his own' (Philippians 3.12).

So off they went. Paul the seafarer, Paul the Roman citizen, the Paul who had lectured to the Areopagus, stood before the

Roman tribunal in Corinth, and thrown all Ephesus into uproar – Paul had his head shaved, paid the expenses of the others, and went off into the Temple to sign the paperwork and set the process in motion.

He must have known it wasn't going to work. The welcome he and his companions had had from Mnason, a Cypriot Jewish Christian living in Jerusalem, was no doubt cheering, but Mnason's was the last friendly roof under which Paul would ever stay.

ACTS 21.27–36

Riot in the Temple

27When the seven days were completed, some Jews from Asia spotted Paul in the Temple. They gathered a crowd and grabbed him.

28'Men of Israel,' they yelled, 'come and help us! This is the man who's been teaching everybody everywhere against our people, our law, and this place! And now, what's more, he's brought some Greeks into the Temple, and he's defiled this holy place!' 29(They had previously seen Trophimus the Ephesian with Paul in the city, and they thought Paul had taken him into the Temple.)

30The whole city was stirred up, and people rushed together from all around. They seized Paul and dragged him outside the Temple, and the gates were shut at once. 31As they were trying to kill him, word reached the tribune of the guard that all Jerusalem was in an uproar. 32At once he took soldiers and centurions and ran down to them. When the crowd saw the tribune and the soldiers, they stopped beating Paul. 33Then the tribune came up, arrested him, ordered him to be bound with two chains, and asked who he was and what he had done. 34Some in the crowd said one thing, some said another. Since he couldn't find out what was really going on because of the uproar, he gave orders for Paul to be brought into the barracks. 35When they got to the steps, the pressure of the crowd was so strong that the soldiers had to carry Paul. 36The great mob of people was following, and shouting, 'Kill him! Kill him!'

On the news every day, as I write this, there is footage of American and British soldiers in Afghanistan and Iraq. Like many others, I was of the opinion that we were wrong to start what we did in that part of the world, and I haven't changed that point of view. But I am full of admiration for the men and women – well, almost all of them, but then there are always some who let the side down in any walk of life – who are out there doing an extraordinarily difficult job under very trying conditions. The British television tends, naturally, to interview British officers, and again and again, even when facing impossible tasks or tragic events, they come across as intelligent, well-educated people with plenty of common sense, free from any bombastic rhetoric. They are there to do a job and they are doing it with professionalism and as much good humour as they can muster. Sometimes they are people who, when the war is over, will change careers and have a powerful future ahead of them.

I think of those young officers, professional and educated but trying to operate within the labyrinthine complexities of Middle-Eastern politics, as I think of the tribune in charge of the guard, up in the fortress Antonia – which the Romans had built overlooking the **Temple** compound precisely so that they could keep an eye on just this kind of disturbance. Tribunes in the Roman army were often young men on their way up the ladder, politically and perhaps socially. This man might well have been aristocratic; he would certainly have been well educated. But nothing in the Roman system could have prepared him for the intricacies of first-century Jewish political and religious life. I once met a university professor in the holy land who said to me, wearily, that it might be just about possible to explain the Palestinian question to an intelligent listener, given enough time and goodwill, but that if I wanted to understand Lebanon I would have to do at least a Master's degree in Middle-Eastern politics first before I could even begin. Jerusalem in the 50s of the first century would take at least that. I once made a large-scale map of all the different factions and groupings, and their leaders, at the start of the Roman–Jewish war (about ten years after the incident we are studying), and it covered nearly my whole desk, with lines criss-crossing and intersecting. And that was just the people that Josephus had thought fit to record. No doubt he, like all historians, massively oversimplified.

So, with Jerusalem at flashpoint during the festival – Luke doesn't say that Paul had in fact made it back for Pentecost, as had been his plan, but it is quite likely, and that would explain the extra presence of Jews from Asia in the city – it wasn't difficult to whip up a crowd and get them excited at the thought of catching a traitor. Forget the purification, the shaved head, the vow: here was the man who was teaching everywhere that Judaism is finished, that our people, our **law**, our Temple are all a waste of time! And, ignoring the facts (that Paul had come into the Temple with four other Jews, all in a state of purification) and making up some of their own (that Paul had brought a **Gentile** fellow Christian, Trophimus from Ephesus, right into the Temple rather than just into the city), these Jews from Asia, probably from Ephesus, were able to do in Jerusalem what Demetrius and his friends had done back where they came from. It can't have been much fun for Paul to reflect ruefully on how clearly his own words were coming true, that the **gospel** of Jesus Christ crucified and risen was a scandal for Jews and folly for Greeks. But come true they did.

The **miracle** is that he survived. If a crowd is intent on killing someone they can often succeed before the time it would take for an officer upstairs in the fort to notice, to call reinforcements, and to hurry down to intervene. By that time they had dragged Paul out of the Temple gate and, says Luke, 'The gates were shut', a sentence heavy with meaning, rather like John's comment that when Judas went out, 'it was night'. That was the last time Paul would see the inside of the beautiful Temple. It was only to be another 15 years or so before it was destroyed, never to be rebuilt.

The tribune, faced with the riot and a battered victim, tried to find out what the problem was, but since the charges were broad, imprecise and in any case inaccurate, it's hardly surprising he couldn't make head or tail of them. So, having secured him with a chain – something else Paul was going to have to get used to in the coming days, months and years – he tried to bring him up into the barracks. Once again the chanting, like the chanting of the mob in Ephesus, or the rhythmic chanting of the angry crowd in E. M. Forster's *A Passage to India*, overwhelms the area, reminding us all too unpleasantly of the scenes as Jesus is brought before Pilate. The chief **priests** have not so far been involved in Paul's case, though they soon will be. Paul is handed over to Roman custody by sheer force of mob violence.

The one note of clarity in the whole scene is the point Luke is making yet again. The mob is trying to kill Paul because of false charges to do with his disloyalty to the Jewish law and customs. And the Roman soldier rescues him. Luke is not, as some have supposed, trying to suck up to Rome, saying that Romans always do the right thing while Jews always do the wrong thing. Remember the proud but stupid Roman magistrates in Philippi! Just wait for those cunning and unscrupulous governors Felix and Festus! No: Luke is trying to establish a pattern, which includes the Gallio scene in Corinth and the town clerk in Ephesus. Give this man a chance and he will show you his innocence. Let cool-headed justice prevail over hot-tempered mobs, and Paul will be vindicated.

Luke is not just trying to make a general point, for a general readership, about Christians in general. He is making a specific point about Paul. Yes, wherever he goes there is a riot. But that is because he is being loyal to the true, if extraordinary and dangerous, purposes of the God of Abraham, Isaac and Jacob, the creator God who will one day call the whole world to account. Every vindication of Paul is another advance signal of that eventual day. The God who called the pagan Cyrus to rescue Israel from Babylon (Isaiah 45.1) can and will use Roman justice, for all its glaring faults, to show in advance that Paul has done nothing worthy of death. Learn to hear the story in these terms, and to wrestle with today's complex problems of **faith**, politics, justice and loyalty with new courage and hope.

ACTS 21.37—22.11

Why Not Hear My Story?

[37]As they were about to go into the barracks, Paul turned to the tribune.

'Am I allowed to say something to you?' he asked.

'Well!' replied the tribune. 'So you know some Greek, do you? [38]Aren't you the Egyptian who raised a revolt some while back and led those four thousand "assassins" into the desert?'

[39]'Actually,' replied Paul, 'I'm a Jew! I'm from Tarsus in Cilicia. That's not an insignificant place to be a citizen of. Please, please, let me speak to the people.'

[40]So he gave him permission. Paul stood on the steps and motioned with his hand to the people. When, eventually, there was silence, he spoke to them in Aramaic.

[22.1]'My brothers and fathers,' he began, 'hear me as I explain myself to you.'

[2]When they heard him speaking in Aramaic they became even quieter.

[3]'I am a Jew', he continued, 'and I was born in Tarsus in Cilicia. I received my education here, in this city, and I studied at the feet of Gamaliel. I was trained in the strictest interpretations of our ancestral laws, and became zealous for God, just as all of you are today. [4]I persecuted this Way, right to the point of killing people, and I bound and handed over to prison both men and women – [5]as the high priest and all the elders can testify. I received letters from them to the Jews of Damascus, where I was going in order to find the heretics who were there, tie them up, and bring them to Jerusalem to face their just deserts.

[6]'Just as I was on the way, and getting near to Damascus, suddenly a bright light shone from heaven all around me. It was about midday. [7]I fell down on the ground and I heard a voice, saying "Saul, Saul, why are you persecuting me?" [8]I answered, "Who are you, Master?" And he said to me, "I am Jesus of Nazareth, and you are persecuting me!"

[9]'The people who were with me saw the light, but they didn't hear the voice of the person speaking to me. [10]So I said, "What shall I do, Master?" And the Lord said to me, "Get up and go into Damascus, and there you will be informed of all the things that have been arranged for you to do."

[11]'So, as I couldn't see because of the brightness of that light, the people with me led me by the hand, and I came to Damascus.'

A story is told of Bishop Kallistos Ware, the Greek Orthodox bishop who for many years taught theology at Oxford. Bishop Ware was born and bred in England (his original name was Timothy), and he converted to Greek Orthodoxy as he was growing up. I don't know if he told the story against himself, or whether it was told about him, but it rings true to other things I and others have heard him say.

He used to go – maybe he still does – to spend time in retreat on a remote island in the Aegean. There are plenty of monasteries where one can get right away from it all and spend time in prayer, fasting and contemplation. At least, almost right away from it all. On this occasion, a visitor from America came upon him, looking very sun-tanned and very Orthodox, very Greek in fact, sitting quietly in the monastery. The visitor asked him one or two questions, and Bishop Ware responded, naturally, in his perfect Oxford English.

'My,' said the visitor, 'you do speak good English.'

'Ah,' replied the bishop, 'one picks it up here and there.'

That is the kind of shock – though not quite the kind of response – that happened to the tribune when he was trying to have Paul carried up the steps, away from the crowd, and into the barracks for questioning. Suddenly the battered prisoner squirms round and asks him a question – in good, educated, stylish Greek. 'Is it permitted for me to speak to you?'

We can just imagine the tribune stepping back in surprise. This man knows *Greek*? And speaks it with flair and polish? He had assumed that he was some ruffian, or trouble-maker, from out in the wild somewhere; perhaps 'the Egyptian' who had led a recent revolt, of which we have evidence elsewhere. The question, and the tribune's assumptions, are somewhat complex, since many if not most Egyptians at this period would be able to speak Greek reasonably fluently, as indeed would many if not most residents of Judaea or Galilee. It seems best to assume that what the tribune knew about 'the Egyptian' included the belief that he was a wild, unlettered man; that he had assumed that this same man, having disappeared after his earlier attempt (reported by Josephus) to perform prophetic signs including making the walls of Jerusalem fall down, had now reappeared and been caught by the angry crowd in the **Temple**. First-century history is not short of characters like that, even if perhaps the tribune has got a little muddled, with the 'assassins' (the 'dagger-men' or *sicarii*) being so far as we can tell a separate movement. But who knows. As I said before, Josephus makes it complex enough, and he is undoubtedly oversimplifying, as we all do.

'No,' replies Paul, revealing the first two things about himself, but keeping the third card up his sleeve in case he needs it later (he will, and soon). He isn't 'the Egyptian'. He is Jewish; but he is a citizen of Tarsus in Cilicia and, as he puts it politely, Tarsus is 'not a trivial place to come from'. It may not have been the leading city in southern Turkey, but it could hold its head up, having about half a million inhabitants at its height (by no means all were citizens; Paul was from the elite), and a fine educational tradition.

But the reason for telling the tribune all this isn't to curry favour, but to ask permission to speak. One might have thought that Paul would not be in much of a fit state to speak, having just been beaten up by a mob; but this is his chance to do in Jerusalem what he had done in so many other places, to speak to his fellow countrymen, his beloved if misguided fellow Jews, the people who, as he had written in a letter only a few weeks before, were 'Israelites, to whom belong the adoption into God's family, the glory, the **covenants**, the **law**, the worship, the promises, the patriarchs and the **Messiah** himself'. He quite probably recognized some faces in the crowd, people he had studied with 20 or more years before, and perhaps there were relatives there as well. This great, angry, violent mob was the people of whom he had said that he had great sorrow and unceasing anguish in his heart, and could wish that he himself would be cut off from the Messiah for their sake (Romans 9.2–5). Of course he wanted to speak to them. He had never stopped praying for them (Romans 10.2). Could he not speak to them of their own Messiah?

It's a risky strategy, but worth a try, especially when you can switch effortlessly, as Paul could, into the ancestral tongue, or at least the current form of it (he used Aramaic, we assume, rather than classical Hebrew, which not all of them would have understood). Sure enough, when they first see him waving his hand for attention, and then hear him speaking the local language, they are ready at least to give him a hearing. Will he be able, then and there, to clear his name, to explain what it's all about, to tell his whole story so they can see why he does what he does and that he isn't guilty of what they are accusing him of?

Well, he will have a go. This is where Luke, too, takes a risk with his readers, since we have already heard this story, back in chapter 9, and will hear another variation on it quite soon, in chapter 26. It is almost as though Luke had included in his **gospel** the 'sermon on the plain' not once, but three times. Either we say that Luke is a very careless editor and hasn't really thought about the effect of all this in a work of such literary artistry, or – which for that very reason is far more likely – he has a strong motive for wanting his readers to understand Paul's own story very well indeed, well enough almost to be able to recite it themselves.

He begins with some important local detail. Yes, Tarsus was his birthplace, but he was brought up in Jerusalem 'at the feet of Gamaliel'. His parents were strict **Pharisees**, and they made sure he had the best that Pharisaic – that is, strict rabbinic – education could provide. We have, of course, met Gamaliel before, in chapter 5, where he was advocating successfully that the Sanhedrin should back off from attacking the Christians in case they might find themselves attacking God, which was, in effect, the very thing of which Jesus accused Paul on the road to Damascus (see verse 8). But Paul was not of the same mind; not all pupils slavishly follow their teachers. Indeed, as he goes on to say, in parallel with his similar autobiographical comments in Galatians 1.13–14 and Philippians 3.5–6, he knew the ancestral law, the Mosaic code, inside out, and was – here it is again – 'zealous for God', righteously indignant against those who blasphemed God in any way, including by belittling or downgrading the law taken at its strictest. Paul pays them a compliment, in Acts 22.4, which he must have known would have applied in a crowd like this to some more than others: zealous for God, he says, 'just like all of you here today'.

Then, again as in Galatians and Philippians, he cites the most important evidence for his solid and unimpeachable early orthodoxy: he had persecuted the church (which, using the old name which Luke stays with here and there, he calls 'the Way'). He adds graphic details: death, bonds, imprisonment. He calls the **high priest** and his whole council to bear him witness; after all, they gave him the official letters to support his punitive trip to Damascus. Not many of the listening crowd would ever have spoken to a high priest, still less received a direct commission from him. This is impressive stuff.

And then, of course, comes the moment when, again within the strict rabbinic tradition, Paul receives a blinding revelation from God. (The **rabbis** were not only passionate about the law; they were passionate about God, which meant about prayer, about mysticism, about a life of holiness; indeed, it was because of all that that they were passionate about the law in the first place.) And, as we saw, the moment of revelation turned out to be a revelation of Jesus. So far, Paul has the crowd in his hand. They are no doubt astonished, perhaps sceptical, and already looking in their minds for explanations, as modernist scholars have done: many people have tried to psychoanalyse Paul and to suggest that he was suffering from some kind of internal delusion which he interpreted as a vision from **heaven**. But the key thing is not the 'how' of what was going on in Paul's psyche, but the 'what' of his belief, the belief which made sense of everything else, the belief that was vindicated in a thousand ways as he went out and acted on it.

Clearly, Jesus was central to that belief; and so, equally clearly, people then and now have tried to find explanations, any explanation other than the one which means that it actually happened, that Jesus really is alive and addresses people, and transforms them from persecutors into preachers. Paul is not finished with his story. But he has staked out the ground. He has spoken the Name. His deeply Jewish, deeply orthodox, deeply respected birth, background, training and zeal led him straight into the path of the Messiah, and he discovered that it was Jesus. And now Jesus had led him to face a mob of people just like the person he himself had been.

ACTS 22.12–22

Out of His Own Mouth

¹²'There was a man named Ananias,' Paul continued. 'He was a devout, law-keeping Jew, and all the Jews living in Damascus would testify to the fact. ¹³He came and stood beside me and said, "Brother Saul, receive your sight." In that very moment I could see, and I looked at him. ¹⁴This is what he said. "The God of our ancestors chose you to know his will, to see the Righteous One, and to hear the word from his mouth. ¹⁵This is because you are going to bear witness for him to all people, telling them what you have seen and heard. ¹⁶Now, then, what are you going to do? Get up, be baptized and wash away your sins by calling on his name."

¹⁷'After I came back to Jerusalem, and was praying in the Temple, I fell into a trance, ¹⁸and I saw him speaking to me. "Hurry up!" he said, "Leave Jerusalem as quickly as possible! They won't accept your testimony about me." ¹⁹"But, Lord," I replied, "they themselves know that in all the synagogues I used to imprison and beat those who believe in you. ²⁰And when they shed the blood of Stephen, your witness, I was myself standing there and giving my approval. I was looking after the cloaks of those who were killing him."

²¹ "No," he said to me. "Go away from here! I'm sending you far away – to the Gentiles!" '

²²Up to this point the crowd listened to Paul. But now they began to shout.

'Away with him from the face of the earth!' they yelled. 'Someone like that has no right to live!'

In British football, the 'manager', or head coach, is often the most important character in the whole unit. Players come and players go, but if the manager is good he can make things happen, win tournaments, put on excellent performances no matter what.

But often, of course, managers move from one club to another. Sometimes this is because they have been sacked by a club that's doing badly; but sometimes it happens because, even though their club was doing well, they have received an offer they can't refuse from elsewhere. And when that happens, you can expect fireworks.

The fireworks come, of course, when the manager turns up with his new team to play against the team he used to manage. The fans go wild. 'Judas' is the mildest thing they are likely to call him. They will come back to him again and again during the game, mocking him, pointing at him, jeering at him if his new team aren't doing as well as they might. Sometimes it's done in fun, but sometimes you can feel the genuine hatred and venom for someone who the fans feel has let them down badly. There was a case in the newspapers the other day of a manager in just that position, getting ready to face his old team in the stadium where he was once the boss and will now be Public Enemy Number One. 'It's going to be an interesting afternoon,' he said, with characteristically British understatement.

Take that sense of betrayal, of local identity and loyalty, of a burning issue which won't go away, of an 'us and them' complex, and then see it cranked up a thousand times hotter. Take a sense of lasting horror at 'the other side', in this case the entire world of paganism, that has been branded into the very soul of an entire people over not a few decades, not even a few centuries, but one or two millennia. Take the stories, not just of the wonderful season when we nearly won the cup, and the awful moment when the referee failed to award an obvious penalty, but of persecutions and pogroms, of **exile** and shame, of vile foreign rulers doing unspeakable things to noble local heroes, of the foul practices reputed to go on behind closed doors in pagan temples, of orgies and blood and dead babies. Take the songs, not just of this or that football team, but of the creator God putting the heathen gods in their place, songs of lament for Israel's shame at the hands of the foreigners and of delight at her victory over them, of YHWH summoning the nations to meet him on Mount Zion and showing them who their true king really is.

Only when you have allowed your mind to dwell on that total sense, on that God-given and God-directed loyalty – and that horror of everything that dishonours this God, everything that lives outside the doors of the synagogue, outside the borders of the holy land; only then will you even begin to understand why Paul had to try to explain what had happened, and why the crowd had to reject it, and reject it with a furious passion. Of course he had to tell them about Ananias, taking great care to stress how devout and orthodox a Jew he was. Of course he had to refer to God as 'the God of our ancestors'. Of course he had to refer to Jesus as 'the Righteous One', the *tzaddik*, a title full of revered overtones for the upright Jew. And of course he had to describe his return to Jerusalem and his moment in the **Temple**. He hadn't come to announce that the Temple was a blasphemous nonsense. He was praying there, and it was there and then that Jesus had spoken to him again. And even when the Lord warned him of the very result which had now come to pass, he had to tell them that he had argued back, on the basis that the folk in Jerusalem knew that he had been there, approving and assisting, at the death of Stephen. Of course Paul had to say all that.

And of course the crowd had to reject it. 'Sending him away to the **Gentiles**' – there it was, they had heard it with their own ears, from his own mouth. He was, after all, the man they thought he was. He was the one who was telling the Gentiles they were all right as they are. (If only they could have read 1 Corinthians, or 1 Thessalonians, or any of the letters, with Paul's careful, often agonized, attempts to make these ex-pagans think and behave Jewishly!) He was the one who was teaching Jews all around the world to live like Gentiles – in other words, teaching them to accept table fellowship with anyone and everyone purely on the basis of **faith** in this '**Messiah**' he was talking about, this blasphemer Jesus who had caused all the trouble in the first place. If Paul thought this was a 'defence', he had another think coming. They were going to show him otherwise. He was guilty, guilty as the Gentiles whose friend he had become, guilty as sin itself.

As we shut our ears to the baying of the crowd, and stop the dust they are throwing up from getting in our eyes, we find ourselves asking: did it have to be like this? Is this what happens, in the long term, when the prodigal comes home and the elder brother refuses to accept him? Was there after all an inevitability about the mutual rejection? Paul himself would say that there was – but that it was not final. In Romans 9—11, written weeks before this uproar but written, almost prophetically, as a description of its theological 'inside', he bears his fellow Jews witness, he says, 'that they have a zeal for God, but it is not enlightened', not 'in accordance with knowledge' (10.2). They are, he says, 'ignorant of God's righteousness', that is, of what God is doing in the world, and in their own history, and supremely in Jesus, as the revelation in action of his own faithfulness to the **covenant**. They are 'seeking to establish their own righteousness', that is, the status of being 'the righteous ones', the people to whom God will say, always and for ever, 'You are my beloved people, with you I am well pleased.' And they will not see (because, like the monkey with his hand grasping the nut inside the trap, they will not release their grip on what they already have, and so cannot get free to take the huge, wonderful thing being offered to them) that God is offering them all of that and more: fulfilment of the covenant, the real and final 'return from exile' promised in Deuteronomy 30, the gift of the **law** not just as a book to be studied but as the very beating of their own hearts, and, above all, the Messiah. The Messiah is the goal, the completion, the crown of it all, bringing to its destination the long, sad story of God's people, taking upon himself all the anger, all the fear, all the bitterness of the centuries, and making an end of it for all except those who are now so identified with and by that anger that they dare not let it go for fear that they won't know who they are any more. That is what Paul is saying in Romans 10.1–11. If only they will believe in this Messiah, who is Lord of all, Jew and Gentile alike, they will find the true fulfilment of all their national and law-based dreams and hopes. But they won't. 'All day long', said God through Isaiah, 'I have stretched out my hands to a disobedient and contrary people' (Romans 10.21, quoting Isaiah 65.2). Having read this far in Acts, we can see why Paul quoted that passage at that point.

But that isn't the end. Perhaps Paul was even hoping – because he always hoped for things far more abundant than most people would ask or expect – that even now he would see something of Romans 11 at work as well. 'Inasmuch as I am the **apostle** to the Gentiles, I magnify my ministry', he wrote, 'in order that I may make *my flesh* jealous, and so save some of them.' 'My flesh' is what he wrote, there in Romans 11.14; and the 'jealousy' of which he spoke, a major motif for him in those chapters, is what he just now experienced in the negative sense, as the mob reacted with fury against his mention of a mission to the Gentiles. But supposing . . . supposing . . . supposing they reflected, just for a moment, that the Gentiles were thereby coming to share in *their* promises, *their* patriarchs, *their* covenants, and *their Messiah*; might they not, as perhaps the older brother in Jesus' story might yet do, become 'jealous' in the positive sense, and decide it was time to stop, and smile, and see the point, and join in?

Only a hope like that can explain the apparent folly of Paul's attempt, and of the fact that, after taking such care over sketching a deeply devout context, he blew it all by the very mention of the Gentiles. And only a hope like that can sustain the church as it reads Acts, and Romans, and tries to make sense of it all in a world where so much more venom has been spat in both directions. Sadly, when the church, ashamed of this tradition, has held Paul at least partly responsible for it, agreeing with the attitude of the mob on that fateful day, it has robbed itself of the deepest thinker who might yet help us to make a new start, to run the speech again, and this time let it be heard through to the end.

ACTS 22.23–30

Roman Citizenship Comes in Useful

[23]The crowd was shouting, tearing their clothes, and throwing dust in the air. [24]The tribune gave orders for Paul to be brought into the barracks, and he told the guards to examine him by flogging, so that he could find out just what was the reason for all the uproar against him.

[25]As they were tying Paul up ready for the whips, Paul spoke to the centurion who was standing beside him.

'Is it lawful', he said, 'to flog a Roman citizen without first finding him guilty?'

[26]When the centurion heard that, he went off to the tribune and spoke to him.

'What d'you think you're doing?' he said. 'This fellow's a Roman citizen!'

[27]The tribune came and spoke to Paul.

'Tell me,' he said. 'Are you a Roman citizen?'

'Yes,' replied Paul.

[28]'It cost me a lot of money to buy this citizenship,' said the tribune.

'Ah,' said Paul, 'but it came to me by birth.'

[29]The people who were about to torture Paul stepped back quickly from him. As for the tribune, he was afraid, discovering that he was a Roman citizen and that he had had him tied up.

[30]On the next day, still wanting to get to the bottom of it all, and to find out what was being alleged by the Jews, he released Paul, and ordered the chief priests to come together, with the whole Sanhedrin. He brought Paul in and presented him to them.

CAN YOU PROVE IT?

The sign in the shop selling alcohol challenges all and sundry. I was once buying a drink in one of the small bars in O'Hare Airport in Chicago and was astonished, as a bald and bearded middle-aged man, to be asked to produce proof of my age before I could be served. (Apparently there was some new crack-down in progress against under-age drinking; as usual with this kind of thing, as with airport security in general, 10,000 people have to go through a tedious and irrelevant ritual because one or two may be up to no good.)

In my own country, the laws get tighter and tighter, and whether it's in a bar or a store with a licence to sell alcohol, there are all kinds of ways of asking the question: are you really old enough to do this? 'If you're lucky enough to look under 18', said one sign, sugaring the pill, 'and you still want to buy alcohol, I'm afraid we shall have to ask you to prove it.'

So the question presses: did Paul have to prove his Roman citizenship? If not, why didn't everyone who was about to be flogged make the same claim, in the hope that they might have been able to escape by the time the truth was discovered?

Well, there were severe punishments on offer for anyone claiming untruthfully to be a citizen. Some sources say you could even be put to death for it. So there might have been simply a scare factor: you wouldn't dare try that one on, would you? But in fact there was a way of proving it. It may seem unlikely that Paul still had it about his person after all he'd just been through, but there was an official badge, a little double-faced tablet, made of bronze most likely, known as a 'diploma'; this functioned both as a birth certificate and as a citizenship token. Maybe we are to understand that Paul might have produced such an object as the conversation was progressing; perhaps, if this were a play instead of a history, there would be an understood stage direction at this point, like someone silently producing a passport. ('"Yes," replied Paul, *feeling under his tunic and producing his diploma.*') This is the kind of thing that a contemporary writer might easily assume (if I say 'When I went through customs', I don't mention that I showed the official my passport unless I want to highlight some question about it). But one way or another, Paul convinced first the centurion, then his commanding officer, the tribune.

The tribune sounds quite doubtful. He is a first-generation citizen, and he had had to pay for the privilege (something quite common under the Emperor Claudius). But Paul, for whatever reason, had not had to go that route; he had been born a citizen. Speculation abounds as to how this came about. Antony had granted some Jews citizenship after they had helped him in his campaigns in the middle of the first century BC. Further back, there is evidence for a Jewish presence in Tarsus in the 170s BC, and for some Jews there becoming Roman citizens at least 100 years before Paul's day. So it is perfectly possible that Paul's citizenship was inherited, not just by him, but by his father and even grandfather before him. Paul was, in short, well qualified for the work God had had for him: a Jew of the strictest pedigree and highest biblical training; a Greek speaker and thinker thoroughly at home with the world of ancient philosophy and rhetoric; and a Roman citizen – who knew his rights under the law and was determined to use them as necessary.

We already saw, discussing the incident in Philippi, what a terrifying thing it could be for a Roman soldier to discover that, even by mistake, he might have tied up, let alone flogged, a Roman citizen. Paul, asking his initial question, rubs the point in by adding 'without being found guilty, too!' This is strictly beside the point, since the flogging was not (at this stage) intended as a punishment, but as simply a means of beating the truth out of the prisoner; but the point was no doubt well taken. Without a trial, still less a condemnation, they should not have been doing *anything* to a Roman citizen. Paul could turn the tables on them good and proper if they carried on and he reported it to higher authority.

And once again we have to ask: why is Luke rubbing this point in so strongly? Why add that final clause, which is an explanation the reader could easily have worked out for himself or herself: 'The tribune also was afraid, *for he realized that Paul was a Roman citizen and that he had had him tied up.*' This is more than merely the general point, 'the Romans tend to vindicate Christians when they're on trial.' This is the very specific point: 'The Romans again and again vindicate *Paul* when charges are against him; and they are careful to treat him properly, as a citizen should be treated.'

Of course, there is a second-order problem which we want to press. The casual way in which torture was accepted as normal, as a way of getting at the truth on the assumption that unless someone was screaming in agony their natural tendency would be to lie, ought to be as shocking to us as it was obvious, a part of daily life, to them. We dread to think of the number of perfectly innocent people, down the years not only of the Roman Empire but of several other regimes ancient and modern, who have been put through terrible suffering for no good reason except that nobody could think of a more sensible way of dealing with whatever problem was pressing. Paul, claiming his exemption as a citizen from this barbarity, must have known that had he not been a citizen, or not been able to prove it, he would have had to go through it; and therefore that lots of other people had done, and would again. There was the rack, the thongs, the whip; they were not, we assume, gathering dust. A normal part of everyday barracks life, perhaps enjoyed all the more by the guards because it meant they could take it out on some local or other as a representative of the stupid people they were supposed to be policing. Might Paul perhaps have pressed home his advantage and told the tribune that actually the system as a whole was rotten and ought to be abandoned?

Forget it. As with the fashionable idea that the New Testament writers approved of slavery itself, on the grounds that if they hadn't they would have protested against it, such suggestions proceed, to be honest, from the comfortable armchairs of people who have never faced the realities of life under pressure on the ground, or have never tried in imagination to live even for a minute in the real world of antiquity. *Of course* Paul and the others disapproved of slavery. Their controlling narrative, the great Jewish **Exodus** story, was precisely a story about a God who, as the supreme revelation of his own character, rescued people from slavery. Of course they disapproved of torture; their even greater controlling narrative, the story of the cross and **resurrection** of Jesus, focused specifically on the cruelty and injustice of his torture and death, and on the victory over the entire system which was declared when he rose from the dead. Yes, there is a time for protest, and a time to drive through reforms whether people are truly ready for them or not. But yes, too, the far greater reform is to teach whole communities so to live by these controlling stories that an inner revulsion will stop them from ever going near such practices again. Would that these stories were having that effect throughout today's world.

ACTS 23.1–11

Paul Before the Sanhedrin

¹Paul looked hard at the Sanhedrin.

'My brothers,' he said. 'I have conducted myself before God in a completely good conscience all my life up to this day.'

²Ananias, the high priest, ordered the bystanders to strike Paul on the mouth.

³'God will strike you, you whitewashed wall!' said Paul to Ananias. 'You are sitting to judge me according to the law, and yet you order me to be struck in violation of the law?'

⁴'You are insulting the high priest?' asked the bystanders.

⁵'My brothers,' replied Paul, 'I didn't know he was the high priest. Scripture says, of course, "You mustn't speak evil of the ruler of your people."'

⁶Paul knew that one part of the gathering were Sadducees, and the other part Pharisees.

'My brothers,' he shouted to the Sanhedrin, 'I am a Pharisee, the son of Pharisees. This trial is about the Hope, about the Resurrection of the Dead!'

⁷At these words, an argument broke out between the Pharisees and Sadducees, and they were split amongst themselves. ⁸(The Sadducees deny that there is any resurrection, or any intermediate state of 'angel' or 'spirit', but the Pharisees affirm them both.) ⁹There was quite an uproar, with some of the scribes from the Pharisees' party standing up and arguing angrily, 'We find nothing wrong in this man! What if a spirit spoke to him, or an angel for that matter?'

¹⁰Faced with another great riot, the tribune was worried that Paul was going to be pulled in pieces between them. He ordered the guard to go down and snatch him out of the midst of them and bring him back up into the barracks.

¹¹On the next night, the Lord stood by him.

'Cheer up!' he said. 'You have given your testimony about me in Jerusalem. Now you have to do it in Rome.'

Ever since the French Revolution, politics has been seen in terms of a left–right spectrum. The further Left you go (it is assumed), the more you will favour freedom from constricting and aristocratic authority, loose structures, plenty of voting about everything and ultimately anarchy. The further Right you go (it is equally assumed), the more you will want a controlling government, producing law and order, proper and firm justice, plenty of people to tell you what to do and ultimately dictatorship.

Of course, pressed too far this doesn't work. When a left-wing government gets into power it quickly passes all kinds of laws to tell people very precisely what they may and may not do. When a right-wing government gets into power they may very well be under pressure to allow for a good measure of 'freedom' for the business community at least, and may want to reject 'big government', which often means government by interfering bureaucrats. Life is never quite as simple as we think.

But when faced with a passage like this one, left and right know pretty well what they think Paul ought to have done. The Left think he should have continued with his denunciation of the **high priest**, and the Right think he should have been more ready to accept proper authority. (Of course, since most modern New Testament scholars have inclined to the left, one tends to hear the former view more frequently.) But, again, things were not that simple. This little passage has the ring of truth – first-century, Jewish, indeed Pharisaic truth. It provides an object lesson in how a Jew like Paul thought about the structures of power in society.

The first and most obvious thing is that someone – this man standing there looking important – has ordered a guard to strike him on the mouth. (This means, by the way, 'You are blaspheming! You're obviously telling lies! You have no right to be speaking in your own defence!') Now Paul knows the Jewish **law** as well as, or perhaps even better than, the man giving the orders, and so he answers him at once, not (I think) with a burst of bad temper, but with a solemn denunciation: 'You are ordering *me* to be struck? If you do that, God will strike you! You are like those people the prophets spoke about, a wall that's rotten inside but which has been whitewashed over to look all right – until the moment you come tumbling down!' Ezekiel 13.8–16 is very instructive on this point, denouncing specifically the prophets who give false promises, saying 'peace, peace' where there is no peace. And Paul rams his point home: you're supposed to be judging me according to the law, but you're cutting off the legal branch you're supposed to be sitting on if you then order me to be struck, because that's against the law.

So far, Paul has right on his side – or so it seems. But he has not considered the possibility that the man giving the orders is actually the high priest himself. We assume that Ananias cannot have been wearing any distinctive sign of his office, and that Paul would not have been expected to know which member of the ruling clan happened to be holding office at the time; it was, after all, a good 20 or more years since he had last had contact with a high priest. But when it is pointed out who Ananias is, with the tart remark that Paul has just insulted the highest official in the Jewish system, he is quick to apologize – not for the sentiment, but because it was expressed to someone whose office ought to be respected. 'I know the law, the scripture; it says you shall not speak evil of the ruler of your people.' Paul respects the office, though clearly not the present holder of it.

Paul thus manages to hold together two things which people often find difficult. On the one hand, he certainly will respect the office. Without that, chaos is come again. That is the long and the short of his famous passage in Romans 13.1–7: God wants the world to be governed, because he wants people to live in peace and justice, and if you don't have structures of justice then the bullies, the extortioners and the rest will always win. The problem, of course, is when those structures become structures of *in*justice; but the present passage meets that question head on. The fact that you must respect the structures does not rule out, but rather actually *includes*, the duty to remind the people currently operating the structures what it is that they ought to be doing, and for that matter not doing. This is not the first, and it will not be the last, time when Paul provides some object lessons in basic political theology.

This in turn gives us a graphic illustration of what it means to say, as Paul does in his opening (and, to Ananias, offensive) remark: I have conducted myself before God in a good conscience my whole life. This does not mean 'I have never done anything wrong'; it means 'Whenever I have done anything wrong I have immediately done whatever was necessary to put it right', including, as here, apologizing for a 'sin of ignorance' (Acts 23.5). That was precisely the kind of thing that the sacrificial system was designed to deal with.

This belief in the calling of God to rulers to do justice in the present was, for a **Pharisee**, grounded ultimately in the future when, so they believed, God would set everything to rights, would restore all things, would make a new creation and would raise the dead to live in it. That would be the final 'judgment', and all other 'judgments' would in some measure or other anticipate that one. That was not, presumably, how the **Sadducees** saw the matter, since they didn't believe in **resurrection**, or indeed in new creation, or indeed, so it seems, in any kind of **life** after death at all, or perhaps only the shadowiest variety. And Paul, knowing this – and perhaps realizing that he's never going to get much of a hearing out of this bunch if they aren't even willing to let him say his first sentence without resorting to what is euphemistically called 'judicial violence' – decides to release his biggest cat into a room full of self-important pigeons. 'Resurrection!' he shouts. 'That's what this trial is all about! That is the great Hope for which we Pharisees have always stood up! The issue before us is the Resurrection of the Dead!'

That is more or less the equivalent of someone in a crowded and heated political meeting in a volatile southern American state suddenly producing a Confederate flag and waving it around. Some will always rally to it, whatever else they think about the person doing the waving. Whatever other substantive issues people might have expected to discuss will be lost in the melee. And this in turn brings us back where we were in 4.2, where the Sadducees were highly annoyed that the **apostles** were teaching resurrection, and saying that it had already begun in Jesus.

But the Pharisees (we don't know what proportion of the court were one or the other) at once see a call to a rallying-point. They can't let the side down. Knowing that Paul claims that Jesus has been raised from the dead, they obviously are not about to go *that* far, but they are prepared to come halfway. Anyone who believes in ultimate resurrection, of course, has to believe that somehow God holds those who have died in some form of continuing life while they await their resurrection. There are various ways of saying this; a famous one is to speak about the '**soul**', as the Wisdom of Solomon (a Jewish book of this period) does in its third chapter. The two options the Pharisees prefer is to talk (as we saw in 12.15) of an 'angelic' existence, or to talk of someone's '**spirit**' still being alive and awaiting resurrection. So, since they certainly won't agree that Jesus has actually already been raised bodily from the dead, they are prepared to allow that maybe the person whom Paul met on the road to Damascus was the 'angel' or the 'spirit' of this person Jesus, still alive and awaiting resurrection (along with everyone else) on the **last day**. And if this is what Paul is standing up for (verse 9), why, then they are prepared to line up and support him.

The tribune realizes it's no good. (He may, we suppose, be a bit exasperated with Paul for precipitating this off-topic discussion, but that's how it goes.) So he brings him back to the barracks to stop him being torn apart, like the child in Solomon's judgment, with the Sadducees and the Pharisees each claiming part of him.

Once again, the moment of crisis becomes the moment of vision. As in Corinth, so now in Jerusalem, the Lord stands by Paul. These moments of realization, of clarity of inner sight, have been all-important for Paul, just as they have been for countless Christians ever since. (It is remarkable, when you start talking about this kind of thing, how many people will say, 'Yes, that's funny, I remember when such-and-such happened . . .' and out they will come with a similar moment when suddenly the clouds rolled away and they *knew*, they heard, they perhaps even saw. We Christians often sell ourselves short by quietly forgetting these moments, or not talking about them for fear other people won't understand or will think we're making it all up.) And the word this time is encouraging indeed, and provides a key turning-point in Luke's plot. Paul is not, after all, to die in Jerusalem. His sense of vocation, to go to Rome, was genuine. He isn't promised a comfortable ride. But he will get there, and must do there what he has done here: bear witness. And the word for 'witness', as we have seen before, is the word from which we get 'martyr'.

ACTS 23.12–22

The Oath and the Plot

¹²The next morning, the Jews made a plot together. They swore an oath, binding themselves not to eat or drink until they had killed Paul. ¹³There were more than forty of them who made this solemn vow with one another. ¹⁴They went to the high priest and the elders.

'We have sworn a solemn and binding oath', they said, 'not to taste anything until we have killed Paul. ¹⁵What you need to do is this: tell the tribune, with the Sanhedrin, to bring him down to you, as if you wanted to make a more careful examination of his case. And then, before he arrives, we'll be ready to dispatch him.'

¹⁶Paul's nephew (his sister's son) heard of the plot. He went off, entered the barracks, and told Paul about it. ¹⁷Paul called one of the centurions.

'Take this young man to the tribune,' he said. 'He's got something to tell him.'

¹⁸So he took him off and brought him to the tribune.

'Paul the prisoner called me and asked me to bring this young man to you,' he said. 'Apparently he's got something to tell you.'

¹⁹So the tribune took the young man by the hand, and led him off into a private room.

'What is it you have to tell me?' he asked.

²⁰'The Judaeans have agreed to ask you to bring Paul down to the Sanhedrin tomorrow,' he said. 'It will look as if they're wanting to make a more thorough investigation about him. ²¹But don't do what they want! There are more than forty men who are setting an ambush for him, and they've sworn a solemn oath not to eat or drink until they've killed him. They are ready right now, waiting for the word from you!'

²²So the tribune dismissed the lad.

'Don't tell anyone at all that you've told me about this,' he said.

Today in the newspapers there was a story about a woman who had a ridiculously narrow escape. She had stepped out of her office for just a moment of fresh air, when a car, whose driver had suddenly fallen ill, came crashing through the window and landed right on the chair she'd been sitting on not a minute before.

Now I am very well aware that every time that sort of thing happens there are other cases where a car, or a crocodile, or an aeroplane, or something, does something which causes someone's death, and there was nothing to stop it. And I am also aware that for everyone who claims the hidden and saving action of providence, there are others who, perhaps rightly, dismiss the claim as coincidence.

I am reminded, though, of the famous saying of Archbishop William Temple: 'When I pray, coincidences happen; when I stop praying, the coincidences stop happening.' But at least this brings us back to the problem we saw in Acts 12: how come James gets killed with the sword, but Peter gets let out of jail free?

That is the shape of the problem but, as with the so-called 'problem of evil' itself, we do not even address, let alone solve, the problem by denying one of its elements. (With 'the problem of evil', the other side of the coin is of course that if you deny any element of divine activity either in making the world or running it you are left with 'the problem of good': why is there so much beauty, love, truth and justice just lying around all over the place?) And, granted that throughout history people have made plots against other people, and have often carried them out all too successfully, isn't it interesting that on this occasion the plot which might so easily have done away with Paul once and for all was scuppered by a little boy?

This tells us, of course, something we didn't know and would love to know more about. Did Paul have lots of family members in Jerusalem? Were they Christians? How much contact did he have with them, and were they enthusiastic supporters of what he was doing or embarrassed by the attention he was drawing to the family? We know none of this. All we know is that the same night that Paul received a vision of the Lord telling him that he would make it safely to Rome, a little boy happened to be at the right place at the right time, pricked up his ears and knew what to do.

It wouldn't be too unlikely, in a crowded city like Jerusalem. I have written elsewhere of one experience I had, leading a pilgrim party, when a guide who had taken photographs of us wanted to meet us later in the day to give us the prints. We didn't know at that stage that the rendezvous we arranged was going to be blocked off by the authorities, and when the time came to meet up we were a good mile or more away, in quite a different part of the city. Nor could we contact him by mobile phone. And yet he showed up. The city was packed with tourists and pilgrims. How had he known where we were? 'Oh,' he said with a smile, 'we call it the Arabic telephone.' Everybody tells everybody else everything that's going on. Look, there's that party from England. Yes, they're staying at the Seven Arches. Oh, are they the people Ahmed was photographing? Yes, and he's meeting them at the Lion Gate. No he won't, it's shut off. Ah yes, Sadiq said they were going round to the Zion Gate instead. And so on. And so on. Westerners, particularly those who insulate themselves in cars and behind glass all day, find it extraordinary, almost spooky.

And of course you can't guarantee that the bit of information that you really need to find out will be found out. But it is extremely easy to suppose that with all those serious men making this solemn oath not to eat . . . well, they wouldn't turn up for dinner, for a start. Where is Abba? Hush, dear, he's doing God's work. Oh, that's exciting, what does God want him to do? Hush, dear, he won't be eating until they've got rid of that troublemaker they caught in the **Temple**. And a little boy tells another little boy down the street, and they hear of someone else who's in it as well, and soon all the little boys realize there's something going on. And one of them just happens to be the nephew of the man whose name is on everyone's lips and who will soon, they hope, be at the point of their knives.

What we all want to know at this point is, of course, what did they all do next, once the plan was thwarted? They could go, perhaps, for several days, getting increasingly hungry and agitated, urging the chief **priests** to do something about it, to find a way to let them get at him. Five days sees Paul already down in Caesarea, but with the chief priests following him down and presenting their case. Perhaps, think the hungry men, perhaps they'll be able to get him for us now? But no. He is in the governor's power, and it will be two years before there is even the slightest chance. I imagine that few of them, if any, starved. I imagine the **high priest** found a legal loophole to absolve them from their silly vow. Or maybe, since they were legal experts, they invented one themselves. It wouldn't be the first or the last time. And – since part of the point of all this is that they were the ultra-orthodox legal experts, concerned above all for the honour of God and his **law** – there would be a nice irony in imagining them cautiously explaining to their own consciences how even that most solemn oath hadn't quite meant what it said.

Is there a lesson to be learned from this splendid little story, straight out of an old-fashioned *Boys' Own Magazine*, with the youngster suddenly becoming the hero and holding the key to the plot? If there is, it can only be a message about God's strange providence. 'No good thing', said the Psalmist, 'will the Lord withhold from those who live an upright life.' That doesn't mean that bad things never happen to good people, or that good people always get what they want. That certainly isn't true, as many other Psalms – to look no further – also declare, and as Acts insists again and again. But it can be claimed as a principle, and then applied, in prayer, to particular situations. If there is danger, let it be averted. If there is malice, let it be thwarted. If there is temptation, give me strength to resist it. If I really need something, let it be provided. And always, Not my will but yours be done. And always, Your **kingdom** come. Funny how the Lord's prayer creeps up on you, as it were, from behind. It's just what we needed.

ACTS 23.23–35

We Have Ways of Keeping You Safe

²³So the tribune summoned two of the centurions.

'Get ready a squad of two hundred,' he said. 'They're going to Caesarea. Take seventy horsemen and two hundred light-armed guards. They leave at nine o'clock tonight. ²⁴Get horses ready for Paul to ride, and take him safely to Felix the governor.'

²⁵He wrote a letter which went like this:

²⁶'Claudius Lysias, to the most excellent governor Felix, greeting. ²⁷This man was seized by the Jews, who were going to kill him. When I learned that he was a Roman citizen I went with the guard and rescued him. ²⁸I wanted to know the charge on which they were accusing him, so I took him into their Sanhedrin. ²⁹There I discovered that he was being accused in relation to disputes about their law, but that he was not being charged with anything for which he would deserve to die or to be imprisoned. ³⁰I then received information that there was to be a plot against him. So I am sending him to you at once. I have told his accusers that they must inform you of their charges against him.'

³¹So the soldiers did what they were told. They took Paul and brought him by night to Antipatris, ³²and the next day they

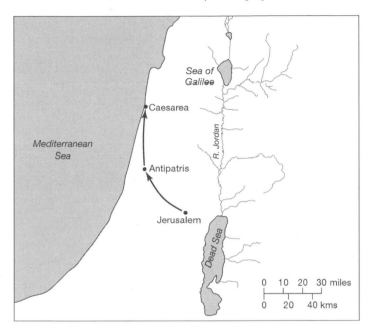

Acts 23.23–35

allowed the horsemen to go on with him while they returned to barracks. [33]The company arrived at Caesarea and handed over the letter to the governor, presenting Paul at the same time. [34]Felix read the letter, and asked which jurisdiction Paul was from. He found out that he was from Cilicia.

[35]'I will hear your case', he said, 'when your accusers arrive.' He ordered that he be kept under guard in Herod's Praetorium.

Richard Adams' celebrated novel *Watership Down* draws the reader into the dramatic and complicated world of a group of rabbits. We follow with increasing sympathy and fascination as Hazel and his companions go on their journey. (Adams was himself a classical scholar, and there are traces of the ancient journeying sagas in his work.) They brave all kinds of hazards, particularly wicked members of their own race on the one hand and, of course, humans on the other. And of all the things that humans do which make rabbits terrified, the car is one of the worst. You never know where you are when crossing one of their roads. These vast and noisy objects come rushing out of nowhere and can kill one or more of your family or friends in an instant.

The rabbits have a word for car: *hrududu*. It is, obviously, a rabbity way of trying to imitate the noise of the engine. They speak of hrududus with a mixture of horror, anger and fear. They avoid them like the plague. So it is one of the book's great moments when Hazel has been lost, far away from the others, and then, astonishingly, is rescued by humans who bring him back. And they bring him, naturally, in a car.

Hazel tells his friends the story, hardly able to contain his excitement, and enjoying to the full the enormous irony of it all.

'How did you get back from the farm?'

'A man brought me in a hrududu . . . nearly all the way.'

Looking back, Paul must have felt exactly like that. He had managed – just – to stay on the right side of the law throughout his travels around Turkey and Greece. He had avoided, to be honest, having too much to do with police, the lawcourts, the military or such eminent persons as provincial governors. He valued his freedom to come and go, the fact that he could stay in one place for two days and another for two years. Throughout much of the story, especially after the brief brush with Roman justice in Philippi, we have a sense that Paul would just as soon stay well away from Roman officials or soldiers. Like Jesus going around Galilee, always keeping on the move, hard to pin down by the anxious, brooding Herod as he heard tales about someone else going about being thought of as 'king of the Jews', so Paul kept on the move, happy that though no doubt various Roman officials had heard about him they were not trying to stop him doing what he had been called to do.

And now he is, so to speak, brought home in a hrududu. A Roman officer rescues him. The plot against him is discovered, and the tribune takes swift action. We now discover the tribune's name: Claudius Lysias, where 'Claudius' may well be a new name added in reference to the emperor under whom he had purchased his citizenship (as in 22.28). And suddenly the full machinery of the Roman army, just what a travelling **apostle** would normally want to avoid if he could, is mustered to rescue him from the plot and to take him to the governor, who will keep him safe in more ways than one. So the guards, who the previous day had been ready to tie Paul up and flog him, are now transformed into his protectors, along with their colleagues. And the plotters, who are getting ready an ambush for the following morning in the hope that the tribune will do what they want and send Paul back from the barracks to the Sanhedrin, hear the clatter of hooves and boots in the night and realize, perhaps, that they are going to have to wait longer than they thought before they can eat and drink again. Two hundred soldiers, 70 horsemen, 200 spearmen; nobody ever accused the Romans of underplaying their hand when it came to military presence. They may not know exactly who Paul is or what the fuss is all about, but soldiering is about doing, not knowing, and doing is what the Romans do best.

So by the small hours Paul is well away from Jerusalem, spending the night under heavy guard in Antipatris. Luke implies that the footsoldiers go all the way there and then return to barracks but, since the likely site of Antipatris is between 30 and 40 miles from Jerusalem, an obvious staging post somewhat more than halfway between Jerusalem and Caesarea, there is no way that infantry could get there and back in a night. The footsoldiers probably escorted Paul well clear of the city and then left the cavalry, with Paul on horseback in the middle of them, to take him on from there through the darkness.

And before they left, the tribune had to rack his brains, do some quick thinking, and write a short but sufficient account of what he was doing and why. It reads a bit like a civil service report, short and to the point – and tidying up some of the inconvenient and embarrassing facts. Claudius Lysias does not want the governor, or anybody else, to know that he had had Paul tied up and ready to be flogged before he found that he was a Roman citizen. So he neatly switches the order of events, makes a virtue out of the problem, and states that it was because he discovered Paul to be a Roman citizen (how?) that he rescued him from the mob in the first place.

The heart of the letter, though, is the point which yet again Luke wants to emphasize. *Paul was accused of things to do with the Jewish law, but my judgment as a Roman official is that he deserves neither death nor imprisonment.* Where have we heard that before? Oh, in Corinth, Philippi, Thessalonica, a variant of it in Ephesus. And we shall hear it again, more than once, before the story is out. Who is Luke really writing for? What is he trying to tell them?

Claudius Lysias, we may hope, slept well that night. He had got the trouble off his desk and onto someone else's. Caesarea was the official centre of Roman government. The governor might well come up to Jerusalem from time to time, as Pontius Pilate had done at that fateful Passover 25 years or so before. But normally he would be down at the coast, at the main port, able to be in touch more easily with the wider world, not least with Rome itself, and away from the over-heated atmosphere that Jerusalem could so easily generate. And the point of all this is that, in being sent to the governor, as a Roman citizen, Paul is now in a much stronger position. He enjoys the full benefit of the official system, such as it was.

Felix, the governor, however, hopes he can play 'pass the parcel'. Having received this tricky character, perhaps he can send him on to somebody else. If Paul comes from a different province altogether he can have him sent there to be tried by his local governor. (Pontius Pilate, we recall, tried a similar move when he sent Jesus off to Herod, as in Luke 23.6–12; it didn't work then, either.) But Paul is from Cilicia, which, like Judaea, comes under the Roman administration centred in Syria. So that won't do. Felix has to face the problem himself; or park it, which is what eventually he decides to do.

We know a bit about Felix from various other sources. Claudius Lysias may have moved up socially quite a step by purchasing his citizenship, but Felix has gone from the bottom of the ladder to near the top. He was born a slave. After being given his freedom he, with his brother Pallas, became favourites of the Emperor Claudius – possibly because Claudius, naturally afraid as many emperors were of envious people in high places, preferred to employ and to trust people whose personal gratitude to him was so great that they would be less likely to rebel. Felix was, then, predictably looked down on by snooty Roman aristocrats, much as we might imagine polite society in Boston reacting to a gas station attendant from rural Massachusetts suddenly being elected mayor. During his term of office in Judaea (roughly AD 52–59, which helps to date this whole episode), things went from bad to worse, as the Jews were given more and more reasons to hate their Roman overlords and to fan the flames of their zeal for God and the law, the zeal which, by the end of the next decade, would bring war and utter ruin.

All this enables us to locate the episode, including the riot in Jerusalem and the anxieties of the chief **priests**, in terms of culture, theology and social pressure. We cannot stress too strongly, or too often, that the 'theology' which Paul worked out in his various letters was not the product of someone sitting at a desk and working out a jigsaw of abstract concepts – though his concepts and doctrines do fit together remarkably well. They were the result of someone struggling with the huge questions of *what God is doing right now* in the midst of a turbulent world where many different answers to that question were on offer. Paul clung to the sheet-anchor: the God he had worshipped from boyhood, the God whose glory he had seen in the face of Jesus **Christ**, was faithful to his promises, and would go on being faithful to those who kept **faith** with him, even if he often seemed to have surprising ways of showing it.

ACTS 24.1–9

Bring on the Barristers

[1]After five days, Ananias the high priest came down to Caesarea with some of the elders, and with a barrister named Tertullus. They told the governor what they had against Paul. [2]Paul was summoned, and Tertullus began his speech of accusation.

'Most excellent Felix! We are enjoying great peace because of you! Through your wise foresight and planning things have greatly improved for this people. [3]We welcome it in every way, in every place, and with every feeling of gratitude. [4]But, so as not to keep you waiting any longer, I beg you, of your forbearance, to listen to us briefly.

179

> 5'We find this fellow to be a public nuisance. He stirs up civil strife among all the Jews, all over the world. He is a ring-leader in the sect of the Nazoreans. 6He even tried to defile the Temple! But we caught him. 8If you examine him yourself you will be able to find out about all these things of which we're accusing him.'
>
> 9The Jews added their voices to this speech, agreeing that it was just as had been said.

Jokes about lawyers are unkind, ungrateful, uncharitable – and often uncannily accurate. I remember listening in horror as a clever and unscrupulous young lawyer, in a meeting of a college governing body, constructed a rhetorically powerful argument out of bits and pieces, scraps of ideas, and made a case which colleagues found hard to refute even though everyone who knew what was in fact going on knew it was nonsense. That is, after all, what lawyers are paid for: to make sure that everything that can be said on one particular side is said. And part of the problem, in the ancient world as in the modern, is that people with money and power can hire extremely clever and effective lawyers, who can not only master their brief but also present it in such a way that a jury, and for that matter a judge, will be led along by it to the conclusion the client wants, and has paid for.

Barristers will of course use flattery if they think it will help, and with someone like Felix it probably would. Many observers at the time, and most historians ever since, would disagree strongly with Tertullus' opening lines. Judaea may have been technically at peace, but there was seething discontent rumbling along just below the surface, ready to burst out at any excuse (such as catching a supposedly renegade Jew, someone who fraternized with pagans, in the **Temple**). Likewise, Felix was not actually a man of wise foresight; nor had he made many great reforms and improvements in Judaea. Nor, in fact, was he especially known for 'forbearance' or, as we might translate it, 'graciousness'. But of course Tertullus was hardly likely to tell the truth, which was that everyone laughed up their sleeves at this slave-turned-governor and his high-handed ways. Truth is a casualty in war;

and a lawcourt can be, and was in this case, the continuation of war by other means.

And it carried on like this. We can see the point to this extent: if you want a quiet life, with things going on much as they have, and everybody going about their business, then you really don't want someone like Paul coming to visit too often. He is, from that point of view, a nuisance and a troublemaker. The problem is, of course, that he is all that *seen from the point of view of people who have the system sewn up to their own advantage.* Everything's just fine; don't make a fuss; just keep paying your taxes, do what we say, and nobody need get hurt. Or even upset. That is, ultimately, the high road that leads to Orwellian brainwashing. Don't worry about making things different. Big Brother will look after you. (For those who think that Big Brother is just a television programme, try looking in a bookshop for George Orwell's famous and chilling book *1984.* The date may be long past, but the theme is still extremely relevant.) The Christian **gospel**, it is often said, is designed to comfort the disturbed and disturb the comfortable. Paul was good at the former, as his pastoral themes in letters like 1 Thessalonians make clear. But it would be fair to say that he specialized in the latter.

The charges against him, then, were the classic themes that a Roman governor might be expected to take notice of. Trouble is something we can do without. The reason we Romans are here in the first place, Felix would have known only too well, is because there is always likely to be trouble on the eastern front. All the great Western empires have looked to the East, out beyond Turkey, and have shuddered at the thought of the massed hordes of barbarians ready to sweep down and take over the West, with their ancient or modern weapons of mass destruction, at a moment's notice. For Rome it was Parthia; for the Middle Ages it was 'The Turk' (meaning, loosely, Turkey and points east, the Muslim hordes); for today . . .

And the second reason we are here, Felix might have reasoned, is because the great imperial capital to the west needs food. Italy can't grow enough grain to feed the crowded city of Rome. Egypt can, however, and it is absolutely vital for the safety, not to mention the luxury, which Rome requires that the supply of ships, full of that precious grain, keeps coming and that nothing, no trouble elsewhere in the Middle East, prevents it. Once again, this sounds strangely familiar, though it isn't of course grain that today's Western empires need from the Middle East, or that makes them so jumpy about the thought of trouble.

So Paul was caught in larger issues not of his own making. The accusation of being an agitator, a nuisance-maker, wasn't just the sort of thing that might earn a rap over the knuckles as a silly or petty criminal; it was more serious, a threat to public order at a place and time when public order mattered rather a lot. He is fomenting civil strife (verse 5): the word is the same as was used in connection with Barabbas in Luke 23.19, and indeed the charges against Paul here have several echoes with that chapter, notably with the accusations against Jesus himself in the first two verses ('perverting the people, forbidding them to give tribute to Caesar, giving himself out to be a king'). So, Tertullus declares, Paul is a ringleader, a central figure and stirrer-up, in this new sect, the Nazoreans (just as the Christians didn't have a standard word for themselves at this period, so nobody else seemed quite to know what to call them, either, but the memory of Jesus of Nazareth opened up the possibility of this loose title).

And, in particular, Tertullus finally came to the charge which had been thrown at Paul in Jerusalem: of defiling the Temple, or at least attempting to do so. (Verse 7, by the way, which is absent here, is an addition in some late manuscripts, adding an explanation about the tribune seizing Paul in the Temple.) This brings us all the way back to Stephen in chapter 7, of course, and the question of early Christian attitudes to the Temple, which haunts Acts but is never fully resolved. At one level, it's clear that the early Christians still went on going to the Temple, and indeed offering **sacrifice** (as in 21.26). But at another level, it's clear – not least from the letters which Paul had written by now to various churches – that the Temple in Jerusalem had been totally upstaged, in their minds, by the new community where the **spirit** was living and active.

Nothing more is said in Acts, after Stephen's speech, about the future of the Temple. But within a few years of Paul's trial

Mark's gospel at least will be written, recording the rather full prophecy of the Temple's destruction (Mark 13, paralleled in Matthew 24 and Luke 21). The first generation of Christians were thus living in a strange time of overlap, with the ancient Temple under judgment but still a major symbol which they weren't prepared to abandon until God made it quite clear, but with the new Temple – the community of which Peter, James and the others were 'pillars' (Galatians 2.9), the community where God's own spirit now lived (1 Corinthians 3.16) and the renewed humans of whom the same was true individually (1 Corinthians 6.19) – already up and running. It was an uncomfortable time, to say the least, and of course it is typical of much early Christian thought, not least Paul's, that one has to say both 'now' and 'not yet' at the same time, in many different areas.

Not that Paul is going to get into all of that in his defence. Indeed, though he does this time make reference to the specific charge about defiling the Temple (verses 11–13, 17–19), he once again shifts the ground to more important matters. But for the moment Tertullus' speech looks damning. We assume Luke has drastically shortened it: no professional barrister would expect to pocket his fee for precisely 50 seconds' worth of work (and that's reading the Greek very slowly and ponderously). There is a build-up of serious accusation. There had, after all, been a riot in Jerusalem; that's why Paul got picked up in the first place. Riots are bad news for the authorities, and they seem to happen where Paul is. And there is no question that he is a member of the 'Nazoreans' or 'Nazarenes'; he won't deny that, or that he is a leader of the group, or that they are in trouble all over the place. We know about these sects, Felix will have thought, and the danger they are to public well-being. And why was there a riot, if he wasn't up to no good in the Temple? So there is a strong prima facie case. This man is a nuisance, a troublemaker, a fomenter of civil unrest, and as a particular example of this general bad behaviour he's been trying to do what we always suspect these Christians of doing, demonstrating their contempt for the whole Jewish way of life in general and the Temple in particular by coming and defiling it.

Only when we allow the weight of these charges, and their prima facie plausibility, do we face the real theological problem that has been looming up behind the rather stylized account of a typical first-century barrister making a sly speech to a typical first-century provincial governor. If this is how the authorities get at 'truth', so that they can do 'justice', is the world threatening to collapse into chaos after all? Would not Paul be better doing what many revolutionaries have done in many places and at many times – and what many people today assume will result from any attempt to 'combine religion and politics' – namely, to deny the validity of the court and declare that he wouldn't have anything to do with it, since obviously it wasn't capable of bringing about God's justice? Was he being merely pragmatic in going with the flow of the hearing? Or are there more important principles at stake, principles such as we find in the thirteenth chapter of his own letter to Rome? And do those principles not flow directly from the deeply Jewish belief that the God with whom we have to do is the God of both creation and providence? These are major issues, of great importance in the early twenty-first century, and Acts has a lot to say about them.

ACTS 24.10–21

A Defence of the Hope

[10]The governor motioned to Paul to speak.

'I understand that you have been governor of this nation for several years', he began, 'and therefore I am all the more pleased to make my defence before you. [11]You will be able to discover that it is not more than twelve days since I came up to worship at Jerusalem. [12]They didn't find me disputing with anybody in the Temple; nor was I stirring up a crowd, either in the synagogues or elsewhere in the city. [13]They can provide no proof of any of the charges they are now bringing against me.

[14]'But this much I will confess to you: that it is true that I do worship the God of my ancestors according to the Way which they call a "sect". I believe everything which is written in the law and the prophets, [15]and I hold to the hope in God, for which they also long, that there will be a resurrection of the righteous

and the unrighteous. [16]For that reason I make it my settled aim always to have a clear conscience before God and all people.

[17]'For several years I have been collecting alms and offerings to bring to my nation. [18]That was the business I was engaged in when they found me purified in the Temple, without any crowds and without any riot. [19]There were some Jews from Asia there; they are the ones who should appear before you and bring any accusations against me that they may have. [20]Or let these people themselves say what wrong they found in me when I stood before the Sanhedrin – [21]unless it is about this one thing, which I shouted out as I was standing among them: "It's because of the resurrection of the dead that I am being judged before you today." '

I am still fascinated by kaleidoscopes. I love watching the shapes as they move around and form themselves into different patterns. They were quite basic when I was a boy, and now that I'm grown up and not supposed to like toys any more I often look, in sneaking admiration, at the sophisticated ones you can get today.

Now kaleidoscopes make abstract patterns. I suppose you can get some now that will form themselves into recognizable objects – anything, it seems, is possible in these high-tech days. But supposing you had an ordinary kaleidoscope, with lots of brightly coloured abstract shapes going round and round; and supposing, as you went on turning it, suddenly the whole thing turned into a shape – a figure – a human form! You might find that alarming. It would certainly be a moment to savour.

That is exactly the sort of moment we are now presented with, in Luke's summary of Paul's defence before Felix. (Once again, we must assume it's a summary. This is only the second time Paul has appeared before a Roman governor; on the previous occasion, before Gallio in Corinth, the case was dismissed before he had a chance to speak. The man who wants to give an address to the mob which was beating him up is not going to want to speak for only a couple of minutes to the representative of Caesar himself.) It would be easy, reading through Acts, to get a little weary by this time, and to think, 'Here he goes again – not guilty about the **Temple** – believing in the prophets – **resurrection** – yes, we've heard all this before.'

Well, we have and we haven't. This is where, quite carefully, Luke turns the kaleidoscope of the various things Paul has been saying and brings them all together in a new, striking and clear form.

First, Paul does indeed provide a refutation of the main, central charge against him, that he had been causing a disturbance in, or trying to defile, the Temple. (To 'refute', by the way, doesn't just mean 'to reject' or 'to dismiss', as in some popular speech today; it means 'to provide a complete and convincing argument against'.) He has only been in the country less than a fortnight, and was thus (since he's already been in Caesarea five days, verse 1) only in Jerusalem for a week. He was taking great care to be quiet, not to speak in public, certainly not to engage in debate or dispute. We can only imagine the self-restraint this must have involved for Paul, but since he had made the effort it was a little hard to be accused of what he had carefully not been doing. He wasn't drawing crowds, either in the Temple, or in the synagogue, or in the city at large (verse 12). He knows that there is no way (barring the presentation of witnesses who lie through their teeth) that they can in fact prove the charges (verse 13).

But before he goes on to the positive explanation (verses 18–19) of what precisely he was doing in the Temple – and he didn't, after all, need to be there, he could have paid a private visit to the church and gone off to Antioch or anywhere else – he wants to explain the framework for what he had been doing. He does indeed plead guilty to the charge of being part of (he doesn't say a leader of) the sect of the Nazoreans, though he doesn't call it that, but prefers the ancient phrase 'the Way' once more (see 9.2; 16.17; 18.25–26; 19.9, 23; and, in the next passage, verse 22). And he admits that the non-believing Jews see 'the Way' as a 'sect' or a 'heresy' – the word means 'faction', or 'party', not necessarily in a bad sense, because the **Pharisees** and **Sadducees** are 'parties' in that sense, but increasingly with the sense of 'dangerous, breakaway, troublesome group' – but he doesn't accept that. 'The Way' isn't just a silly option, a strange, distorted group within Judaism, an odd little party off on the side with a particular bee in its bonnet. This is the main line: 'according to the Way (which they call a sect), I worship the God of my ancestors, believing everything in the **law** and the prophets.'

In other words, Paul is claiming the moral, theological and biblical high ground. For him, following Jesus is not an odd hobby that might lead him away from scripture and tradition, but it is the way, indeed the Way, by which the one true God has fulfilled all that the scriptures had said. Paul, in other words, is claiming to be a loyal and faithful Jew. That was his boast throughout, that Jesus had not made him stop being true to his ancestral faith, but that Jesus had revealed who the God of Abraham had been all along and what he had been up to. Remember his verdict on his own former life, and those who still sat where he once sat: they have a zeal for God, but it is not in accordance with knowledge (Romans 10.2). For Paul, the knowledge of God in the face of Jesus the **Messiah** meant not that he was abandoning the faith of his ancestors but that he was penetrating to its very heart.

In particular – and this is the point where the present speech picks up what Paul had said in his brief speech to the Sanhedrin in the previous chapter – he believes in the main-stream, standard hope. Actually, it was controversial, as Paul well knew, and as we saw he had used the fact to his advantage in the earlier scene. It must be slightly tongue in cheek, as though challenging the Sadducean chief **priests** who are listening to this to disagree in public if they dare, to say that 'they long for this hope as well'. But the hope of Israel remains, expressed in Psalms and prophets, and growing directly out of the belief of ancient Judaism that Abraham's God was 'the judge of all the earth' (Genesis 18.25) who will judge justly, that this creator God will one day sort the whole world out, restore all things (Acts 3.21), overturn corruption, injustice, decay and death itself. 'The resurrection of both the righteous and the unrighteous' is not, then, simply a miscellaneous, and rather bizarre or outlandish, doctrine, a kind of extra shib-boleth of belief tacked onto an otherwise more easily believ-able creed. It is all about God's final sorting out of everything, about God's ultimate judgment of the whole world. That is the great hope of Israel. According to Israel's classic poetry, it is the great hope of the whole creation (Psalm 96.10–13; 98.7–8).

And that is why Paul will entrust himself to this court. Not because he thinks for a moment that the Roman system is flawless, or will always do the right thing. Paul knows perfectly well it won't. Not because, as a Roman citizen, he has a dewy-eyed and naive faith that Caesar and his underlings will get it right eventually. He knows that Caesar is a blaspheming pagan, demanding worship which belongs to Jesus alone. Rather, because God is the creator who will one day call the whole world to account, and who has entrusted human authorities with the task of bringing a measure of that calling-to-account into the world in advance. They will go on getting it sometimes right and sometimes wrong, which is why it remains the task of God's people not only to make their defence but also to remind the authorities, as we have already seen Paul do, of what their job is supposed to be. The resurrection is not only at the heart of Christian **faith**. It is also the driving force behind a Christian understanding of what magistrates, at every level, are there for.

This may make it a little bit clearer what Luke seems to be up to, in writing the story of the early church, and particularly Paul, in terms of a succession of 'trials'. The **gospel** is all about God putting the world right – his doing so in Jesus, his doing so at the end, and his doing so for individuals in between, as both a sign and a means of what is to come. Luke wants his readers to see the life of the church itself in that same way. We shouldn't expect a comfortable ride. We shouldn't imagine that people will leave us alone, will not challenge us as to what we are doing, as to how our faith belongs in the public world. If we are the people in and through whom God is putting into effect the setting-right that happened in Jesus, and anticipating the setting-right that will happen at the end, we should expect to see that uncomfortable but necessary setting-right going on all over the place, sometimes in martyrdom and sometimes in vindication and acquittal, as the church makes its way in the world.

And this explains, too, why Paul repeats in verse 16 what he said before the Sanhedrin (23.1): he always does his best to live with a clear conscience. There will come a day when everything is put right, so you need to live without shadows on the conscience now, in the present. This doesn't of course mean you never do anything wrong, but that you always aim to recognize, confess and make amends for sin. Paul has always done that, and he would not dream of deliberately doing anything which would offend either God or other people. This may come as a surprise to people who see Paul as a troublemaker; but listen to what he says in 1 Corinthians 10.31–33: 'Whether you eat or drink or whatever you do, do all to the glory of God. Give no offence to Jews, or to Greeks, or to God's church, just as I try to please everyone in everything I do.' That is the rule he has always tried to follow. And that is why the charges against him are ridiculous before we even get to the details.

When he comes to those details (verses 18–19) we find a circle closed at last. Luke has not mentioned, before this point, the collection which weighed so heavily on Paul's mind when he was writing 2 Corinthians. Now he declares that this has been what has occupied him out in the wider world: to bring alms and offerings to his nation. (The word 'offerings' can mean '**sacrifices**', but though Paul did share in offering a sacrifice back in 21.26 he uses this same language, in this context, in a more general sense in Romans 15.16.) This, we realize with a shock, is Paul's summary, before Felix and with the chief priests listening, of his whole **Gentile** mission! And it all ended up with Paul back in the Temple, purified and worshipping (Acts 24.18).

Therefore, he concludes, there is nothing in their accusations. Yes, some Jews from Asia did accuse me of defiling the Temple by bringing a Gentile into it, but they are not here and as a citizen I have the right to have accusers face me in person. Yes, these chief priests listened to me in their council, but the only thing I said which anyone might regard as inflammatory was my reaffirmation of our ancestral hope. And (he might have added in his heart) that hope is the reason I have hope here and now; because God's final hope has come forward to meet us in the person of Jesus **Christ**, so that we live by a hope already realized and a hope yet to come.

The speech is stunning, rhetorically, historically, theologically, politically, personally. It ranks with anything Paul himself wrote in his letters. He will speak once more in Acts, in the full-dress statement before Agrippa II in chapter 26. But here we see the groundwork, the solid rock on which Paul stood. It gives, not just a series of glittering themes, but a full picture of the man. It stands as a testimony, an example, a promise.

ACTS 24.22–27

Felix Calms (and Slows) Things Down

²²Felix was quite well informed about the Way. He adjourned the hearing.

'When Lysias the tribune comes down,' he said, 'then I will make my decision about your business.'

²³He told the centurion to keep Paul under guard, to allow him some freedom, and not to stop any of his companions from looking after him.

²⁴After some days, Felix came with Drusilla his wife, who was Jewish. They sent for Paul and listened to him speaking about faith in the Messiah Jesus. ²⁵As he talked about justice, and self-control, and the judgment to come, Felix became afraid.

'That's quite enough for now,' he said. 'You can go. When I get a good opportunity I'll call for you again another time.'

²⁶At the same time he was hoping that Paul would give him money, and so he sent for him frequently and talked with him. ²⁷After two years Felix handed over the reins of office to Porcius Festus. He wanted to do the Jews a favour, and so he left Paul in prison.

A friend of mine preached a sermon, as my guest, on radiators and drains. Some people, he said, are radiators, and other people are drains. Some people, that is, naturally give energy and warmth to others. People like having them around, because they make you feel more alive. Others, however, suck up what's around them and give little or nothing back. They drain you of energy. They make you feel exhausted, mentally and emotionally and perhaps physically.

The sermon went on to ask the very interesting question whether God is a radiator or a drain, and to point out that though many people persist in thinking of God as a drain (always wanting us to do things, never satisfied, always ready to criticize and find fault) God is in fact the radiator par excellence. It was a fascinating sermon; the fact that I can remember it without effort several years later tells its own story. But it is with people as radiators and drains that I am now concerned.

Felix was a drain. He had taken all that the Emperor Claudius had given him and used it for his own ends. He had lusted after someone else's wife and had taken her for himself. Luke doesn't draw attention to Drusilla's past, but many of the first readers of his book would know it well. She was the sister of Agrippa II, whom we shall shortly meet, and the first-century scandal-industry was just as effective when it came to the rich, the royal or the otherwise famous as is our own. It was quite a coup for a jumped-up ex-slave to grab a princess, especially when she was already married to someone else. Like many provincial governors, he was in it for what he could get.

Everything Felix does in this little episode has 'drain' written all over it. Even when he seems to be doing something right, it's not difficult to see 'what's in it for me' oozing out of every pore. Of course, Felix knows he's in a tight spot. The Jewish authorities were under his ultimate control, but only so far. Local leaders would often press charges against a governor for maladministration, and there were several instances of them doing so, not least in a famous case, in Judaea itself, half a century earlier. Even if they didn't accuse him during his time in office, Felix couldn't stay in Judaea for ever, and when he left there might well be questions people wanted to raise. So it is definitely not in his interest to dismiss the case, let Paul go free, and hear howls of protest all the way from Jerusalem to Caesarea – and perhaps out beyond, to Himself Across the Sea.

Equally, it is not in his interest at all to do an injustice to a Roman citizen who is obviously well aware of his legal rights and knows exactly what's going on. Paul's brilliant speech had argued convincingly against the main charges, pointing out that some of them were invalid since the accusers were not present, and establishing the larger framework within which what he was doing made (as Felix could very well see) excellent sense in its own terms, and perhaps in Jewish terms as a whole.

The matter was complex. What was a drain to do? Adjourn the case, of course. Cool things down. Slow things down. Stop them dead, in fact. 'Let's wait till Lysias the tribune comes and deal with it then.' But he doesn't. And it wouldn't have made any difference if he had.

So Felix is left with a famous Roman citizen on his hands. Imprisonment wasn't in itself a punishment in Roman law; it was a way of holding onto someone while you thought what to do with them, or to keep them from being a nuisance – or, as in this case, to protect them from people who would gladly have harmed them or killed them. The situation is delicate. Will Paul complain that Felix is holding him unjustly? Well, that's a danger; so he allows him a measure of freedom, and lets his friends come and look after him. That's important, too, because the Roman system didn't provide food or anything else for prisoners. Either people brought them what they needed, or they starved (see Philippians 2.25; 4.10–20). And, to give Paul the impression that he was still considering what to do with him, he sent for him quite often, let him talk, and discussed things with him. But it's still 'what's in it for me'. Felix has heard Paul speaking about collecting money from around the world, and about paying the expenses of **sacrifices**. He may suspect that Paul has access to funds. He may not actually have said, in so many words, 'Ten thousand talents and you're a free man.' That would, of course, have been illegal, which didn't stop people doing it but which would probably leak out, and the authorities, again, would have him on toast. But he knew that Paul would know that it was on offer. And he probably realized that Paul was frustrated at not being able to talk about Jesus day by day like he used to, and would be glad of an opportunity to bear witness before the governor and his wife . . . So the drain wins. For the moment.

And again, at the end. Finally his term of office finishes, most likely in AD 58 (we know this not least because of coins which successive governors issued, with their own name and that of the emperor on them). Well, here's a fine opportunity: perhaps he will want to clear the desk, to leave his successor a clean sheet, to do the decent thing at last. But no. Drains don't change. During his final years in office he had provoked the

Jewish authorities in various ways, and he knew he might be in trouble. (He was, actually, and it was only through the pleas of his brother Pallas that he was let off by Nero.) So it was better, on a what's-in-it-for-me basis, to give the Jews a final sop. So he left Paul in prison. If anyone ever imagines that Luke is trying to paint a picture of noble Roman authorities always behaving impeccably, always trusted to do the right thing, they can pour that silly idea down the drain.

But, in the middle of the scene, we have a fascinating picture of Paul, rather like **John the Baptist** before Herod in Mark 6.20, being summoned to the man in charge and told to talk. Paul seems to have exercised, as John did for Herod, a kind of fearful fascination: the twisted, crooked ruler found the straight talking extraordinary and even appealing but of course frightening at the same time. If what Paul was saying was true, his own life was a tangled mess indeed. **Faith** in the **Messiah**, Jesus, would mean coming to terms with justice, self-control, and the coming judgment, and on each of those scores Felix must have realized that he was, to say the least, doing rather badly. So he plays a kind of cat-and-mouse game with Paul, in which, though he may have thought to begin with he was the cat, he ends up being the frightened mouse. Go away for now, he says; oh, come back again and talk some more; go away again; come back; and so on.

And of course, from Luke's point of view, the Cat in question isn't Paul. It's Jesus the Messiah, the real Lord, the one Paul can't stop talking about as he points away from himself to his Master; Jesus, the one who will indeed straighten everything out, the one who therefore longs to see justice in our public dealings, self-control in our private worlds, who died at the hands of Roman 'justice' and was raised again to set this new world in motion. We must never forget that Acts is the book in which Luke describes all that Jesus *continued* to do and to teach (1.1). This is what that continuing ministry looks like, as the living Jesus once more confronts a Roman governor and puts him straight on matters of truth, justice and the **kingdom of God** (John 18.33—19.12).

The two years Paul spent in custody in Caesarea must have been, at one level, pure torture for him. Like an eagle with its wings clipped, he could see the wider world out there. The sea-coast and the harbour, where he had put in more than once, were just a few minutes' walk from where he was confined, but he couldn't reach them. What had happened to his own sense of vocation about going to Rome? He had sent a letter to the church there, telling them he was on his way after a brief visit to Jerusalem . . . and now this. What had happened, too, to Jesus' clear promise to him, that he would get to Rome in the end?

No answer came. No doubt, as Paul prayed the Psalms, he regularly found their invocation of God's promise and power very relevant: Wake up, YHWH! Why don't you do something? Can't you see that the pagans are having it all their own way? It's your own honour that's at stake here! Perhaps those Psalms are there for precisely that reason. Or perhaps God's people are allowed to get into the position where they need to pray them quite personally and angrily, so that in doing that they can come to the place where much of the human race is for much of the time, facing a puzzling, grey world with only occasional little flashes of a divine possibility, and can bring that unspoken sorrow, that dull ache, into speech, into prayer, into the presence of God. Perhaps that is part of how Jesus is straightening the world out.

Perhaps, too, Paul was aware of other things going on around him. Some have even suggested that this was the time, with unexpected forced leisure, when his anonymous companion, the one who writes 'we' from time to time in the present book, was busy on another project.

ACTS 25.1–12

To Caesar You Shall Go

¹So Festus arrived in the province, and after three days he went up from Caesarea to Jerusalem. ²The high priests and the leading men of the Jews appeared before him, laying charges against Paul, and putting a request to him. ³They wanted him to do a special favour for them and against Paul, by sending for him to be brought up to Jerusalem. They were making a

plan to kill him on the way. ⁴But Festus answered that he was keeping Paul at Caesarea, and that he himself would shortly be going back there.

⁵'So', he said, 'your officials should come down with me. They can put any accusations of wrongdoing they may have against the man.'

⁶He stayed with them for a few days (about eight or ten) and then went down to Caesarea. On the next day he took his seat on the tribunal and ordered Paul to be brought to him. ⁷When he appeared, the Jews who had come down from Jerusalem surrounded him and hurled many serious accusations at him, which they were not able to substantiate. ⁸Paul made his response:

'I have offended neither against the Jews' law, nor against the Temple, nor against Caesar.'

⁹Festus, however, wanted to do a favour to the Jews.

'Tell me', he said to Paul in reply, 'how would you like to go up to Jerusalem and be tried by me there about these things?'

¹⁰'I am standing before Caesar's tribunal', said Paul, 'which is where I ought to be tried. I have done no wrong to the Jews, as you well know. ¹¹If I have committed any wrong, or if I have done something which means I deserve to die, I'm not trying to escape death. But if I have done none of the things they are accusing me of, nobody can hand me over to them. I appeal to Caesar.'

¹²Felix consulted with his advisors.

'You have appealed to Caesar', he said, 'and to Caesar you shall go.'

There is a kind of wistfulness about the royal Psalms. We imagine them being sung in the first Temple in Jerusalem, some of the Western world's oldest and still finest poetry. 'Give the king your judgments, O God, and your justice to the king's son! Then shall he judge the people according unto right, and defend the poor with equity! Then shall the mountains yield prosperity for the people, and the hills their justice.' That's what we want, say the singers. A king who will sort everything out. Someone who will at last give the poor their rights. Someone through whose reign the land will be at peace, and the fields will give their proper harvests. And with each successive king, as the songs were sung again and the prayers ascended in hope, there must have been plenty in the Temple who were thinking: We said all this last time, and it didn't work. We pinned our hopes on the last king for whom we sang these songs, and he let us down. Will it be any different this time?

Now of course the New Testament writers would answer that these hopes had been fulfilled at last in the person and through the achievement of Jesus; but that's not the point I'm making here. The point here is that very often, when a new Roman emperor came to the throne or a new provincial governor arrived in place of the previous one, people would lift up their heads in hope, just as they do today when a new President or Prime Minister is elected. Maybe this time we'll get something sorted out! Maybe this is the person who will at last do what needs to be done! And the answer usually is, well, they do and they don't. And in a few more years we'll be saying the same about someone else.

So we shouldn't be surprised, either at the high hopes that greeted the arrival of Festus in AD 59, or at the frustrations on all sides when, like his predecessor, he vacillates. He goes up to begin with, as would be normal, to Jerusalem, to pay his respects and to get to know the senior Jewish officials on their own territory. Here we discover that any fears Paul might have had about their continuing desire to go after him were fully justified; it's two years since they faced him at Felix's tribunal, but his is one of the first matters they want to raise with Festus. Suspecting they may not get anywhere if they go down to Caesarea again – Paul would say the same as he had before, with predictably similar results – they suggest to Festus that he might bring Paul up to Jerusalem instead. We can see, and presumably Festus was intelligent enough to see, what they had in mind, namely, another potential ambush (verse 3). So, initially, he recommends that they follow him down to Caesarea and start the process off again there.

And now at least someone has arrived who wants to get on with things. A new provincial governor, arriving after what was probably several months of interregnum, would have, literally or metaphorically, a great number of things on his desk, all clamouring for attention. There would be secretaries, slaves, messengers from Syria, goodness knows what to attend to, quite apart from domestic priorities, settling into the governor's residence, getting to know the local dignitaries, and so forth. But on the very first morning after arrival at his official abode, Festus takes his seat at the tribunal and orders Paul to be brought before him. There are the Jewish leaders who have come down with Festus from Jerusalem, surrounding Paul Luke implies that they are not behaving in an orderly manner but, having not sighted their quarry for two years, are now aroused to great passion once more and come all about him in the courtroom – and throwing all kinds of accusations against him. This, again, seems to imply that the list of accusations had grown during the time of waiting. Paul was now going to be accused of everything from planning to destroy the Temple to selling drugs to teenagers and failing to stop at a red light.

Paul, once more, will have spoken, we imagine, for considerably longer than the very clipped 15 words Luke gives him. The substance of what is here summarized is more or less the same as his speech in chapter 24 (I have not offended against the Jews, or against the Temple), with one important extra addition: *nor against Caesar*. This implies, of course, that, like some of those who accused him in places like Philippi and Thessalonica, his enemies were suggesting charges not only of anti-Jewish behaviour but also of anti-Roman teaching or practice. Paul might have replied that they were contradicting themselves, since the kind of anti-Jewish charges they had in mind were what you'd expect from a pagan, and the kind of anti-Roman charges they might have brought were what you'd expect from a Jew; the two might cancel each other out. But perhaps, again, he might have remembered what he'd written to the Corinthians about the **gospel** being a scandal to Jews and folly to Greeks, and might have reflected that, inconsistent though the charges were, they were typical of the sort of thing someone preaching the gospel might expect to meet.

Did Paul know what was likely to happen next? He'd had two years to think and pray about it. It is highly likely that he had thought through all the different possible scenarios. He knew well enough that he was in a strong position, since however much Festus wanted to please his new province he wouldn't want to do anything, or be seen to do anything, to effect injustice on a Roman citizen. Festus could of course

simply acquit and release him, in which case he would still be
at serious risk from plots against his life, as soon as he was out
of the security – however frustrating it must have been! – of
Roman custody. Assuming he's unlikely to do that, Paul has
him in something of a cleft stick. But he knows how to break
the stalemate.

Festus tries one last time to do something which would buy
him a lot of political credit with the Jewish authorities and
indeed the population as a whole. He had made his point to
the leading Jews by forcing them to come down to Caesarea
to his official court. Why not see if we could now do them a
favour? But he has to ask for Paul's consent, as he and Paul
both know well. 'Would you be willing to go up to Jerusalem
and be tried there before me?' Worth asking the question if
only to show the Jewish authorities that he was trying, belated-
ly, to do them the favour they had requested. But he must have
known what the answer would be – at least the first part.

Paul knows his rights. He is standing at Caesar's tribunal,
before Caesar's delegated officer, and this is where as a citizen
of Caesar's empire he ought to be tried. Once again he protests
his innocence; he is not afraid to die if he deserves to, but
he knows very well that going up to Jerusalem would be tanta-
mount to Festus 'handing him over' to the Jewish officials
(verse 11), with only one possible result. He insists not only on
justice, but on properly constituted officials doing their properly authorized job, just as he insisted on getting his public
apology from the magistrates at Philippi. And so, with all other
cards in his hand exhausted, he finally plays his ace of trumps.
'I appeal to Caesar.'

It is just possible that what he meant by this was, 'I appeal to
Caesar in the person of you, his official representative', in other
words, 'No, I insist on being tried here and here only.' In that
case, Festus would be trumping him back, getting out of his
problem by referring the case up to His Majesty. But it is far
more likely that what Paul himself intended was to go direct to
Caesar himself.

The 'appeal', of course, was not like an 'appeal' today, when
a verdict has already been reached and a sentence already
imposed, and the convicted person appeals against one or

both. The case against Paul has still not been tried, and has still not reached a verdict, far less a sentence. What Paul is appealing for is for the case to be tried elsewhere, in the highest court in the empire. This is his right as a citizen (though not many citizens would dare disturb His Majesty with such a request, and might expect the cards to be stacked against them if they tried it). Paul has been promised by God through his sense of vocation (19.21), and has been promised by Jesus through a special vision (23.11), that he would get to Rome. What Luke has now told us is that Paul himself has had to take responsibility, at one level, for making this happen.

This is an important point about the interaction between God's purposes and our praying. Sometimes, when we pray and wait for God to act, part of the answer is that God is indeed going to act, but that he will do so through our taking proper human responsibility in the matter. It's hard to tell in advance what the answer will be. There are times when it is 'The Lord will fight for you, and you have only to keep still' (Exodus 14.14), and other times when it is 'Be strong and very courageous, for you shall put this people in possession of the land I swore to give them' (Joshua 1.6). Discerning and discovering which applies in which case – and note that even in the latter case God is giving the people the land which Joshua is giving them – is a major element in the discernment to which all Christians, and especially all Christian leaders, are called.

The appeal that the case should be tried elsewhere, i.e. before Caesar himself, makes us ask once more about Luke's motives in writing the book. What he reports in chapters 21 to 26 is not, strictly speaking, a sequence of trials as such, but a sequence of abortive hearings and of *preparations for* a trial still to come, which remains tantalizingly out of sight.

ACTS 25.13–27

Agrippa and Bernice

> [13]After some days King Agrippa came to Caesarea, with Bernice, to greet Festus. [14]They spent several days there, and during that time Festus put to the king the whole matter of Paul and the case against him.

'I have a man here', he said, 'who was left by Felix as a prisoner. ¹⁵When I was up in Jerusalem, the chief priests and the Jewish elders came before me and charged him with wrongdoing. ¹⁶My response was that it is not our Roman custom to hand anyone over until the accused has had a chance to look his accusers in the face and make a defence against the charges. ¹⁷So they came down here, and I didn't postpone the business, but sat in court the next day and commanded the man to be brought. ¹⁸His accusers stood there and brought charges – but not of the sort of wrongdoing I had been expecting. ¹⁹It turned out to have to do with various wranglings concerning their own religion, and about some dead man called Jesus whom Paul asserted was alive. ²⁰I simply didn't know what to do about all this dispute, and so I asked him if he would like to go up to Jerusalem and be judged there about these things. ²¹But Paul then appealed for his case to be sent up to His Majesty! So I gave the order that he should be kept under guard until I can send him to Caesar.'

²²'I should like to hear this man for myself,' said Agrippa to Festus.

'Very well,' said Festus. 'You shall do so tomorrow.'

²³On the next day, Agrippa and Bernice came with great ceremony, and entered the audience chamber. With them came the tribunes and the leading men of the city. Festus gave the order, and Paul was brought in.

²⁴'King Agrippa', said Festus, 'and all of you assembled here, you see this man. The whole multitude of the Jews appealed to me about him, both in Jerusalem and here. They shouted that it wasn't right to let him live. ²⁵But I found that he had done nothing to deserve death, and since he then himself appealed to His Majesty I decided to send him. ²⁶I don't have anything definite to write to our Lord and Master about him, and so I've brought him here to you, and particularly before you, King Agrippa, so that I may know what to write once we have had a judicial hearing. ²⁷There seems no sense to me in sending a prisoner without giving some indication of the charges against him.'

'To see ourselves as others see us.' That telling line from Burns (actually, he wrote 'oursels'; but someone would think it was a misprint if I had put that) sums up a good deal of the task of human communication. I am in correspondence, as I speak, with a man I have not met who has read a good deal of what I write, and yet when I read what he says, which is kindly and wisely expressed, I have a sense that I am seeing myself from an angle I do not recognize and, obviously, from which I need to learn something. And a great part of the task of mutual discussion between the great communities of religious **faith** in the world is the challenge, which must perhaps come before anything else, to see ourselves through one another's eyes. This is not just politeness, good manners, though it is that too. It is part of effective communication.

So it is all the more fascinating to see Paul and his beliefs and preaching through the eyes of a Roman official. One of the things that newly appointed public office-holders will normally do is to greet, and be greeted by, the local dignitaries and, in this case, the local royalty. The Romans liked to govern through local aristocracies where possible, since it meant getting other people to do the dirty work and take any rap that might come. Part of the difficulty they had faced in Judaea was the incompetence of Herod the Great's family, which was why they had sent in prefects and procurators, and why his kingdom had been divided and subdivided, then recombined in new ways, with the map chopping and changing like the Balkans in the 1990s. We already met Herod Agrippa I in chapter 12, where we saw him attack the church and then meet a swift and horrible end. This is his son, Herod Agrippa II, a great-grandson of Herod the Great, and popular both with the Romans and with the Jews. His power was of course severely circumscribed, and it was always a nice question as to which matters fell directly to the king, which to the Roman governor, and which to the **high priest**, and which should be sorted out between them. So it was important that Agrippa should meet a new governor as soon as possible.

Bernice, meanwhile, was the sort of figure whose photograph, had she lived in our times, would seldom have been out of the glossy magazines. She was Agrippa's sister, but they travelled together and lived together and many tongues wagged about them. She had been married to their uncle, another Herod, Herod of Chalcis, and after his death had set up house with

Agrippa. At one point, perhaps to silence the whispers, she married the king of Cilicia, a man by the name of Polemo, but then went back to Agrippa, which of course started the whispers going again. At one point it was rumoured that she had become the mistress of Titus, the adopted son of Vespasian, the conqueror of Jerusalem in AD 70, and Vespasian's successor as emperor. Though Luke mentions none of this, the fact that he just says 'and Bernice' in verse 13 may tell its own story; most of his first hearers or readers would raise at least one eyebrow at the thought of this fashionable and powerful woman coming into contact with Paul. It is as though, reading the story of some travelling evangelist, we were to come upon a photograph of the preacher shaking hands with Marilyn Monroe.

The thought of a Roman governor enquiring from a Herod what to do about an important prisoner does of course echo Luke 23.6–12, and Luke will no doubt be well aware of that – as well as of the fact that Agrippa's marital or non-marital arrangements may have some echoes in the domestic arrangements of his great-uncle, Herod Antipas (Luke 3.19). It may be, as I have suggested already, that Luke wants his readers to understand the story as being in some significant ways parallel to the passion narrative in the **gospel**, not in that it leads to Paul's death, which would be both rather obvious and bad theology, but in more subtle and interesting ways, which we shall explore in due course.

So how does Paul appear, seen through the eyes of the puzzled Festus who, on his first meeting with this flamboyant couple, decided to ask them about Paul? There was no question what to do; he must be sent to Caesar; but, as he says at the end of Acts 25, it may be that Agrippa could help him write to the emperor something about what the charges really were. It would look extremely odd for a prisoner to arrive under heavy guard in Rome but with no statement of the accusation against him. Festus' summary of what it was all about is telling indeed. This is how the Christian faith appeared to one outsider, at least. Paul was not charged with the sort of crimes one might have imagined. Instead, it was a matter of disputes about the Jewish religion, 'and about some dead man called Jesus whom Paul asserted was alive'.

There we have it: **resurrection** from the pagan viewpoint. At least it shows Festus had been listening; and it shows, too, how 'resurrection' appeared. It wasn't 'about some dead man called Jesus who had gone to **heaven** and with whom one might have a relationship'. It was about a dead man – no question of that in Festus' mind – and about the fact that Paul said he was alive – no question of that either. And 'alive' meant 'alive', bodily of course. It's not quite clear whether Festus' conclusion was that Paul was simply asserting that Jesus hadn't died after all, or whether he'd grasped the full enormity of the actual Easter claim.

Festus, like Lysias the tribune in his letter to Felix, subtly changes in his own favour the account of what had happened, as Luke no doubt intends us to pick up. Earlier he had suggested taking Paul back to Jerusalem because he wanted to do the Jews a good turn. Now he says that it seemed a good idea because he wanted to get straight in his mind just what the charges against him were all about, charges which concerned Jewish **law** and customs rather than ordinary wrongdoing (verse 20).

There is, of course, no question of Paul now being put on trial before Agrippa. What is being set up is simply an informal interview in the hope of enabling Festus to write his official letter. But once again Luke has made it quite clear where the land lies, exactly in line with one 'verdict' after another, whether formal or informal, which has been issued over Paul in the preceding years and months. Has he done anything wrong from the standpoint of Roman law? No. Has he done anything wrong from the standpoint of Jewish law? No, but his claims (that the law and the prophets have been fulfilled in Jesus, and particularly in his resurrection) are extremely controversial both in themselves and in their implications, and there is continuing angry dispute over that (verse 24). What should be done with him? Well, strange as it may seem with someone to whom trouble seems to stick like sand to a wet foot, nothing. He could be released.

Luke describes the arrival of Agrippa and Bernice with a caustic eye (verse 23). He is not going to describe the arrival of Caesar himself at his tribunal in Rome, but maybe he wants us to think ahead to that moment. And maybe, just maybe, he is hinting at the arrival of a still greater King, whose coming Paul and his friends eagerly awaited, one at whose name every knee, not least the petty princelings of this earth, would bow.

ACTS 26.1–11

Paul Before Agrippa

¹Agrippa addressed Paul.

'You are permitted', he said, 'to speak for yourself.'

Paul stretched out his hand and began his defence.

²'I consider myself blessed, King Agrippa,' he said, 'to have the chance to speak before you today in my defence concerning all the things of which the Jews have charged me, ³in particular because I know you are an expert on all matters of Jewish customs and disputes. I beg you, therefore, to give me a generous hearing.

⁴'All the Jews know my manner of life. I lived from my earliest days among my own people and in Jerusalem. ⁵They have known already for a long time (if they are willing to testify!) that I lived as a Pharisee, according to the strictest sect of our religion. ⁶And now I stand accused because of the hope of the promise made by God to our ancestors, ⁷the hope for which our twelve tribes wait with earnest longing in their worship night and day. And it is this hope, O king, for which I am now accused by the Jews! ⁸Why should any of you judge it unbelievable that God would raise the dead?

⁹'I thought I was under obligation to do many things against the name of Jesus of Nazareth, ¹⁰and that is what I did in Jerusalem. I received authority from the chief priests to shut up many of God's people in prison, and when they were condemned to death I cast my vote against them. ¹¹I punished them many times in all the synagogues, and forced many of them to blaspheme. I became more and more furious against them, and even pursued them to cities in other lands.'

One of the great, though controversial, bishops of Durham in the first half of the twentieth century was Hensley Henson. He was a brilliant speaker and writer, a much loved (though sharp-tongued) pastor, and a great campaigner on all kinds of social, political, cultural and especially religious and theological issues. He was not afraid of controversy. Once, when he had spoken out against a labour dispute, the miners decided to set upon him in Durham and throw him in the river. Fortunately for Henson but unfortunately for the dean of the cathedral, they got the wrong man, and it was the dean who ended up getting a soaking.

One of Henson's great topics was the establishment of the Church of England – something which many in England, and (in my experience) most Christians outside it, simply don't understand. That's another topic for another time. But Henson was interesting. Up to a certain point, he had been strongly in favour of retaining the establishment: that is, of the monarch being the head of the Church of England, of keeping bishops in the House of Lords, and of each parish church being seen as, in principle, the place of worship (and other events like weddings) for the whole community, and not merely for those who happened to be fully paid up members. But then, quite suddenly, he changed. A great debate about new liturgy took the church into deep and controversial waters. The church had decided in 1928 that it wanted the new prayer book; but Parliament, which in those days still had the power to do such a thing, voted against; and the proposal had to be shelved. Henson, a strong supporter of the new book, was furious. If this was what establishment meant, he was now against it – on quite similar grounds to the previous reasons why he had been for it. His concern was for the worshipping health of the whole nation. If that, as he used to think, could be furthered by establishment, so be it; but if not, then it should go.

Now Henson would, I think, regard it as a huge joke that he of all people, whose theological views were by no means always as orthodox as they might have been, should be regarded as a model for St Paul making his defence before Herod Agrippa II. Here we are again: the church coming before the state to plead its case! But my point is a rather different one. Henson would have claimed, and did claim, that in changing his mind so drastically on the issue of establishment he was being fully consistent on a deeper principle, the principle of providing forms of worship for the whole country in appropriate language and style.

And my point is this. When we read the defence of Paul before Agrippa, it would be easy to imagine that the present passage, with Paul simply rehearsing all the ways in which he had been such an obviously zealous Jew in his early, pre-Damascus Road, days, was aimed at showing that at least he knew what regular, ultra-orthodox Judaism was all about. If he was now thought to be speaking against Judaism, at least nobody could accuse him of not knowing what he was talking about. Like an ex-drug addict going into a hospital and talking to patients who were trying to kick the habit, he wouldn't just be speaking from theory and general humanitarian concern, but from the position of insider knowledge. If we read the passage this way, it makes a lot of sense, in parallel with what he says in Galatians 1.13–14 and Philippians 3.5–6, and with other passages like Romans 10.2 hovering in the wings not far behind. He wasn't rejecting something he didn't really know. He wasn't teaching odd things because he'd only picked up a garbled version of Judaism, out there in the Diaspora perhaps, ending up rejecting something no well-taught Jew would have embraced in the first place. This is an important point; it was important in the first century, and it has been important in recent debates, too. It is indeed one element in what the passage is all about.

But only one. At another level, this passage is saying, at its heart, that though there was an obvious break between Saul of Tarsus prior to his **conversion** and Paul the **apostle** afterwards, *there was a strong line of continuity making a bridge between the two.* This is, in fact, where the language of 'conversion' may be misleading because, as Paul himself would have put it, and indeed did put it frequently to anyone who would listen, at no point did he waver in his belief that the God of Abraham, Isaac and Jacob was and is the true God, the one and only creator God. He didn't change Gods. From his point of view, he didn't even, really, change religions. Rather, he followed (so he would have said) the one God, the creator, Abraham's God, down the line he had always promised to lead his people, the line that would lead to **resurrection**. And the main break that had occurred was that he had become convinced that resurrection had already occurred, in one single case, while everyone else (apart from those on the Way) was still expecting it as a solely future event.

This is so important that Paul spells it out in three rapid-fire points. First, it is rooted in the promise made to the ancestors. The Sadducees, as we have noticed, regarded resurrection as a new-fangled doctrine, dangerous in its implications. But Paul insists, with the mainstream **Pharisees**, that it was at least solidly implied in the promises to Abraham and the others at the beginning.

Second, it is the promise that all Jews everywhere now cling to, and that they celebrate in their worship. Paul is not saying, 'Jews worship like this, but I'm saying something different', but rather, 'The message I believe and preach is rooted in the worshipping life of Israel itself.' Again, the Sadducees would have disagreed, since they wouldn't have allowed mention of resurrection in worship. But Paul knew his Judaism, in Jerusalem and the Diaspora; and historical studies, not least of the developing synagogue liturgy at this point, bear him out in saying that resurrection was indeed the mainstream view at this period. (Quite what he means by 'the twelve tribes' in verse 7 is a nice question, since nine of the tribes had been exiled 800 years earlier, but we can't solve that here.)

Third, it is for this hope that he is accused! This has been Paul's main point all along, in his brief and stormy hearing before the Sanhedrin in chapter 23 and in his defence before Felix in chapter 24. Of course, he knows as well as we and they do that there are many other charges festooned around his neck, but this is, for him, at the heart of it. His preaching of resurrection is not, as we have said, an odd extra dogma bolted onto the outside of everything else he believes and teaches, related only extraneously to the other things which his contemporaries among non-believing Jews find so offensive. His message about resurrection – (a) that it is what we were all waiting for, and (b) that it has happened, to our enormous surprise, in Jesus – is at the heart of his claim that this changes everything at the same moment as fulfilling everything. It is the changes, of course, which are the controversial bits, but Paul's point would be that they are not changes for change's sake, nor changes because there was something wrong with the old ways, but changes *because God's new world had arrived*, fulfilling the promises to bless all nations through Abraham, and that in this new world it appeared that some things which Jews, himself included, had thought were fixed for ever had turned out to be, quite deliberately from God's point of view, only temporary. This, indeed, is the argument he makes with great care in Galatians 3.

Paul is thus stressing *both* the fact that he had been an ultra-orthodox, ultra-zealous Jew himself, educated to the highest pitch of Jewish learning (verses 4–5), righteously indignant for God and his law, persecuting the followers of Jesus to prison and to death, pursuing them even in foreign lands (verses 9–11); in other words, that he knew what Judaism was all about from the inside; *and* that it was the hope which nestles at the very heart of that ancient and venerable faith which formed the bridge from what he was to what he had become. And the heart of his appeal – even in this part of the speech, it isn't just an autobiographical account, it is an appeal – is then couched in verse 8: why should any of you not believe that God raises the dead?

The answer might well be, especially from Festus: well, we all know it doesn't happen and won't happen. All ancient pagan philosophers, like all modern ones, are adamant on the point. But Paul is primarily addressing Jews, albeit Jews like the urbane, cosmopolitan man-of-the-world Agrippa II. And Jews are supposed to believe, as primary rock-bottom doctrine, that God is the creator, the lifegiver. Why not, then, resurrection? And why not, then, the resurrection of Jesus as the fulfilment of that promise?

This is the basis of Paul's account of himself, which obviously goes far beyond what Festus was hoping for, that is, some indication of what charges Paul ought to face in Rome. Paul is far from finished. But already what he has said ought to be worked out and thought through carefully by Christians of all sorts. It is all too easy to present conversion, our own or Paul's, as a black-and-white change from one religion (or no religion at all) to another. But what Paul had believed as a zealous Jew, and what he then believed as a zealous Christian, were both alike grounded in God the creator. In the same way – this is a different point, but an important one – the human lives people lead, whether they realize it or not and whether they live by faith or not, are in fact rooted in God the creator. When they come, if they do, to faith in Jesus Christ, this is not a turning away from the God who has actually been the source of everything they are and have all along. To learn from Paul the deeper meaning of conversion may be delicate and difficult, but it would be worthwhile to try.

ACTS 26.12–23

Paul's Conversion (One More Time)

[12]'While I was busy on this work', Paul continued, 'I was travelling to Damascus with authority and commission from the chief priests. [13]Around midday, while I was on the road, O king, I saw a light from heaven, brighter than the light of the sun, and shining all around me and my companions on the road. [14]We all fell to the ground, and I heard a voice speaking to me in Aramaic.

' "Saul, Saul," he said, "why are you persecuting me? It's hard for you, this kicking against the goads."

[15]' "Who are you, Lord?" I said.

' "I am Jesus", said the Lord, "and you are persecuting me. [16]But get up and stand on your feet. I'm going to tell you why I have appeared to you. I am going to establish you as a servant, as a witness both of the things you have already seen and of the occasions I will appear to you in the future. [17]I will rescue you from the people, and from the nations to whom I am going to send you [18]so that you can open their eyes to enable them to turn from darkness to light, and from the power of the satan to God – so that they can have forgiveness of sins, and an inheritance among those who are made holy by their faith in me."

[19]'So then, King Agrippa, I didn't disobey this vision from heaven. [20]I preached that people should repent, and turn to God, and do the works that demonstrate repentance. I preached it first to those in Damascus, then also in Jerusalem, in the whole countryside of Judaea, and among the nations. [21]That is the reason the Jews seized me in the Temple and tried to slaughter me. [22]But I have had help from God, right up to this very day. And so I stand here to bear witness, to small and great alike, of

nothing except what the prophets, and Moses too, said would happen: [23]namely, that the Messiah would suffer, that he would be the first to rise from the dead, and that he would proclaim light to the people and to the nations.'

'Listen to the tune,' says the music teacher.

The children sit round her, spellbound. They love this bit.

'Now sing it back to me – Johnny!'

Johnny does his best. Then Sophie. Then Philip.

'Well,' says the teacher, 'you're not doing badly. Listen to it again.'

They sit, quietly, listening to the music again.

'Now, Sam, your turn.'

Sam is confident. He sings it right through.

'That's it! You're all getting it.'

One by one they try, until they all know it right through.

'Now, think very hard and listen very hard,' says the teacher. 'And I want you to listen for the other bit that's playing as well as the tune.'

This time the tune is loud and clear, the bit they all know; but there's a descant as well. There's another tune which goes on top of the first tune, sweet and soaring and fitting in all along, coming to rest just above the main theme.

'What about it, Sarah?' asks the teacher.

Sarah has a go, but she keeps coming back to the main tune. So do one or two of the others.

'Listen one more time,' says the teacher.

This time they are ready for it. One by one they try it, until it's more or less there.

'Now!' says the teacher. 'Now I want the boys to sing the tune and the girls to sing the descant.'

Absolute chaos first time. Listen again, try again.

Gradually there dawns on the room that most wonderful of sounds: harmony, with everyone inside the room part of it.

When Luke plays a tune no fewer than three times, as we have already remarked, he clearly wants us to learn it by heart. When he then plays it, the third time through, with some descants as well, he clearly thinks that the descants really do go with the tune, but wants us to be able to hear, and perhaps sing back to him, both the tune and the descants and then the whole thing together.

Because this time, in making this final great set-piece speech before Agrippa, Bernice, Festus and the assembled great and good of Judaea and the surrounding regions (though Paul keeps his eye on Agrippa throughout, addressing him as if he were the only person in the hall), Paul has built into his account of his **conversion** the various elements that are needed to answer the charges against him. He has done this not simply by saying (a) I was converted like this, and then (b) this is my teaching about **Gentiles** and Jews, but by running them together as a statement of what Jesus himself had said to him on the road.

The main thrust of the address comes in verse 19: I didn't disobey the vision I had from **heaven**. At this point Paul is saying what Peter, John and the others said two or three times in the early chapters of the book: we must obey God rather than human authority (4.19; 5.29). For Paul this isn't just the occasional orders of a court, but the 'human authority' of the entire tradition of Judaism as he, along with the rest, had received it. If God has revealed himself to me in a fresh way (though of course, to stress again, in full continuity with what had been promised long ago), and if he has given me a vision from heaven with direct commands, then I can hardly be blamed, precisely as a loyal Jew, if I do my best to follow those commands to the letter.

So what were the commands? The main part of the speech divides into two, after the introduction we looked at in the previous section. Verses 12–18 describe the vision on the road to Damascus, the 'tune' we heard in chapter 9 and then, with only small variations, in chapter 22. Now, however, it has an extra part: the 'descant' which forms, naturally, the part Luke wants us to focus on particularly. Then verses 19–23, beginning with that disclaimer about obeying God, describe what Paul has done precisely in obedience to that vision, taking him up to and including the things about which specific charges have been laid against him. Once more, we must assume that this is a summary. It is, as it stands, brief and tight-packed. But the elements it contains are enough for us to see the full sweep of Paul's **gospel** and the way it not only derived from his initial vision on the road to Damascus but also played out in his missionary work.

The main 'descant' in verses 12–18, running on top of what we have heard before about the event, is of course the extra words of Jesus. To begin with, he warns Paul about the difficulty of 'kicking against the goads' (verse 14) like an ox, angry at the metal prods that are pushing it in the right direction and kicking out at them, thereby making things worse. The point is not simply that God is wanting Paul to do something and, like an obstinate ox, he is refusing. The point is that the crucified Jesus is himself doing a new work through his **resurrection**, and that Paul, in persecuting the church, is like an ox kicking against the direction the Driver intends the whole ox-train, plough and all, to be travelling.

There then follows an advance statement of what Paul is being called *for*. This is why some people have referred to his 'conversion' as a 'call'. To an extent that is right since, as we have seen, Paul wasn't 'converted' *away from* one God or religion, but 'called' *to* a radical new understanding of that same God as the basis for a radical new fulfilment of that same religion. He is to do two things, according to this vision. First (verse 16), he is to bear witness, as a servant of Jesus himself, to tell people what he has seen and heard and what he will see and hear in subsequent visions. Second (verses 17–18), he is being sent specifically to the Gentiles. This in turn subdivides into four – and we should remember, as Paul certainly remembered, that it was exactly in this area that he had got into most trouble with Jewish mobs and authorities all around Greece and Turkey and now in Jerusalem as well.

First, it would be his task to open the eyes of the Gentiles (Paul of course had his eyes opened as part of his Damascus experience), so that they may turn from darkness to light. This is a summary of what Paul says in 1 Thessalonians 1.9 and elsewhere, and the point is not just that the Gentiles should, in some general sense, 'see the light', but that they should turn away from idols and come to acknowledge the one true God – in other words, that they should become, in heart though not in body, just like good Jews.

This is reinforced, second, in the turning of Gentiles away from the power of the **satanic enemy**, however that is understood, and their turning to God himself, to the 'living and true God' of whom Paul speaks elsewhere. We should note that in both these first two themes the point is that they should *turn,* that is, that they should 'repent' (reinforced in Acts 26.21). And the point of turning, within this context, is once again to meet the underlying objection of Jews to the coming of Gentiles into the family of Abraham: that these pagans are idolaters, they are in league with the devil, they are unclean. No, they aren't, says Paul (actually, No they aren't, says Jesus according to Paul according to Luke); they will have turned, turned away from all that, put it behind them. The thought that Gentiles could receive **repentance** as a gift from God was the big surprise that the church had had to face in 11.18. According to Paul here, it was something that Jesus had promised from the start.

Third, therefore, they will receive **forgiveness** of sins, one of the main central blessings of the whole gospel. And, once more, the point about forgiveness is not just that this will give the individual a clear conscience, a sense of God's presence close by without criticism or condemnation, but much more that if the Gentiles have had their sins forgiven there is no reason whatever why they should not be full members of Jesus' extended family.

That, in fact, is precisely the fourth point: 'an inheritance among those who are made holy by their **faith** in me' (verse 18). This is where it was all going. *The Gentiles, according to Jesus himself, belong within the same family as believing Jews.* 'Those who are holy', within Judaism and without further qualification, would obviously mean 'those who are made holy within the Jewish system, including **Temple**-purity, the sacrificial system, and so on'. But holiness or purity is itself, it seems, in process of being redefined: true holiness is what happens 'when hearts are cleansed by faith' (see 15.9, in a similar context). That can happen to Jews; and it can also happen to Gentiles.

And it isn't just that Jesus said it, so it must be so. Paul's experience as a missionary has more than filled out this promise (verses 20–23). Paul told the Gentiles to repent – and for this Jewish people wanted to kill him! Yes, this is a telescoping together of several things, but from Paul's point of view it made good sense. The main Jewish objection to Gentiles was that they were automatically sinners, 'lesser breeds outside the **law**'. Paul's work has consisted in dealing with that sin, by repentance and faith. Surely, then, Jews, God's people, Abraham's children, should celebrate! But no, they are angry. But God has been with Paul, and the sum and substance of his whole **message** is this, drawn together in a packed formula in verses 22b and 23. This time there are five elements (it's Luke's fault this is so dense, by the way).

First, Paul's message is *a message rooted in Israel's scriptures*. The prophets, and Moses, told the story, and the story has now reached its climax.

Second, Paul's message is (of course!) *a message about Jesus as **Messiah***. He is the fulfilment of Israel's hopes, great David's greater son. Psalms, prophets and all are called in to bear witness to this.

Third, it is *a message about the suffering Messiah*, both the necessity of that suffering, within the long plan of God set out in the scriptures, and its interpretation. He 'must' suffer, as Jesus insisted both before and after his death (Luke 9.22; 24.26, and elsewhere); and that suffering will, 'according to the scriptures', be redemptive and atoning.

Fourth, *he would be the first to rise from the dead*. Luke never tires of reminding us that the point of Easter is that it is the beginning of God's new world. The first **apostles** were announcing 'the resurrection of the dead – in Jesus' (4.2). That was Paul's message too.

Fifth, and most importantly, this was *a message about God's light shining on all people alike*. This is not simply an addendum to 'the gospel', a bit of 'outworking' which doesn't really affect, or doesn't deserve to stand with, the central statement of the whole. The point of the good news, for Paul, Luke and the whole New Testament, is precisely that, since this is the fulfilment of the Israel-shaped plan of the creator God, the whole created order is at last summoned to worship.

Oh, and sixth, not stated in this list but foundational to the whole, because it is how it all came to Paul in the first place: *this Jesus, the scripturally promised, suffering, risen and mission-*

ary Messiah, is the human, glorious face of the one true and living God. What we call 'christology' – the question about how we are to speak of Jesus and God in the same breath – had been second nature to Paul ever since the day he met Jesus.

I do not know how long Paul's original address went on. I do know that he had packed into it all the main things he wanted to say – and that Luke has telescoped them together densely and drastically but still so as to leave their clear detail visible. The thrust of the whole thing, by way of total defence against all the charges that the Jews, official and unofficial, might lay against him, is this: (a) I am doing only what comes straight out of the scriptures we share; and (b) I am being obedient to a heavenly vision which shows, in considerable detail, how it is that when God welcomes the Gentiles into his family he does so righteously. And therefore (c) I am not guilty. I am only doing what I was told, and in so doing – not least in the welcome to the Gentiles for which, in a distorted version, I have been accused of infidelity to Israel – I am actually fulfilling, rather than undermining, the most ancient traditions and the richest hope of my people.

It is a form of defence still well worth employing. And it is worth, too, checking out Paul's letters to notice just how remarkably well this close-packed statement corresponds to most of his main themes.

ACTS 26.24–32

'Paul, You're Mad!'

[24]As Paul was making his defence in this way, Festus roared out at the top of his voice,

'Paul, you're mad! All this learning of yours has driven you crazy!'

[25]'I'm not mad, most excellent Festus,' responded Paul. 'On the contrary, I am speaking words full of truth and good sense. [26]The king knows about these things, and it is to him that I am speaking so boldly. I cannot believe that any of this has escaped his notice. After all, these things didn't happen in a corner. [27]Do you believe the prophets, King Agrippa? I know you believe them.'

²⁸'You reckon you're going to make *me* a Christian, then,' said Agrippa to Paul, 'and pretty quick, too, by the sound of it!'

²⁹'Whether quick or slow,' replied Paul, 'I pray to God that not only you but also all who hear me today will become just as I am – apart, of course, from these chains.'

³⁰The king, the governor and Bernice, and those sitting with them, got up. ³¹As they were going away, they talked to one another about it.

'This man', they were saying, 'has done nothing to deserve death or chains.'

³²And Agrippa commented to Festus,

'This man could have been set free, if only he hadn't gone and appealed to Caesar.'

I was once lecturing to a group of students in Oxford. We were just getting to the point at the centre of the lecture – I think it was dealing with Romans 8.3 – where I wanted to explain as clearly as I could the full Pauline meaning of the death of Jesus. I have been and am aware that at this moment in any such lecture, or indeed sermon, there is a certain tension. One is dealing with things that are so important and so sensitive that you have to prepare carefully in **spirit** as well as mind.

Just as I was launching into the key sentence, suddenly a lawnmower started up on the lawn right outside the window where we were sitting. We all jumped. The spell was broken. We lost the train of thought and had to start again. And I explained to them that I wasn't surprised, because this has happened to me quite a lot. Once, at the decisive moment in a lecture in Canada, I and the class were coming to the critical point, and just as we reached it a student got up to open a window (well, maybe I was generating a lot of hot air). Another time, as I reached the critical point in an evening address to several thousand people in a huge tent, the electrics all failed and my microphone went dead. I raised my voice and finished the talk at full, but unamplified, volume. I have become used to explaining to people, when this happens, that though I don't engineer this, and would in many ways prefer the quiet life of lecturing and teaching about things that don't touch on such sensitive nerve centres, the things I have to deal with do seem to strike uncomfortable chords in what, for want of a better word, we call 'the atmosphere'.

So when I hear that just as Paul's address reached its peak, the newly arrived Roman governor had had quite enough, I am not surprised. (Not, please, that I am comparing myself to St Paul, like a mouse drawing itself up to its full height beside the elephant.) Some translations say Festus 'exclaimed', which sounds like someone saying, testily, 'Really, really, Paul, I think that's a bit over the top.' But the Greek says he shouted at the top of his voice – an embarrassing thing to do, perhaps, in front of his distinguished guests, but then this Roman official, who was new to Jews and their ways and who certainly had never dreamed of anything remotely like this in his life before, was bound to find Paul's explosive material too, well, explosive. 'PAUL, YOU'RE OUT OF YOUR MIND! YOU'VE DONE TOO MUCH STUDYING!' (Always a good move for those who don't like what the scholar is saying.) And the speech, and the meeting, is over.

But not before Paul has made a final appeal, direct, and also embarrassing the way such appeals are, to Agrippa. Agrippa was, after all, known to be not only a 'friend of the Romans' but also very much *persona grata* with the Jewish people. He wasn't violent in the way that some of his forebears had been. He understood the Jewish traditions, as Paul gave him credit for back in verses 2–3, and presumably knew all about the present movement, as Paul assumes here in verse 26.

So, naturally, Paul can ask him a simple question, can't he? Agrippa, you are a loyal Jew, aren't you? You do believe the prophets, don't you? Of course you do!

Agrippa knows there is no way he can simply avoid the question, with a sudden hush coming over the gathering and everyone craning their heads round to see what answer the king will make to this extraordinary mad-or-perhaps-not-mad scholar who has had the temerity to put him on the spot. Agrippa sees well enough, of course, where it's going. It's either got to be 'No, I don't believe them', in which case he has well and truly lost his street credibility, for ever, with a good swathe of his own people. Or it's going to be 'Yes, I do believe them', in which case Paul will clinch the point and say, 'So you do believe in **resurrection**! So why can't you believe in Jesus?' That was the point he was setting up for in verse 8. He is ready, and Agrippa knows he is ready, to close the deal then and there.

It's a bold move, of course, and one that is perhaps not to be copied too readily in ordinary evangelism. Not, of course, because one shouldn't put people on the spot; that is up to the **holy spirit** and the individual evangelist. Rather, because I would not, myself, first get people to agree that resurrection is something they are prepared to believe in and then try to fit Jesus into the picture. But then I don't normally lecture to orthodox, or would-be orthodox, Jews for whom 'resurrection' is, at least officially, an article of **faith**. For the people I normally speak with, I would assume that it's better to make the case the other way round. But the spirit leads one speaker this way, and another one that, and the important thing is not to follow a logically correct order of argument but to make sure you get to the right point at the end.

And Agrippa isn't having it. 'So, you reckon you're going to make me a Christian here and now?' He's off the hook, but he's a bit embarrassed as well, because (I think) he sort of believes the prophets, even though the life he's led has been a clever riding of both horses, the Jewish one and the pagan one, and he doesn't really want to give either of them up. There may just be a wistfulness about his response. 'In another life, if I hadn't bought so heavily into this thing, and that thing, and the other thing . . . then maybe it might have all made sense. I can see where you're coming from. But . . . not today, thank you.'

And Paul, picking up Agrippa's clever if embarrassed response, turns it neatly round and sends it back with a joke. 'Actually, yes, I'd like everyone here to be just like me' – and then, glancing down in mock surprise at the clunky shackles round his ankles – 'except for these chains, of course.'

The defence is over. The king and the governor walk out together. The whisper round the hall is that Paul hasn't done anything to deserve death, or for that matter those chains. And Agrippa, speaking (as far as Luke is concerned) for what all wise Jews ought to say to all listening Romans, says to Festus, 'What a pity the fellow went and appealed to Caesar. He could have been set free if he hadn't done that.'

Of course, Festus could have taken his courage in both hands and released Paul. Word would not yet have reached Caesar that he had a strange Jewish prisoner coming his way; why not just abort the process then and there? But if Caesar discovered that Festus had had such a man in custody, that the man had appealed to the emperor, and that he, Festus, had overriden it, Caesar might be displeased on two counts: partly that Paul might after all be a genuinely seditious man who had managed to pull the wool over the governor's eyes ('If you let this man go', said the crowd to Pilate, 'you are not Caesar's friend!' [John 19.12]), and partly that when a citizen appeals to the emperor he should be able, no, be *made*, to follow it through. Not to do so would only encourage frivolous half-hearted appeals which people might then try to back out of. And of course, if Festus had let Paul go he would hardly have pleased the Jewish authorities, who might not have taken much notice of Agrippa's generous comment.

Equally, all this left the way now clear for Paul to be taken to Rome as His Majesty's guest. There were some inconveniences about this, not to mention dangers, as we shall see. But he was safe from potential Jewish assassins, and didn't even have to organize his own passage. He was going to Rome at last, but in a characteristically upside down and inside out fashion. His writings, not least 2 Corinthians, suggest that he might have seen the funny side of this, too.

ACTS 27.1–12

All at Sea

¹When it was decided that we should sail to Italy, they handed Paul over, along with some other prisoners, to a centurion named Julius, who belonged to the Imperial Cohort. ²They got into a ship from Adramyttium, which was intending to sail to various places along the coast of Asia. So off we set. Aristarchus, a Macedonian from Thessalonica, came too.

³Next day we put in at Sidon. Julius was kind to Paul, and allowed him to go to his friends to be cared for. ⁴When we left Sidon, we sailed under the lee of Cyprus, because the winds were against us, ⁵and then crossed the sea off the coast of Cilicia

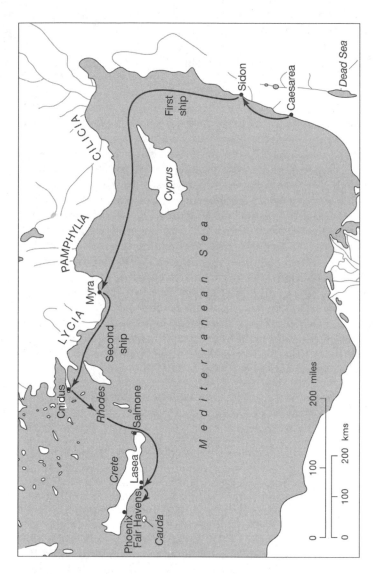

Acts 27.1–12

and Pamphylia, arriving at Myra in Lycia. ⁶There the centurion found a ship going from Alexandria to Italy, and we got on board.

⁷After a few days we were making very heavy weather of it, and only got to the shore at Cnidus. Since the wind was not helping us, we sailed under the lee of Crete, off the coast from Salmone. ⁸Getting past that point with some difficulty, we came to a place which is called 'Fair Havens', not far from the town of Lasea.

⁹Quite a bit of time had now elapsed, and sailing was becoming dangerous. The Fast had already come and gone. Paul gave his advice.

¹⁰'Men,' he said, 'I can see we're going to have trouble on this voyage. It's going to be dangerous. We may well sustain heavy losses both to the cargo and to the ship, not to mention to human life.'

¹¹But the centurion put his faith in the helmsman and the ship-owner rather than in what Paul had said. ¹²Unfortunately, the harbour was not suitable for wintering in, so most people were in favour of going on from there to see if they could get to Phoenix, a harbour on Crete which faces both south-west and north-west. They would then be able to spend the winter there.

In John Fowles' novel, *The French Lieutenant's Woman*, the reader getting near the end receives a shock. There are two endings. You can choose. Would you like the story to finish like this, or like that? What are you saying about yourself, or about the book, if you go this way or that way? This is a classic post-modern move, turning the tables as it were on the reader who has been basking in the safety of the observer, the bird's-eye view from which, though you are involved, of course – otherwise you wouldn't have read this far – you can pretend to be detached. No, says the author, admit it, you are involved, and now you have to choose. You thought you were looking through a window, but suddenly it turns into a mirror.

Luke hasn't given us two endings to Acts. Of course, we are involved in the story, and anyone with an atom of imagination will be involved up to the neck in the chapter now beginning. But Luke is now taking us in a direction that, unless you vaguely knew the book before and so had an idea what was coming, you might well think was extremely bizarre. Especially if you knew Luke's **gospel**, as Luke's theoretical 'ideal reader', Theophilus, was expected to (Acts 1.1 with Luke 1.3); and especially if you had been picking up the parallels, particularly in the last few chapters. Jesus went on a journey and eventually arrived in Jerusalem; so did Paul. Jesus was picked up by the Jewish authorities and handed over to the Romans; so was Paul. Jesus was interrogated by the Roman governor, who at one point brought him before Herod Antipas; Paul was interrogated by two Roman governors and brought before Herod Agrippa. And so on.

But Jesus was sent to his death, and Paul was sent to Rome. Or rather, as becomes increasingly clear, Paul was sent off to sea. And at this point we have to remind ourselves about Jewish attitudes to the sea.

The Jews were not a seafaring race. They left that to the Egyptians, to the south, and the Phoenicians, to the north, not to mention the Greeks, who were never happier than when messing about in island-hopping boats, and ferries, and seaborne businesses, and temples to Poseidon (or Neptune, as the Romans called him). But for the Jews, the sea was a monster.

Yes, the one God had made it just as he made everything else (he made the sea, insisted the Psalmist, and everything in it [Psalm 146.6]), and it was his, and did his bidding. But all the same the sea was regularly seen as a dark force, a power in its own right and a place from which dark powers might emerge. The **Exodus** was marked by YHWH's astonishing parting of the sea, later celebrated as his victory in battle over a monster (Psalm 93.3–4). And when Daniel saw his great, central vision, describing the history of God's people in terms of wicked world empires rising up against them and eventually being overthrown, he talks of four monsters *coming up out of the sea* (Daniel 7.3). Well, they would, wouldn't they?

There is much more about the sea than this in Jewish tradition – the book of Jonah, for example! – but this will do for a start. Paul, of course, unusually for a Jew, was a seasoned sea-traveller, used to jumping on and off boats, putting in at ports while a storm went by, watching and waiting as cargoes were loaded and unloaded, listening to the local dialects, getting to know the seafarers' jargon. He had already been shipwrecked no fewer than three times, as he tells us in 2 Corinthians 11.25, written of course before this present journey. Once, he says in the same passage, he had been adrift at sea for a night and a day, perhaps clinging to a lump of wood. (2 Corinthians 11 is one of many passages in Paul's own letters which make us wish Luke had had the time or energy to write a biography of Paul several times the length of Acts.) He would have been under no illusions about what might await him on the long voyage to get to the imperial capital from one of its farthest outposts.

He had lived much of the last few years in that in-between stage, knowing that the sea was still potentially a great enemy while believing that all enemies had been defeated by Jesus the **Messiah**. The sea still carries the signs, and the memories, of the battles of old. One day, to be sure, it will roar out its deep joy, along with the songs of the trees and the fields, when YHWH comes to set the earth right for ever (Psalm 96.11; 98.7), with the very sea-monsters themselves joining in the song of celebration (Psalm 148.7). But at the moment it still tosses up our losses, as T. S. Eliot put it, and there are always some who will face what he called 'the trial and judgment of the sea'. And that, perhaps, is what Luke has in mind.

Acts 27 is, in other words, the equivalent within the present narrative of Luke 23 within Luke's first volume. Paul's ship-wreck, coming up soon now, corresponds to Jesus' crucifixion within Luke's narrative structure. That is a large claim, and I probably can't ever prove it. But it fits, and it works, and it makes sense of something which has puzzled many genera-tions of readers of both the gospel and Acts: that Luke seems not to make very much, except for sudden odd references like Acts 20.28, of the abstract meaning of the death of Jesus. He believes, to be sure, that Jesus died because that was central to God's plan, even though the people who brought about his death carry their responsibility for one of the most wicked actions ever (Acts 2.23; 3.14–15, 18; 4.27–28). But he doesn't give us a formula by which to catch, so to speak, 'how it works'. He doesn't even give us an equivalent of Mark 10.45, 'The **son of man** came not to be served but to serve, and to give his **life** as a ransom for many.' I am suggesting that this is partly at least because the meaning of the cross, so far from being absent or largely so, is woven into the very texture of his entire narrative.

That's how he did it in the gospel, after all. There is a long build-up of warnings against Israel. Then we discover that Jesus is coming to the place where Israel is, identifying with the nation as its Messiah. Then, to our horror, we watch as the judgment Jesus had prophesied for the nation – the literal, physical, judgment-at-the-hands-of-Rome – falls on Jesus himself. You don't get that by a single verse, or a formula. You only get it through the story, read as a whole and picking up the clues.

Suppose Luke is doing the same here – but not with Paul's death, because that as I said earlier would make exactly the wrong point, would imply (perhaps) either that Paul's death was redemptive too, which is ridiculous, or that Jesus' death was merely exemplary, showing the way that everyone else would have to go. That is less ridiculous, but it doesn't begin to do justice even to the hints that we have of a much deeper, richer meaning ('the church of God which he bought with the blood of his own Dear One', Acts 20.28). Rather, Luke is asking us to watch as the story unfolds, to see this narrative as it were superimposed on the story of the cross, not as just another example of suffering and vindication but as a sign of *the way the unique event of Jesus' death is implemented in the mission of the church to the world, the world as it yearns for its new creation.* Just as the magicians of Samaria, Cyprus and Ephesus opposed the gospel as it set off on the different stages of its journey, so now the dark power itself, the mysterious depths that lent themselves so readily to the apocalyptic musings of Jewish mythology, will oppose the gospel, in the person of its archetypal representative, as it arrives on the doorstep of Caesar himself. Paul won't get to Rome, in other words, without going through fire and water, the first as metaphor, the second as fact.

We can already feel the shipwreck coming towards us in the threatening tone of these introductory verses, full of detail about ports and cargoes and destinations and winds, much like Luke's detail about all the people Jesus passes on the way to the cross, and with a brooding wintry feel already making us shiver. The Fast (the day of atonement, which was on 5 October in AD 59, the likely date of the journey) has come and gone; winter is not far away; sailing started to get dangerous in the eastern Mediterranean in mid-September, and normally stopped altogether by mid-November. Ships ought to be making for land, and reckoning on a long stay before the seas are safe again in the spring. What are we still doing out here? you feel them thinking. Paul can see it coming, with a practised sailor's eye and prophetic insight coming together. Those in charge take no notice. 'This is your hour', said Jesus, 'and the power of darkness' (Luke 22.53). We can hear Luke saying the same to the sea itself, with its many gods and many voices. 'If you want to come after me', Jesus had said, 'you must deny yourself, take up your cross, and follow me.' The last rays of the sun, before the storm closed in, will have cast a familiar shadow from the ship's mast on to the dark and threatening waters.

ACTS 27.13–32

The Storm and the Angel

¹³Well, a moderate southerly breeze sprang up, and they thought they had the result they wanted. So they lifted the anchor and sailed along, hugging the shore of Crete. ¹⁴But before long a great typhoon – they call it 'Eurakylon', the Northeaster – swept down from Crete, ¹⁵and the ship was caught up by it. Since the ship couldn't turn and face into the wind, it had to give way and was carried along.

¹⁶When we came in behind an island called Cauda, we were just able to get the ship's boat under control. ¹⁷They pulled it up, and did what was necessary to undergird the ship. Then, because they were afraid that we would crash into the Syrtis sandbanks, they lowered the sea-anchor and allowed the ship to be driven along. ¹⁸The storm was so severe that on the next day they began to throw cargo overboard, ¹⁹and on the third day they threw the ship's tackle overboard as well, with their own hands. ²⁰We then went for a good many days without seeing either the sun or the stars, with a major storm raging. All hope of safety was finally abandoned.

²¹We had gone without food a long time. Then Paul stood up in the middle of them all.

'It does seem to me, my good people,' he said, 'that you should have taken my advice not to leave Crete. We could have managed without this damage and loss. ²²But now I want to tell you: take heart! No lives will be lost – only the ship. ²³This last night, you see, an angel of the God to whom I belong, and whom I worship, stood beside me. ²⁴"Don't be afraid, Paul", he said. "You must appear before Caesar, and let me tell you this: God has granted you all your travelling companions." ²⁵So take heart, my friends. I believe God, that it will be as he said to me. ²⁶We must, however, be cast up on some island or other.'

²⁷On the fourteenth night we were being carried across the sea of Adria when, around the middle of the night, the sailors reckoned that we were getting near some land. ²⁸They took soundings and found twenty fathoms; then, a little bit further, they took soundings again and found fifteen fathoms. ²⁹They were afraid that we might crash into a rocky place, so they let down four anchors from the stern and prayed for day to come. ³⁰The sailors wanted to escape from the ship, and let down the boat into the sea under the pretence of going to put out anchors from the bow. ³¹But Paul spoke to the centurion and the soldiers.

'If these men don't stay in the ship', he said, 'there is no chance of safety.'

³²Then the soldiers cut the ropes of the boat, and let it fall away.

It's a long time since I've been seasick, but the last time I came close to it I was more or less in the same place as Paul in the middle of this storm. I was doing some guest lectures, and taking some services, on a cruise ship (the things clergy will do for a vacation!), and I was scheduled to speak precisely about Paul's voyages and the shipwreck in particular. But during the lecture before mine, the ship began to heave and roll this way and that. At one point the grand piano in the lecture room slipped its moorings and came sliding across the floor, only being stopped from crashing into the audience by some quick-thinking crew members. It was exciting and a bit frightening. I had been taking detailed notes on the lecture before mine,

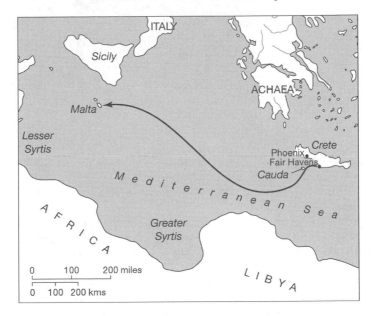

Acts 27.13–32

which was on the ancient archaeology of the Tunisian Roman sites, which we were due to visit after we had been to Malta. And my concentration on my own scribbles, written on a table that was coming and going, up and down, and moving from side to side, did to my sense of balance what you might expect. I went off to the cabin and lay down for a while. Fortunately I was able to get up and stay on my feet for my own lecture.

Even modern boats, with all their sophisticated equipment, can get into trouble at a moment's notice. Only the other day there was a sad article in the paper about a splendid yacht off the coast of Australia that had been found with its engine running, with food on the cabin table, with every sign of normal on-board life – but no people. It looked as though a giant wave had swept them off. It happens. And we don't need to know very much about the detail of ancient trade ships, plying to and fro between the grain harvest of Egypt and the hungry unemployed mob in Rome, to guess what life must have been like on board at the best of times. And this was not the best of times. In a storm at sea there is nowhere to hide. Paul had been right (even if saying 'I told you so' was hardly the best way to win friends or influence people; it's interesting that Paul doesn't list 'tact' as a fruit of the **spirit**) in saying that they should have stopped at Fair Havens, even though the town wasn't the best for wintering in. Instead, they had gambled and lost. They were reduced to taking such precautions as they could, strapping ropes or thongs under the ship to guard it against breaking up under pressure of heavy seas, and lowering a sea-anchor to try to slow down the headlong rush towards the famous, and dreaded, shifting sandbanks of the Syrtis, off the Libyan coast.

The whole point of the voyage, as far as the captain and the owner were concerned, was to get a good price for the cargo at the other end. But when the ship is in danger, you throw the cargo overboard. The point then is to enable the ship to sail as efficiently as you can, and for that you need all kinds of tackle: ropes, extra sails, especially the extremely heavy mainyard. But when things get really tough, all that has to go as well.

At this point a reader with an alert biblical memory may be thinking, where have I heard something like this before? And the answer (which Luke certainly intends us to pick up) is: Yes! Jonah! He was running away to Tarshish to avoid having to go and preach to the great imperial city of Nineveh. When the great storm came, the sailors did what Paul's sailors did: they threw the cargo into the sea (Jonah 1.4–5). At that point Jonah was in the hold, fast asleep, but they woke him up, asked him what was going on, and ended up throwing him overboard, which quelled the storm (and provided a sea-monster with an unexpected dinner).

And of course part of Luke's point is precisely that Paul is *not* Jonah; he is not running away; he is being faithful to his calling to preach in the great imperial capital to which he is bound; and he is certainly not going to be thrown overboard. Instead, in a dramatic reversal, he tells the ship's company to cheer up. He has had a vision (and we, the readers, know what the sailors probably didn't, that when Paul says he's had a vision it's worth listening). An angel has stood beside him during the night, an angel 'of the God to whom I belong and whom I worship', a wonderfully localized and personalized description of God for an audience who knew of many gods. The angel has told Paul that he must indeed stand before Caesar. That's what this voyage is all about. And all the rest of them will be safe along with him. They are going to be shipwrecked 'on some island'; it sounds as though Paul has seen a glimpse, in his vision, of an island with them crashing on the shore, though he doesn't know which island this will be.

Soon the sailors reach a similar conclusion, since the sea is getting rapidly shallower and shallower (verse 28). They follow the normal practice: let down an anchor to slow everything down, then when it is straining unbearably, cut it off and let down another one; and so on. Archaeologists have found sequences of anchors like this: one, two, three, four, in a line, some distance apart, and finally there is the wrecked ship, but a wrecked ship that might have crashed into the rocks much more fiercely without being slowed down in this way. Paul, by now, seems to have more or less taken charge, and when the sailors try a clever plan to save their own skins and leave the ship to its own fate he spots what is going on and gets the centurion to put a stop to it (verses 30–31).

Paul's vision is the turning-point in the story. Up to then they were going down into the darkness; now things are still bad, but there is a light shining, albeit a light visible only to **faith**. The story has got to the point where, in the story of Jesus, 'death could not hold him' (Acts 2.24). Paul has had to go, one more time, through the process he describes in 2 Corinthians 4, immediately after his description of seeing 'the light of the knowledge of the glory of God in the face of Jesus the **Messiah**'. We have, he says (4.7, 10), this treasure in clay jars; we are always carrying in the body the death of Jesus, so that the **life** of Jesus may always be made visible in our bodies. That is the pattern of apostolic life. That is how the **gospel** works through, taking on the cosmic forces of evil, which do the worst they can to Jesus' followers and servants as they struggle ahead in obedience to their vocation. It is as though what Paul wrote two chapters later was a prophecy rather than a report: 'As servants of God we commend ourselves in every way: through great endurance, in affliction, hardships, calamities, beatings, imprisonments, riots, labours, sleepless nights, hunger . . . as dying, and see – we are alive!' (2 Corinthians 6.4–5, 9). Paul's own understanding of the cross, etched into the story of his own apostolic ministry, helps us to see what, at a level too deep for theological formulae, Luke is saying throughout this tale.

There are many Christians who have been taught that once they have faith everything ought to flow smoothly. Acts replies: you have not yet considered what it means to take up the cross. If the gospel of Jesus the crucified and risen Messiah means anything at all, it means that those who carry it will have it branded into their own **souls**. The idea of the church as a little ship was probably not invented at this stage, but Luke was there already. The storms do not mean that the journey is futile. They merely mean that Jesus is claiming the world as his own, and that the powers of the world will do their best to resist. Those who are caught up in the middle of it all must recognize the mark of the cross for what it is, and claim the victory already won in the unique events of Calvary. 'Don't be afraid, Paul. You must appear before Caesar.'

ACTS 27.33–44

Shipwreck

³³When it was nearly daytime, Paul urged all of them to eat something.

'It's now all of fourteen days', he said, 'that you've been hanging on without food, not eating a thing. ³⁴So let me encourage you to have something to eat. This will help you get rescued. No hair of any of your heads will be lost.'

³⁵So saying, he took some bread, gave thanks to God in front of them all, broke the bread and ate it. ³⁶Then all of them were eager to have some food. ³⁷The whole company on board was two hundred and seventy-six. ³⁸When we had eaten enough food, they threw the grain overboard to lighten the ship.

³⁹When day came, they didn't recognize the land. It appeared to have a bay with a sandy shore, and that was where they hoped, if possible, to beach the ship. ⁴⁰They let the anchors drop

away into the sea, and at the same time slackened the ropes on the rudders, hoisted the foresail, and headed for the beach. [41]But they crashed into a reef and ran the ship aground. The prow stuck fast and wouldn't budge, while the strong waves were smashing the stern to bits. [42]The soldiers planned to kill the prisoners so that none of them would swim away and escape. [43]But the centurion wanted to rescue Paul, and refused permission for them to carry out their intention. Instead, he ordered all who were able to swim to leap overboard first and head for land, [44]while the rest were to come after, some on boards and some on bits and pieces of the ship. And so everyone ended up safely on land.

We were already horribly late for the service. It was nobody's fault, really; the traffic had been far, far worse than anyone could have imagined. I had phoned through and told people how it was, but it was really important, still, that we got there as quickly as we could.

We got into the town and approached the church. I was counting every second, thinking all the time where things would have got to, how long it would take to change into my robes, how I could adjust my sermon to weave in a wry apology. (This, by the way, is the stuff of clergy nightmares. But sometimes it really happens like this.) Nearly there now. There was the church, looming up in the distance. It was a strange town, and the friend who was driving (also a clergyman) and I hadn't been there before, but we had been told, in classic fashion, 'You can't miss it.' Well, we couldn't and there it was. But . . . the street between us and it, a matter of 30 yards or so, was a one-way street. In the wrong direction. 'Never mind,' I said, claiming privilege of clergy over traffic rules; there was nobody about, everything was quiet, we could see the church gate just there . . .

And my friend, without a word, turned the car and set off into the unknown territory of a complex one-way system. I was horrified. The clock was ticking. Another minute, two minutes . . . 'What's the matter? Why couldn't you have gone down there?' He gave me a look. He didn't want more points on his driving licence. It wasn't worth it.

He was right, of course. At least in Britain (I have seen people driving the wrong way down one-way streets in Italy and Greece, and nobody much seems to mind). Rules are rules. But sometimes, perhaps – a dangerously Italian attitude, I know, but there it is – the rules need to be balanced off against common sense. Or even something stronger. And that is where the centurion comes in. I always get cross when I read verse 42. For goodness' sake, I want to say to the soldiers, you've all been through so much together; you've got to know one another these last weeks, you've helped throw things overboard side by side, you've had moments of teasing and grumbling and sharing memories, you've become friends in an odd sort of way. How can you now, when rescue is within reach, turn round and kill these prisoners in cold blood?

Part of the answer was, of course: they were Roman soldiers. That's what Roman soldiers did, killing people in cold blood, hot blood, any temperature of blood you care to name. If they didn't, and if the prisoners got away, it's not just points on a driving licence; it's their turn to be killed instead. We recall the Philippian jailer, ready to kill himself because he thought his prisoners had escaped. That's how the system worked. No sentimentality, no common sense, no fellow feeling allowed. Rome hadn't got where it had by allowing people to go soft round the edges at the critical moment. It is only the centurion, who has realized that he has one of the most unusual prisoners he's ever met in his care, who saves the day. He treated Paul kindly right from the start (verse 3), and has not regretted it, even though he didn't take his advice at Fair Havens. And now he sees a larger vision than his myopic subordinates. He does the wrong thing which is also the right thing. He takes the risk and drives the wrong way up the one-way street.

This final twist, just when we were heaving a sigh of relief and thinking all was going to be well, reminds us yet again of the fragility of the whole project, the sheer risk involved. It is, of course, the same risk as the risk of incarnation itself. What if Jesus had died of influenza in his teens? What if he'd been kicked by a camel and never recovered? Ridiculous? No; that's the risk God takes in everything he does, the risk of creation itself, the risk of making a world which is other than himself, the risk of deciding to rescue it by using a human family, by *becoming himself* as a human being.

And if we say that the risk isn't really that great because God remains in control, I think Luke would say emphatically that that is both thoroughly true and thoroughly misleading. The apparent clash of overruling providence and utter human wickedness, seen so graphically in those references to the crucifixion in 2.24 and 3.13, is worked out, not through everything being cheerfully determined in advance, so that all we have to do is sit back and watch it unfold (if we still think like that, after living through Acts 27, we are indeed impervious to literature, never mind theology). Nor is it worked out through a dark, unrelieved, groping around in which we have no certain hope, no security, no assurance, no strong sense of God's living and rescuing presence with us. That, too, is well and truly ruled out by Luke's whole narrative. Somehow, the answer to the puzzle of divine sovereignty and human responsibility is not to be found in a formula, but in flesh and blood. In Jesus' flesh and Jesus' blood. And in our flesh and our blood. Maybe all true doctrines are, in the last analysis, like that.

Yes, we need to believe them. That is the sign that our hearts and our heads have been drawn by the **spirit** to the **faith** which is the badge of all Jesus' followers. But we need to live them; or perhaps we should say, they need to live us, to live in us, to leap into the sea in us, to catch hold of such bits and pieces of broken ship as we can and head for the shore. That, perhaps, is what '**salvation**' is all about.

Because, in this story, that is the word that is used. All hope of being 'saved' had been lost (verse 20). If the sailors had carried out their secret plan to slip away in the ship's boat, they could none of them be 'saved' (verse 31). Taking some food – involving the breaking of bread! – will be 'for your salvation' (verse 34). The centurion wished to 'save' Paul (verse 43). And the end result is that all were 'utterly saved' in coming to land (verse 44). Luke could hardly make it clearer. As in Philippi, yet again, the meaning 'rescued' is clear, and the meaning 'saved – in a far, far deeper sense' corresponds to Luke's larger intention throughout this chapter. Through the waters to safety: that's the Noah story, the **Exodus** story, the **John-the-Baptist** story, the Jesus story. The Paul story. Our story. We have just lived through the crucifixion narrative, like someone kneeling with Luke 23 and meditating on it so that it was as if they were really there, as if it were really happening. 'I am crucified with the **Messiah**,' wrote Paul in what was probably his very first letter, 'nevertheless I live; yet not I, but the Messiah lives in me' (Galatians 2.19–20). 'As many of you as are baptized into the Messiah', he continued a chapter later, 'have put on the Messiah' (3.27). Through the cross, through the waters, to salvation. This is at the heart of Paul's own understanding of Jesus' death, and, I suggest, Luke's as well.

ACTS 28.1–10

The Snake on Malta

[1]When we reached safety, we discovered that the island was called Malta. [2]The local inhabitants treated us with unusual kindness: they set to and built a fire for us all, since it was cold and had started to rain. [3]Paul had collected quite a bundle of brushwood, and was putting it on the fire, when a viper, escaping the heat, fastened onto his hand. [4]The natives saw the animal clinging to his hand.

'Aha!' they said to one another. 'This man must be a murderer! He's been rescued from the sea, but Justice hasn't allowed him to live.'

[5]Paul, however, shook off the snake into the fire and suffered no harm. [6]They kept watching him to see if he would swell up or suddenly fall down dead. But when they had waited and watched for quite some time, and nothing untoward had happened to him, they changed their minds.

'He must be a god,' they said.

[7]Publius, the leading man of the island, owned lands in the region where we were. He welcomed us, and entertained us in a most friendly fashion for three days. [8]Publius' father was lying sick in bed with a fever and with dysentery. Paul went in to see him and prayed; then he laid his hands on him and cured him. [9]At this, everyone else on the island who was sick came and was cured. [10]They gave us many honours, and when we were getting ready to sail away they gave us everything we needed.

234

It was only when I got back from the walk that I realized I was foolish not to have taken a stick. The hills up by the Scottish border, where I was walking by myself, were known to have plenty of adders, and the fact that the previous year they had been closed off to walkers because of the foot-and-mouth disease meant, so I had been told, that all kinds of wildlife had been having a wonderful time, an entire year without being disturbed by humans. I had just grabbed the chance of an odd day off, put on my boots, and gone up into the wild, tramping through long grass where there used to be footpaths. Only when I was right back at the car, four hours or so later, did I think: I might have been like Paul on Malta. Without a stick I wouldn't have had a clue what to do. And it wouldn't be fair to expect Acts 28 to help me out.

If the sea is a classic symbol of evil, the snake is if anything even more so. Whole cults, religions even, have been built around the strange power of the serpent, both for ill and sometimes (as in the famous healing sign of the snake on the pole) for good. The snake in the Garden of Eden is one of the most talked-about animals in all literature. Moses lifts up the serpent in the wilderness (Numbers 21.9) and those who have been bitten are healed. And so on. And now, when Acts 27 has been, in a sense, the equivalent within this story of Jesus' crucifixion at the climax of Luke's gospel, this story is the equivalent of the odd goings-on early in the morning of the third day, as people realize that something extraordinary has taken place but aren't yet sure what it is. Acts 28 is, in a strange way, the equivalent, within the story Luke is now telling, of the **resurrection**. The gospel, like the risen Jesus, is alive and active, and is now reaching out to the ends of the earth.

The story is both shocking – all those riots, beatings, stonings and finally shipwreck, and then Paul might be carried off by a *snake!* – and also funny. The locals on Malta, an ancient culture which today boasts no snakes and a beach called 'St Paul's Bay', not to mention numerous churches and other reminders of this, one of the most famous moments in their history, go through a range of reactions to Paul which more or less mirror those of the crowd in Lystra in Acts 14. There, Paul heals a disabled man; they think he is a god; but when he disagrees with them, they stone him. Here, Paul is bitten by a poisonous snake; the locals think he must be a criminal (whom the abstract but powerful force of Justice has not allowed to live); but when nothing happens to him (though they keep watching him to see, a charming picture of curious locals grouped round the fire staring at this strange bedraggled **apostle**) they conclude he's a god. Very satisfactory all round.

Not least for Luke, for whom, of course, there is no such thing as an abstract force of 'Justice', because there is a God of justice, a God who does indeed put all things right, eventually, and it is this God who has made sure that Paul does indeed get safely to land. Luke simply cannot help, now, allowing the pattern of accusation-and-vindication to run through story after story. 'This man could have been set free,' declares Agrippa. The storm does its worst but Paul and his companions are 'saved'. The snake and 'Justice' do their worst and Paul is hailed as a god. Even though of course neither Paul nor Luke would approve of this, there is no suggestion, as in Lystra, of a **priest** coming to offer **sacrifice**. More important to get warm from the makeshift bonfire and to find somewhere to stay, to sort out arrangements for the rest of the winter, which is now coming on fast.

The centurion, we may assume, would have pulled rank to make sure that his prisoner en route for Caesar was both kept safe and, since he was going to have to share quarters with him, looked after comfortably. Having stopped his soldiers killing the prisoners, he was unlikely to let them far out of his sight now. That is presumably how Paul and the author of the 'we' in verse 7 and elsewhere get to stay with the leading man of the island, Publius (clearly a Roman name). Here history more or less repeats itself, not merely with the opening scene of chapter 13 on Cyprus where the apostles get to meet Sergius Paulus and impress him with Paul's denunciation of the magician Elymas, but with the various healing scenes in the gospel, in Luke 4 and elsewhere. Publius' father is ill; Paul cures him; and then the to-be-expected procession begins, of people coming from all over the island to be healed.

Paul must have felt quite at home. It must have been bizarre to be back at this kind of work once more, not only after the adventure at sea but after his long enforced imprisonment in Caesarea. We are not told that Publius or his father become believers, which is unusual for Luke if it were the case. But the island as a whole is delighted to have had Paul and his friends with them, and actually loads honours on them when they go. What precisely Luke means by 'honours' is not clear, and some people think it's a tactful way of saying 'honoraria', i.e. money in a sort of payment for the healings received.

The whole scene, of course, provides yet another example, before Italy itself is finally reached, of an official finding that Paul was a man to be trusted and valued, on top of the islanders finding that, despite an apparent accusation (via the snake) he was in fact innocent. This sets the narrative up for the final voyage, and the theology for its full meaning. The sea and the snake have done their worst and are overcome. New creation is happening, and the powers of evil cannot stop it. Paul may arrive in Rome a more bedraggled figure than he would have liked, but the gospel which he brings is flourishing, and nobody can stop it.

ACTS 28.11–22

To Rome at Last

[11]After three months we set sail on a ship that had been spending the winter on the island. It was from Alexandria, and had the insignia of the Heavenly Twins. [12]We arrived at Syracuse, and stayed three days. [13]From there we raised anchor and sailed across to Rhegium. After one day there, a south wind arose, and on the second day we arrived at Puteoli, [14]where we found Christians. That was a great encouragement to us, and we stayed there seven days.

And so we came to Rome. [15]Christians from there, hearing about us, came to meet us as far as Appian Forum and Three Taverns. When Paul saw them, he thanked God and took heart.

[16]When we arrived in Rome, Paul was allowed to lodge privately. He had a soldier to guard him.

[17]After three days, Paul called together the leading men of the Jews. When they arrived, he began to speak.

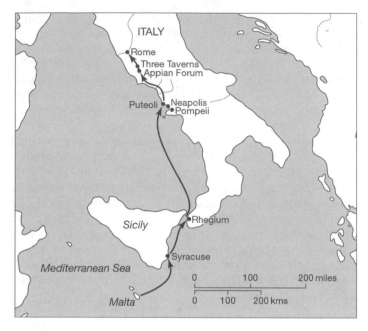

Acts 28.11–22

'My brothers,' he said, 'I have done nothing against our people or our ancestral customs. Yet I was made a prisoner in Jerusalem and handed over to the Romans. [18]The Romans put me on trial and wanted to let me go, because they couldn't find me guilty of any capital crime. [19]But the Judaeans opposed this, and forced me to appeal to Caesar. This had nothing to do with my bringing any charges against my nation! [20]So that's why I have asked to see you and talk with you. It is because of the hope of Israel, you see, that I am wearing this chain.'

[21]'For our part', they responded, 'we haven't received any letters about you from Judaea. Nor has anyone of our nation come here to tell us anything, or to say anything bad about you. [22]We want to hear from your own lips what you have in mind. However, as for this new sect, the one thing we know is that people everywhere are speaking out against it.'

It has been a long voyage, and the biblical commentator, in this, one of the three longest books of the New Testament (Matthew, Luke and Acts are more or less the same length), may well feel on arrival at Puteoli, Appian Forum and Three Taverns that the end is in sight for the writing as well as for Paul. Indeed, anyone who has followed Luke's narrative thus far – and there is a great deal to be said for taking a deep breath and reading the whole thing straight through at a single sitting, instead of taking 10 or 20 verses a day – may well feel as breathless, and grateful for the signs of the destination, as Paul himself must have done.

And yet for Paul of course the story was only just beginning. Everything he had done in his life was a preparation for this moment . . . when he was going to stand before Caesar. The final details of the sailing, the dedication of the ship from Malta to Syracuse and thence to Rhegium (the 'heavenly twins', Castor and Pollux, also known as the Gemini zodiac sign, were often to be seen carved on ships' prows), all function as so much local colour, as a way of Luke letting us know that he has not lost interest in this journey *as a journey*, even if we and perhaps Paul are eager for its end. But we are of course agog to know, what happened when he arrived?

Luke keeps us waiting. And, in the meantime, he gives us, and Paul, the great encouragement: there are Christians already in Rome (of course there are; Paul wrote to them more than two years before), and they hear of Paul's arrival and come to see him, doing with him what citizens of a great city would do for a visiting emperor or a returning princeling: they come out some distance to meet him, to escort him with them into their city. Already on the way they have found other believers in the port of Puteoli; though Rome's official port was Ostia, travellers would often dock at Puteoli and complete the remaining hundred miles or so over land, perhaps because Ostia would be so full of ships and business. Interestingly, they are able to stay with the Christians in Puteoli for a week; what the centurion, or the other prisoners, will have thought of being put up by local Christians we have no idea, but they must by now have realized that they were either dreaming or taking part in a very strange journey with an exceedingly strange prisoner. Anyway, when they get near Rome the believers come several miles to meet Paul at two towns further south, and for Paul this is a real sign of God's grace and blessing. They had read his letter; they have been waiting for him; they are here to welcome him.

And, in Rome itself, Paul is able to rent accommodation for himself. He has to have a soldier living with him, and we learn in his meeting with Jewish leaders that he has to wear a chain all the time (verse 20). But it is a measure of freedom.

But now we have what at first seems like an interlude, and then turns out to be the major closing scene of the book. Paul invites the Jewish leaders in Rome – Rome was a major centre of Jewish population, with dozens of synagogues, many of them accommodating Jews from different parts of the empire, and with different language groups, rather like 'ethnic' churches in London or New York – and they come to his house. Why? What is going on?

The answer must be that he wants, at all costs, to avoid any chance of a further uproar. Not just for his own sake; what is going to happen to him is going to happen to him, and the God who has rescued him from the sea and the snake is well capable of looking after him even when face to face with Nero. No: for the sake of the **gospel**. Whatever conclusion we draw about the report of Claudius expelling the Jews from Rome because of rioting to do with 'Chrestus' (see 18.2, and the discussion there), the Jews were now well and truly back in Rome, and had been presumably for five or six years by now. The chances are that Paul arrived in Rome in AD 60. Nero had succeeded Claudius, and cancelled his banning order, in 54. It was desperately important not to go through a similar cycle again. Nero, though his reign had started in a blaze of glory and new hopes, was already proving unstable, and nobody quite knew what he was likely to do, in between playing his lyre, acting on stage, swaggering around with the troops, patronizing the Senate, orchestrating orgies . . .

So Paul gets his explanation in first. No point in avoiding the Jewish leaders and then being accused, by someone hearing of his arrival, of all kinds of things which would put him on the back foot. You might think there is a danger of *qui s'ex-*

cuse, s'accuse. Inviting people to your home, and then beginning by saying, 'Look here; you need to know that I have done
nothing against our people or our customs', does seem rather
to draw attention to the fact that some people might think
you had, after all. But Paul had no means of knowing, without
facing the problem straight out, whether reports had already
reached the Jews in Rome of what he had been doing, what
he had been charged with, or what he had been informally
accused of. Standing directly in line with what he had said to
the Roman Christians in chapter 11 of his great letter, he
insists to his fellow Jews that he too is a Jew, that though he is
of course a follower of Jesus as **Messiah** he has no charge to
bring against his nation (verse 19).

We would surely be right to see here the dark cloud, which
the early Christians seem to have been aware of, that Jerusalem
was under threat of judgment, at the hands (obviously) of Rome,
and (less obviously, but this was what Jesus had warned) of
God. Faced with that, some of the early Christians, particularly
some early **Gentile** Christians, particularly perhaps some
people who had heard some of what Paul had said but not fully
grasped it all, might have thought: Good! They deserve it.
They've got it coming to them. *And Paul is deeply concerned
lest anyone should think he takes that view.* The idea (which
has been put about here and there in recent years) that Luke
betrays an anti-Jewish cast of mind is an example of failing
to see the complexity, theological and political, of the actual
situation which Paul faced and which Luke is writing up. No
one could tell what was likely to happen in the coming months
and years. We know with hindsight that Jerusalem had
another 10 years to go before the disaster, but it could easily
have happened sooner, and any suggestion in the Jewish community in Rome that the Christians had been somehow egging
the Romans on, or were secretly gloating, would have been
worse than disastrous.

So Paul insists to the Jewish leaders in Rome what he had
insisted to the crowd in Jerusalem, to the Sanhedrin, to Felix
and to Agrippa and the entire entourage in that great scene:
it is because of Israel's hope that I am here, that I am bound,
that I am awaiting my fateful visit with His Majesty. Paul has

had many difficulties with his fellow Jews, as we have seen. But when all is said and done, from the larger perspective, he and they are still close cousins facing the callous, dark might of the pagan world. And it is vital, for both of their sakes, that they do not fall out. Paul certainly doesn't want them showing up with new accusations when, eventually, he stands before Caesar.

Fortunately for Paul, the Jewish leaders seem both remarkably ill-informed and remarkably unconcerned. They have not heard anything from Judaea about him. Nobody has warned them what a pestilent fellow he is. But they have heard about the Christian movement (heard about it? If Suetonius is right, they were expelled from Rome 10 or more years before because of rioting about it), and the one thing they know about the whole business is that nobody has a good word for it. So to be approached in this way by a highly educated fellow Jew who, it seems, is not only a Christian but is coming to trial before the emperor for something to do with it, is an opportunity they cannot pass up. They invite themselves once more.

How Luke might have loved to finish his book with reconciliation between the older and the younger brother. But, as in chapter 15 of his gospel, the story is going to finish too soon – in all sorts of ways. Perhaps this too is deliberate. An unfinished story leaves the reader facing a question: what are *you* going to do about this?

ACTS 28.23–31

The End Is Where We Start From

²³So they fixed a day and came in large numbers to Paul's lodgings. He spoke to them and gave his testimony about the kingdom of God. From morning to night, he explained to them the things about Jesus, from the law of Moses and the prophets.

²⁴Some were persuaded by what he said, and others did not believe. ²⁵They disagreed among themselves. So, as they were getting ready to leave, Paul said one last thing.

'The holy spirit', he said, 'spoke truly through the prophet Isaiah to your ancestors, ²⁶when he said,

Go to this people and say to them:
Listen and listen, but never hear;
Look and look, but never see!
[27]For this people's heart has grown dull,
And their ears are dim with hearing,
And they have closed their eyes –
So that they might not see with their eyes,
And hear with their ears,
And understand with their heart,
And turn, and I would heal them.

[28]'Let it then be known to you that this salvation from God has been sent to the Gentiles. They will listen.'

[30]Paul lived there for two whole years at his own expense, and welcomed everyone who came to see him. [31]He announced the kingdom of God, and taught the things about the Lord Jesus, the Messiah, with all boldness, and with no one stopping him.

When I was an undergraduate, I played the trombone (badly) in various instant home-made orchestras. There were plenty of budding conductors around, eager to try out their skills, and they would organize concerts at a couple of weeks' notice, rally us all round (there were only a few trombonist undergraduates at the time, so we were all in demand), have a couple of rehearsals, and run a friendly concert. We made up in energy and enthusiasm what we lacked in the coherence (not to mention skill) of a regular orchestra.

It was in some of those concerts, organized by a friend in Magdalen College, Oxford, that I learnt to love the symphonies of Antonin Dvorák. I knew the 'New World', of course, his ninth symphony. Everybody did, with its famous cor anglais solo in the second movement, and the great tunes which had not, at that stage, been turned into television commercials. But we also played the fourth, the fifth, the sixth, and the glorious seventh and eighth. Even now, when I hear them, there arise, unbidden, before my mind, clear visual memories of a summer's evening in an old stone chapel, the excitement of the strong, vibrant music, and the poignant sense of central

Europe and its noble cultural traditions, which at that stage – the late 1960s – were of course under heavy Soviet rule.

And I think it was after those concerts that I came back to the 'New World' and realized that, though it is indeed hackneyed, it has something to say that is worth listening to, behind the obvious facade. Two things come to mind which resonate for me with this final scene in Acts, one of the strangest endings to any biblical book (Mark doesn't count, because the ending is almost certainly missing).

First, throughout the 'New World' symphony there is a coming together of cultures, with a kind of question mark between them. The mood is the mood of America, but the tunes are the tunes of central Europe. Are we in fact in the 'new world'? Or are we in the old, but living on foreign soil? Or is it a bit of both? There is sorrow there, and longing, as well as energy and vision.

That is the mood I detect at the close of Acts. Paul has arrived at the gates of 'the ends of the earth', as in the programme set out in 1.8. There is no question that that is how Luke intends us to understand his arrival in Rome: the agenda set for the young church by its Lord has, in principle, been accomplished. But here are his kinsfolk according to the flesh, doing their best to sing the songs of the God of Israel in a strange and pagan land. They have known persecution and danger, by no means always or even usually of their own making. They have known prejudice and suspicion. There is a longing for God's justice to come at last, a passion for God's **law** to be fulfilled once and for all. How can they be at home in this new world?

And Paul knows the answer, but they – or at least some of them – cannot hear it. He spends all day, from morning to night, in yet another of those lengthy Bible expositions we have come to know so well since Peter gave the first one in Acts 2 and Paul did another long one in Acts 13, with many repeat performances which Luke records much more briefly. We could probably map out Paul's lines for him, with Psalms and prophets and Moses and Abraham all telling the great story, and the various smaller stories that contribute to it, and all leading the eye up to a **Messiah** who had to suffer and rise from the dead, a Messiah who was sending the message of his sovereign lordship to all peoples precisely in fulfilment of his promise to Abraham, a Messiah in whose face Paul had glimpsed the glory of the living God.

And, in and through it all, somewhat unusually in terms of the detail of Acts but central in terms of Luke's providing a framework for everything else, the question of God's **kingdom**, highlighted in the first chapter, comes back into its own as we close. That was what he talked to his fellow Jews about (verse 23); that was what he proclaimed 'openly and unhindered' (verse 31). This was, after all, the point of the **message**: that Israel's God, the creator, the God of Abraham, had, in the Messiah, Jesus, claimed his throne as Lord of the world, the one of whom Caesar was simply a low-grade parody. 'Kingdom of God' had always been a political – no, a revolutionary – concept in first-century Judaism. There might, perhaps, be some of Paul's hearers who would already be thinking anxiously what a **rabbi** about 100 years later eventually declared: better to study and keep the law in private than to get involved in talk of the kingdom. That will only get you into trouble. Well, it had, for Paul, but he was still saying it because there wasn't anything else to say. If you believe that Jesus is risen, ascended, and glorified, you have no choice. Jesus is not a distant divine being to whom one might fly off ('the flight of the Alone to the Alone') in an escapist spirituality. If he is Messiah, he is the world's true King.

And even when they cannot hear it, that, too, is sadly part of the scriptural story, as we saw in 13.26–43. This passage from Isaiah 6.9–10 is quoted in Matthew, Mark, Luke and John as well as here, and Paul has something similar in Romans. (That makes it all the more bizarre that, when Isaiah 6 is read in church, people tend to stop immediately before this passage, which was obviously extremely important to the leading New Testament authors.) Somehow, the strange purposes of God to save the world involved the call of a people through whom his message and plan of **salvation** would be carried forwards for the benefit of all. But this people, being naturally themselves composed of sinful human beings, were bound to take this vocation and distort it for their own benefit. Anything else would constitute mere favouritism on God's part. But that is why, in the note that is struck in Romans 11 though not here, Paul insists that though Isaiah 6 and passages like it do indeed stand for the moment as the sorrowful, puzzling, poignant note over the majority of Abraham's physical offspring, that cannot be the last word. And it will be precisely Paul's preaching to the **Gentiles** that will alert the Jewish people to their plight and make some at least want to come back and believe (Romans 11.11–32). The Gentiles will indeed listen to the message of salvation (verse 28); but Paul has already told the church in Rome that this will itself be the means of Israel's 'full inclusion'. The light to lighten the Gentiles must also be the glory of God's people Israel.

I said there were two things about the 'New World' symphony which made new sense to me in relation to the closing passage of this great book. The second of them is the final chord. It isn't an ending, a big crash, a great, satisfying, crunching chord which sends the audience into rapturous applause. The final chord of the 'New World' lingers on the woodwind and strings, pointing away over the horizon, asking questions as much as answering them, beckoning, suggesting, enquiring. Only by the form, the pattern, can words or music reach the stillness. Dvořák does that with his music right there, leaving us with the stillness, the silence at the end, shaped in a new way by the form of what he has told us. And Luke does exactly the same in his last two verses.

We want to know – of course we want to know! – what happened next. And he does not tell us. There are, basically, two (or two and a half) explanations.

The half: Luke lived a long time later and simply didn't know. That is incredible. He knew so much about Paul (or if, according to the sceptics, he didn't, he was prepared to make quite a lot up). He has talked about Paul's death frequently; he has told us, again and again, that he was going to have to stand before Caesar; indeed he has told us that Jesus had told him that he would meet Caesar face to face. If he lived much later, either he knew what happened next or he could have invented something.

So the first real explanation is that Luke knew, but chose deliberately not to tell us. This could have been because, despite the long build-up of acquittals and vindications throughout the book, what happened next was a terrible reversal; or it could have been in order to avoid even hinting at the idea that Paul's death could somehow be in any way a parallel to that of Jesus; it could have been because, even though Paul was vindicated before Nero, Luke for whatever reason didn't want to make that fact the final coping-stone of the book. He has, as we have seen, carefully structured his story so that it is the shipwreck, not Paul's eventual fate, which forms the climax, with 'salvation' woven into it every few verses.

The second real explanation is one which many have rejected, on the grounds that Luke was writing at least 20 years after the event. But we do not know that for certain (though there are strong arguments which many see as telling in that direction). And I have had the sense, working through Acts, of this second explanation as the most likely one *in terms of the form and pattern of what Luke is obviously trying to do*. He has not just been saying, 'Look: the Roman officials will normally do the decent thing, while the Jews will normally try to start a fuss, so go with the Romans rather than with the Jews.' People have tried that line of thought, but it doesn't work. I think it is much more likely that Luke was writing this book, quite deliberately, in order for it to be primary, detailed and very powerful evidence available for when Paul himself came before Caesar. The key point in the narrative, in other words, comes just after the end of the book. A colleague of mine, who lectured in engineering, once came into lunch laughing at an exam script he had just been marking, in which the student had obviously spent hours drawing a very complex diagram only to conclude that the key point was located just off the edge of the page. (The student had written 'and that just about sums up the way life is right now'.) But it isn't that Luke failed to leave room for the key moment in his story. It is, rather, that it hasn't happened yet.

This very old-fashioned view has many problems, as all guesses do, but what it has going for it is the theme of accusation and vindication which we have seen in virtually every chapter from 13 onwards, and in the extraordinary way that Luke has Paul repeat his personal story no fewer than three times. Again and again Roman officials are initially inclined to be hostile to Paul, but eventually end up apologizing, being surprised that he is a citizen and hasn't done anything wrong, dismissing the case, quelling the riot, rescuing him from danger. If Luke's words, after his long book is over, reach into the silence, it is a silence shaped by the theme, deeply germane to Paul's own preaching, of a judgment yet to come which has nevertheless already been anticipated in the present. It is as though Luke has been writing about justification by **faith** (God's eventual judgment of the whole world and all people, whose verdict of 'not guilty' is pronounced in advance over all those who believe, Jew and Gentile alike), but in the concrete and political sense rather than the personal and theological. Caesar will pronounce judgment eventually; that is why Paul has come, why God has commissioned him to come and has protected him to make sure he arrives; but Caesar's judgment can be known in advance in every single judgment that every single Roman or near equivalent official has pronounced, and indeed in such other 'judgments' as the rescue from the sea, the snake and the abstract 'Justice'. That is what I hear in the silence after the end of the book, the pregnant pause as the final chord lingers on and points into the unknown future. Maybe the two years which Luke mentions as the time Paul lived there in his rented accommodation – a mention of time which of course shouts loudly, 'and then what happened?' – corresponds to the two years in Caesarea, a period in which an assiduous writer might assemble his material and write another book.

But that is not how Luke wants us to end our reflection. The book may (or may not) have been written to serve a particular purpose in relation to Paul. But the real hero of the whole book is of course the Jesus who was enthroned as the world's Lord at the beginning, and is now proclaimed, at the end, 'openly and unhindered', that is, with all 'boldness' (a technical term, as elsewhere, not just for moral courage but for a readiness to speak out in public on matters of importance) and with nobody stopping him. And here, for once, Luke gives a full 'Pauline' title to Jesus: 'the Lord Jesus, the Messiah'. King of the Jews; Lord of the World: Jesus of Nazareth, continuing to do and to teach, continuing to announce the kingdom of God which has been decisively inaugurated on earth as in **heaven**.

Jesus of Nazareth, Messiah and Lord: through his servants, through their journeys and their trials, through their pains and their puzzles and their sufferings and their shipwrecks, still reaching out into the future, out beyond Rome and the first century, out across the tracts of time and geography, still confronting men, women and children, rulers, disabled people, local authorities, artisans, governors of islands, wandering tent-makers, philosophers in the market-place, and young men nodding off on windowsills. Luke has brought them all before us, in a dazzling display both of writing and of theology, drawing us in, reminding us once more that this is a drama in which we ourselves have been called to belong to the cast. The journey is ours, the trials and vindications are ours, the sovereign presence of Jesus is ours, the story is ours to pick up and carry on. Luke's writing, like Paul's journey, has reached its end, but in his end is our beginning.

GLOSSARY

age to come, *see* present age

apostle, disciple, the Twelve

'Apostle' means 'one who is sent'. It could be used of an ambassador or official delegate. In the New Testament it is sometimes used specifically of Jesus' inner circle of twelve; but Paul sees not only himself but several others outside the Twelve as 'apostles', the criterion being whether the person had personally seen the risen Jesus. Jesus' own choice of twelve close associates symbolized his plan to renew God's people, Israel (who traditionally thought of themselves as having twelve tribes); after the death of Judas Iscariot (Matthew 27.5; Acts 1.18) Matthias was chosen by lot to take his place, preserving the symbolic meaning. During Jesus' lifetime they, and many other followers, were seen as his 'disciples', which means 'pupils' or 'apprentices'.

ascension

At the end of Luke's **gospel** and the start of Acts, Luke describes Jesus 'going up' from earth into **heaven**. To understand this, we have to remember that 'heaven' isn't a 'place' within our own world of space, time and matter, but a different *dimension* of reality – God's dimension, which intersects and interacts with our own (which we call 'earth', meaning both the planet where we live and the entire space-time universe). For Jesus to 'ascend', therefore, doesn't mean that he's a long way away, but rather that he can be, and is, intimately present to all his people all the time. What's more, because in the Bible 'heaven' is (as it were) the control room for 'earth', it means that Jesus is actually in charge of what goes on here and now. The way his sovereign rule works out is of course very different from the way earthly rulers get their way: as in his own life, he accomplishes his saving purposes through faithful obedience, including suffering. The life and witness of the early church, therefore, resulting in the spread of the gospel around the world, shows what it means to say that Jesus has ascended and that he is the world's rightful Lord.

baptism

Literally, 'plunging' people into water. From within a wider Jewish tradition of ritual washings and bathings, **John the Baptist** undertook a vocation of baptizing people in the Jordan, not as one ritual among others but as a unique moment of **repentance**, preparing them for the coming of the **kingdom of God**. Jesus himself was baptized by John, identifying himself with this renewal movement and developing it in his own way. His followers in turn baptized others. After his **resurrection**, and the sending of the **holy spirit**, baptism became the normal sign and means of entry into the community of Jesus' people. As early as Paul it was aligned both with the **Exodus** from Egypt (1 Corinthians 10.2) and with Jesus' death and resurrection (Romans 6.2–11).

Christ, *see* Messiah

circumcision

The cutting off of the foreskin. Male circumcision was a major mark of identity for Jews, following its initial commandment to Abraham (Genesis 17) reinforced by Joshua (Joshua 5.2–9). Other peoples, e.g. the Egyptians, also circumcised male children. A line of thought from Deuteronomy (e.g. 30.6), through Jeremiah (e.g. 31.33), to the **Dead Sea Scrolls** and the New Testament (e.g. Romans 2.29) speaks of 'circumcision of the heart' as God's real desire, by which one may become inwardly what the male Jew is outwardly, that is, marked out as part of God's people. At periods of Jewish assimilation into the surrounding culture, some Jews tried to remove the marks of circumcision (e.g. 1 Maccabees 1.11–15).

conversion

Conversion means 'turning round', so that you are now going in the opposite direction. In Christian terms, it refers to someone who was going their own way in life (even if they thought it was God's way) being turned round by God, and beginning to follow God's way instead. Theologians have analysed what precisely happens in 'conversion', and how it relates to 'regeneration' (the 'new birth' as in John 3) and 'justification' (God's declaration that this person is 'in the right' with him). The main thing to stress is that conversion is God's work in someone's life, and that it involves a complete personal transformation by God's **spirit**. Sometimes conversion happens suddenly and dramatically, as with Saul of Tarsus (i.e. St Paul); sometimes it is gentle and quiet, though equally effective, as with Lydia in Acts 16.

covenant

At the heart of Jewish belief is the conviction that the one God, YHWH, who had made the whole world, had called Abraham and his family to belong to him in a special way. The promises God made to Abraham and his family, and the requirements that were laid on them as a result, came to be seen in terms either of the agreement that a king would make with a subject people, or of the marriage bond between husband and wife. One regular way of describing this relationship was 'covenant', which can thus include both promise and law. The covenant was renewed at Mount Sinai with the giving of the Torah; in Deuteronomy before the entry to the promised land; and, in a more focused way, with David (e.g. Psalm 89). Jeremiah 31 promised that after the punishment of exile God would make a 'new covenant' with his people, forgiving them and binding them to him more intimately. Jesus believed that this was coming true through his kingdom-proclamation and his death and resurrection. The early Christians developed these ideas in various ways, believing that in Jesus the promises had at last been fulfilled.

day of Pentecost

A major Jewish festival, 50 days after Passover and the feast of Unleavened Bread (Leviticus 23.9–14). By the first century this had become associated with the time, 50 days after the Israelites left Egypt, when Moses went up Mount Sinai and came down with the law. It was on the day of Pentecost that the holy spirit came powerfully upon the early disciples, 50 days after the Passover at which Jesus had died and been raised (Acts 2). Whether or not we say that this was 'the birthday of the church' (some would use that description for the call of Abraham in Genesis 12, or at least the call of the first disciples in Mark 1), it was certainly the time when Jesus' followers discovered the power to tell people about his resurrection and lordship and to order their common life to reflect his saving kingdom.

Dead Sea Scrolls

A collection of texts, some in remarkably good repair, some extremely fragmentary, found in the late 1940s around Qumran (near the northwest corner of the Dead Sea), and virtually all now edited, translated and in the public domain. They formed all or part of the library of a strict monastic group, most likely Essenes, founded in the mid-second century BC and lasting until the Jewish–Roman war of AD 66–70. The scrolls include the earliest existing manuscripts of the Hebrew and Aramaic scriptures, and several other important documents of community regulations, scriptural exegesis, hymns, wisdom writings, and other literature. They shed a flood of light on one small segment within the Judaism of Jesus' day, helping us to understand how some Jews at least were thinking, praying and reading scripture. Despite attempts to prove the contrary, they make no reference to **John the Baptist,** Jesus, Paul, James or early Christianity in general.

demons, *see* **the satan**

disciple, *see* **apostle**

Essenes, *see* **Dead Sea Scrolls**

eternal life, *see* **present age**

exile

Deuteronomy (29—30) warned that if Israel disobeyed YHWH, he would send his people into exile, but that if they then repented he would bring them back. When the Babylonians sacked Jerusalem and took the people into exile, prophets such as Jeremiah interpreted this as the fulfilment of this prophecy, and made further promises about how long exile would last (70 years, according to Jeremiah 25.12; 29.10). Sure enough, exiles began to return in the late sixth century BC (Ezra 1.1). However, the post-exilic period was largely a disappointment, since the people were still enslaved to foreigners (Nehemiah 9.36); and at the height of persecution by the Syrians Daniel 9.2, 24 spoke of the 'real' exile lasting not for 70 years but for 70 *weeks* of years, i.e. 490 years. Longing for the real 'return from exile', when the prophecies of Isaiah, Jeremiah, etc. would be fulfilled, and **redemption** from pagan oppression accomplished, continued to characterize many Jewish movements, and was a major theme in Jesus' proclamation and his summons to **repentance.**

Exodus

The Exodus from Egypt took place, according to the book of that name, under the leadership of Moses, after long years in which the

Israelites had been enslaved there. (According to Genesis 15.13f., this was itself part of God's covenanted promise to Abraham.) It demonstrated, to them and to Pharaoh, King of Egypt, that Israel was God's special child (Exodus 4.22). They then wandered through the Sinai wilderness for 40 years, led by God in a pillar of cloud and fire; early on in this time they were given the **Torah** on Mount Sinai itself. Finally, after the death of Moses and under the leadership of Joshua, they crossed the Jordan and entered, and eventually conquered, the promised land of Canaan. This event, commemorated annually in the Passover and other Jewish festivals, gave the Israelites not only a powerful memory of what had made them a people, but also a particular shape and content to their **faith** in ʏʜᴡʜ as not only creator but also redeemer; and in subsequent enslavements, particularly the **exile,** they looked for a further **redemption** which would be, in effect, a new Exodus. Probably no other past event so dominated the imagination of first-century Jews; among them the early Christians, following the lead of Jesus himself, continually referred back to the Exodus to give meaning and shape to their own critical events, most particularly Jesus' death and **resurrection.**

faith

Faith in the New Testament covers a wide area of human trust and trustworthiness, merging into love at one end of the scale and loyalty at the other. Within Jewish and Christian thinking faith in God also includes *belief*, accepting certain things as true about God, and what he has done in the world (e.g. bringing Israel out of Egypt; raising Jesus from the dead). For Jesus, 'faith' often seems to mean 'recognizing that God is decisively at work to bring the **kingdom** through Jesus'. For Paul, 'faith' is both the specific belief that Jesus is Lord and that God raised him from the dead (Romans 10.9) and the response of grateful human love to sovereign divine love (Galatians 2.20). This faith is, for Paul, the solitary badge of membership in God's people in **Christ,** marking them out in a way that **Torah,** and the works it prescribes, can never do.

fellowship

The word we often translate 'fellowship' can mean a business partnership (in the ancient world, businesses were often run by families, so there's a sense of family loyalty as well), or it can mean a sense of mutual belonging and sharing in some other corporate enterprise.

Within early Christianity, 'fellowship' acquired the sense not just of belonging to one another as Christians, but of a shared belonging to Jesus **Christ**, and a participation in his life through the **spirit**, expressed in such actions as the 'breaking of bread' and the sharing of property with those in need.

forgiveness

Jesus made forgiveness central to his **message** and ministry, not least because he was claiming to be launching God's long-awaited 'new **covenant**' (Jeremiah 31.31–34) in which sins would at last be forgiven (Matthew 26.28). Forgiveness doesn't mean God, or someone else, saying, of some particular fault or sin, 'it didn't really matter' or 'I didn't really mind'. The point of forgiveness is that it *did* matter, God (and/or other people) really *did* mind, but they are not going to hold it against the offender. It isn't, in other words, the same thing as 'tolerance': to forgive is not to tolerate sin, but to see clearly that it was wrong and then to treat the offender as though it hadn't happened. The early Christian answer to the obvious question, 'How could a holy and righteous God do that?' is 'through the death of Jesus'. What's more, Jesus commanded his followers to extend the same forgiveness to one another (Matthew 6.12). Not to do so is to shut up the same door through which forgiveness is received for oneself (Matthew 18.21–35).

Gentiles

The Jews divided the world into Jews and non-Jews. The Hebrew word for non-Jews, *goyim*, carries overtones both of family identity (i.e. not of Jewish ancestry) and of worship (i.e. of idols, not of the one true god YHWH). Though many Jews established good relations with Gentiles, not least in the Jewish Diaspora (the dispersion of Jews away from Palestine), officially there were taboos against the contact such as intermarriage. In the New Testament the Greek word *ethne*, 'nations', carries the same meanings as *goyim*. Part of Paul's overmastering agenda was to insist that Gentiles who believed in Jesus had full rights in the Christian community alongside believing Jews, without having to become **circumcised**.

good news, gospel, message, word

The idea of 'good news', for which an older English word is 'gospel', had two principal meanings for first-century Jews. First, with roots in Isaiah, it meant the news of YHWH's long-awaited victory over evil and rescue of his people. Second, it was used in the Roman world for the accession, or birthday, of the emperor. Since for Jesus and Paul the announcement of God's inbreaking **kingdom** was both the fulfilment of prophecy and a challenge to the world's present rules, 'gospel' became an important shorthand for both the message of Jesus himself and the apostolic message about him. Paul saw this message as itself the vehicle of God's saving power (Romans 1.16; 1 Thessalonians 2.13).

gospel, *see* **good news**

heaven

Heaven is God's dimension of the created order (Genesis 1.1; Psalm 115.16; Matthew 6.9), whereas 'earth' is the world of space, time and matter that we know. 'Heaven' thus sometimes stands, reverentially, for 'God' (as in Matthew's regular '**kingdom** of heaven'). Normally hidden from human sight, heaven is occasionally revealed or unveiled so that people can see God's dimension of ordinary life (e.g. 2 Kings 6.17; Revelation 1, 4—5). Heaven in the New Testament is thus not usually seen as the place where God's people go after death; at the end, the New Jerusalem descends *from* heaven *to* earth, joining the two dimensions for ever. 'Entering the kingdom of heaven' does not mean 'going to heaven after death', but belonging in the present to the people who steer their earthly course by the standards and purposes of heaven (cf. the Lord's Prayer; 'on earth as in heaven', Matthew 6.10), and who are assured of membership in the **age to come.**

high priest, *see* **priests**

holy spirit

In Genesis 1.2, the spirit is God's presence and power *within* creation, without God being identified with creation. The same spirit entered people, notably the prophets, enabling them to speak and act for God. At his **baptism** by **John,** Jesus was specially equipped with the spirit, resulting in his remarkable public career (Acts 10.38). After his **resurrection**, his followers were themselves filled (Acts 2) by the same spirit, now identified as Jesus' own spirit; the creator God was acting afresh, remaking the world and them too. The spirit enabled them to live out a holiness which the **Torah** could not, producing 'fruit' in their lives, giving them 'gifts' with which to serve God, the world, and the church, and assuring them of future **resurrection** (Romans 8;

Galatians 4—5; 1 Corinthians 12—14). From very early in Christianity (e.g. Galatians 4.1–7), the spirit became part of the new revolutionary definition of God himself: 'the one who sends the son and the spirit of the son'.

John (the Baptist)
Jesus' cousin on his mother's side, born a few months before Jesus; his father was a **priest**. He acted as a prophet, baptizing in the Jordan – dramatically re-enacting the **Exodus** from Egypt – to prepare people, by **repentance**, for God's coming judgment. He may have had some contact with the **Essenes**, though his eventual public message was different from theirs. Jesus' own vocation was decisively confirmed at his **baptism** by John. As part of John's message of the **kingdom**, he outspokenly criticized Herod Antipas for marrying his brother's wife. Herod had him imprisoned, and then beheaded him at his wife's request (Mark 6.14–29). Groups of John's disciples continued a separate existence, without merging into Christianity, for some time afterwards (e.g. Acts 19.1–7).

jubilee
The ancient Israelites were commanded to keep a 'jubilee' every fiftieth year (i.e. following the sequence of seven 'sabbatical' years). Leviticus 25 provides the basic rules, which were expanded by later teachers: land was to be restored to its original owners or their heirs, and any fellow Jews who had been enslaved because of debt were to be set free. It was also to be a year without sowing, reaping or harvesting. The point was that YHWH owned the land, and that the Israelites were to see it not as a private possession but as something held in trust. People debate whether the jubilee principle was ever put into practice as thoroughly as Leviticus demands, but the underlying promise of a great remission of debts was repeated by Isaiah (61.1–2) and then decisively by Jesus (Luke 4.16–21). It is likely that this underlies the action of the first Christians in sharing property and giving to those in need (Acts 4.32–35, etc.).

kingdom of God, kingdom of heaven
Best understood as the king*ship*, or sovereign and saving rule, of Israel's God YHWH, as celebrated in several Psalms (e.g. 99.1) and prophecies (e.g. Daniel 6.26–27). Because YHWH was the creator God, when he finally became king in the way he intended this would involve

setting the world to rights, and particularly rescuing Israel from its enemies. 'Kingdom of God' and various equivalents (e.g. 'No king but God!') became revolutionary slogans around the time of Jesus. Jesus' own announcement of God's kingdom redefined these expectations around his own very different plan and vocation. His invitation to people to 'enter' the kingdom was a way of summoning them to allegiance to himself and his programme, seen as the start of God's long-awaited saving reign. For Jesus, the kingdom was coming not in a single move, but in stages, of which his own public career was one, his death and **resurrection** another, and a still future consummation another. Note that 'kingdom of **heaven**' is Matthew's preferred form for the same phrase, following a regular Jewish practice of saying 'heaven' rather than 'God'. It does not refer to a place ('heaven'), but to the fact of God's becoming king in and through Jesus and his achievement. Paul speaks of Jesus as **Messiah**, already in possession of his kingdom, waiting to hand it over finally to the father (1 Corinthians 15.23–28; cf. Ephesians 5.5).

last days

Ancient Jews thought of world history as divided into two periods: 'the **present age**' and 'the **age to come**'. The present age was a time when evil was still at large in its many forms; the age to come would usher in God's final reign of justice, peace, joy and love. Ancient prophets had spoken of the transition from the one age to the other in terms of the 'last days', meaning either the final moments of the 'present age' or the eventual dawning of the 'age to come'. When Peter quotes Joel in Acts 2.17, he perhaps means both: the two ages have overlapped, so that Christians live in the 'last days', the time between God's **kingdom** being launched in and through Jesus and it being completed at Jesus' return. The New Testament gives no encouragement to the idea that we can calculate a precise timetable for the latter event, or that the period of history immediately before Jesus' return will be significantly different (e.g. more violent) than any other (see Matthew 24.36–39).

law, *see* Torah

life, soul, spirit

Ancient people held many different views about what made human beings the special creatures they are. Some, including many Jews, believed that to be complete, humans needed bodies as well as inner selves. Others, including many influenced by the philosophy of Plato (fourth century BC), believed that the important part of a human was the 'soul' (Gk: *psyche*), which at death would be happily freed from its bodily prison. Confusingly for us, the same word *psyche* is often used in the New Testament within a Jewish framework where it clearly means 'life' or 'true self', without implying a body/soul dualism that devalues the body. Human inwardness of experience and understanding can also be referred to as 'spirit'. *See also* **holy spirit; resurrection.**

message, *see* **good news**

Messiah

The Hebrew word means literally 'anointed one', hence in theory a prophet, **priest** or king. In Greek this translates as *Christos*; 'Christ' in early Christianity was a title, and only gradually became an alternative proper name for Jesus. In practice 'Messiah' is mostly restricted to the notion, which took various forms in ancient Judaism, of the coming king who would be David's true heir, through whom YHWH would rescue Israel from pagan enemies. There was no single template of expectations. Scriptural stories and promises contributed to different ideals and movements, often focused on (a) decisive military defeat of Israel's enemies and (b) rebuilding or cleansing the **Temple.** The **Dead Sea Scrolls** speak of two 'Messiahs', one a priest and the other a king. The universal early Christian belief that Jesus was Messiah is only explicable, granted his crucifixion by the Romans (which would have been seen as a clear sign that he was not the Messiah), by their belief that God had raised him from the dead, so vindicating the implicit messianic claims of his earlier ministry.

miracles

Like some of the old prophets, notably Elijah and Elisha, Jesus performed many deeds of remarkable power, particularly healings. The **gospels** refer to these as 'deeds of power', 'signs', 'marvels', or 'paradoxes'. Our world 'miracle' tends to imply that God, normally 'outside' the closed system of the world, sometimes 'intervenes'; miracles have then frequently been denied by sceptics as a matter of principle. However, in the Bible God is always present, however strangely, and 'deeds of power' are seen as *special* acts of a *present* God rather than *intrusive* acts of an *absent* one. Jesus' own 'mighty works' are seen particularly, following prophecy, as evidence of his messiahship (e.g. Matthew 11.2–6).

Mishnah

The main codification of Jewish law (**Torah**) by the **rabbis**, produced in about AD 200, reducing to writing the 'oral Torah' which in Jesus' day ran parallel to the 'written Torah'. The Mishnah is itself the basis of the much larger collection of tradition in the two Talmuds (roughly AD 400).

parables

From the Old Testament onwards, prophets and other teachers used various story-telling devices as vehicles for their challenge to Israel (e.g. 2 Samuel 12.1–7). Sometimes they appeared as visions with interpretations (e.g. Daniel 7). Similar techniques were used by the **rabbis**. Jesus made his own creative adaptation of these traditions, in order to break open the worldview of his contemporaries and to invite them to share his vision of God's **kingdom** instead. His stories portrayed this as something that was happening, not just a timeless truth, and enabled his hearers to step inside the story and make it their own. As with some Old Testament visions, some of Jesus' parables have their own interpretations (e.g. the sower, Mark 4); others are thinly disguised retellings of the prophetic story of Israel (e.g. the wicked tenants, Mark 12).

Pharisees, rabbis

The Pharisees were an unofficial but powerful Jewish pressure group through most of the first centuries BC and AD. Largely lay-led, though including some of the **priests**, their aim was to purify Israel through intensified observance of the Jewish law (**Torah**), developing their own traditions about the precise meaning and application of scripture, their own patterns of prayer and other devotion, and their own calculations of the national hope. Though not all legal experts were Pharisees, most Pharisees were legal experts.

They effected a democratization of Israel's life, since for them the study and practice of Torah was equivalent to worshipping in the **Temple** – though they were adamant in pressing their own rules for the Temple liturgy on an unwilling (and often Sadducean) priesthood. This enabled them to survive AD 70 and, merging in to the early Rabbinic movement, to develop new ways forward. Politically they stood up for ancestral traditions, and were at the forefront of various movements of revolt against both pagan overlordship and compromised Jewish leaders. By Jesus' day there were two distinct schools, the stricter one of Shammai, more inclined towards armed revolt, and the more lenient one of Hillel, ready to live and let live.

Jesus' debates with the Pharisees are at least as much a matter of agenda and policy (Jesus strongly opposed their separatist national- ism) as about details of theology and piety. Saul of Tarsus was a fervent right-wing Pharisee, presumably a Shammaite, until his **conversion**.

After the disastrous war of AD 66–70, these schools of Hillel and Shammai continued bitter debate on appropriate policy. Following the further disaster of AD 135 (the failed Bar-Kochba revolt against Rome) their traditions were carried on by the rabbis who, though looking to the earlier Pharisees for inspiration, developed a Torah-piety in which personal holiness and purity took the place of political agendas.

present age, age to come, eternal life

By the time of Jesus many Jewish thinkers divided history into two periods: 'the present age' and 'the age to come' – the latter being the time when YHWH would at last act decisively to judge evil, to rescue Israel, and to create a new world of justice and peace. The early Christians believed that, though the full blessings of the coming age lay still in the future, it had already begun with Jesus, particularly with his death and **resurrection**, and that by **faith** and **baptism** they were able to enter it already. 'Eternal life' does not mean simply 'existence con- tinuing without end', but 'the life of the age to come'.

priests, high priest

Aaron, the older brother of Moses, was appointed Israel's first high priest (Exodus 28—29), and in theory his descendants were Israel's priests thereafter. Other members of his tribe (Levi) were 'Levites', per- forming other liturgical duties but not sacrificing. Priests lived among the people all around the country, having a local teaching role (Leviticus 10.11; Malachi 2.7), and going to Jerusalem by rotation to perform the **Temple** liturgy (e.g. Luke 2.8).

David appointed Zadok (whose Aaronic ancestry is sometimes questioned) as high priest, and his family remained thereafter the senior priests in Jerusalem, probably the ancestors of the **Sadducees**. One explanation of the origin of the Qumran **Essenes** is that they were a dissident group who believed themselves to be the rightful chief priests.

rabbis, *see* **Pharisees**

redemption

Literally, 'redemption' means 'buying-back', and was often used in the ancient world of slaves buying their freedom, or having it bought for them. The great 'redemption' in the Bible, which coloured the way the word was heard ever afterwards, was when God 'bought' his people Israel from slavery in Egypt to give them freedom in the promised land. When, later, the Jews were exiled in Babylon (and even after they returned to their land), they described themselves as undergoing a new slavery and hence being in need of a new redemption. Jesus, and the early Christians, interpreted this continuing slavery in its most radical terms, as slavery to sin and death, and understood 'redemption' likewise in terms of the rescue from this multiple and tyrannous slavery which God provided through the death of Jesus (Romans 3.24).

repentance

Literally, this means 'turning back'. It is widely used in Old Testament and subsequent Jewish literature to indicate both a personal turning away from sin and Israel's corporate turning away from idolatry and back to YHWH. Through both meanings, it is linked to the idea of 'return from **exile**'; if Israel is to 'return' in all senses, it must 'return' to YHWH. This is at the heart of the summons of both **John the Baptist** and Jesus. In Paul's writings it is mostly used for **Gentiles** turning away from idols to serve the true God; also for sinning Christians who need to return to Jesus.

resurrection

In most biblical thought, human bodies matter and are not merely disposable prisons for the **soul**. When ancient Israelites wrestled with the goodness and justice of YHWH, the creator, they ultimately came to insist he must raise the dead (Isaiah 26.19; Daniel 12.2–3) – a suggestion firmly resisted by classical pagan thought. The longed-for return from **exile** was also spoken of in terms of YHWH raising dry bones to new **life** (Ezekiel 37.1–14). These ideas were developed in the second-**Temple** period, not least at times of martyrdom (e.g. 2 Maccabees 7). Resurrection was not just 'life after death', but a newly embodied life *after* 'life after death'; those at present dead were either 'asleep' or seen as 'souls', 'angels' or 'spirits', awaiting new embodiment.

The early Christian belief that Jesus had been raised from the dead was not that he had 'gone to **heaven**', or that he had been 'exalted', or was 'divine'; they believed all those as well, but each could have been expressed without mention of resurrection. Only the bodily resurrection of Jesus explains the rise of the early church, particularly its belief in Jesus' messiahship (which his crucifixion would have called into question). The early Christians believed that they themselves would be raised to a new, transformed bodily life at the time of the Lord's return or parousia (e.g. Philippians 3.20f.).

sabbath

The Jewish sabbath, the seventh day of the week, was a regular reminder both of creation (Genesis 2.3; Exodus 20.8–11) and of the **Exodus** (Deuteronomy 5.15). Along with **circumcision** and the food laws, it was one of the badges of Jewish identity within the pagan world of late antiquity, and a considerable body of Jewish **law** and custom grew up around its observance.

sacrifice

Like all ancient people, the Israelites offered animal and vegetable sacrifices to their God. Unlike others, they possessed a highly detailed written code (mostly in Leviticus) for what to offer and how to offer it; this in turn was developed in the **Mishnah** (c. AD 200). The Old Testament specifies that sacrifices can only be offered in the Jerusalem **Temple**; after this was destroyed in AD 70, sacrifices ceased, and Judaism developed further the idea, already present in some teachings, of prayer, fasting and almsgiving as alternative forms of sacrifice. The early Christians used the language of sacrifice in connection with such things as holiness, evangelism and the eucharist.

Sadducees

By Jesus' day, the Sadducees were the aristocracy of Judaism, possibly tracing their origins to the family of Zadok, David's **high priest**. Based in Jerusalem, and including most of the leading priestly families, they had their own traditions and attempted to resist the pressure of the **Pharisees** to conform to theirs. They claimed to rely only on the Pentateuch (the first five books of the Old Testament), and denied any doctrine of a future life, particularly of the **resurrection** and other ideas associated with it, presumably because of the encouragement such beliefs gave to revolutionary movements. No writings from the

Sadducees have survived, unless the apocryphal book of Ben-Sirach (Ecclesiasticus) comes from them. The Sadducees themselves did not survive the destruction of Jerusalem and the **Temple** in AD 70.

salvation

Salvation means 'rescue', and the meanings of the word have depended on what people thought needed rescuing, and from what. Thus, where people have imagined that the human plight was best seen in terms of an immortal **soul** being trapped in a mortal and corrupt body, 'salvation' was seen in terms of the rescue of this soul from such a prison. But for most Jews, and all early Christians, it was death itself, the ending of God-given bodily **life**, that was the real enemy, so that 'salvation' was bound to mean being rescued from death itself – in other words, the **resurrection** of the body for those who had died, and the transformation of the body for those still alive at the Lord's return (e.g. 1 Corinthians 15.50–57). For Paul and others, this 'salvation' was extended to the whole of creation (Romans 8.18–26). But if 'salvation' refers to this ultimate rescue of God's created order, and our created bodies, from all that distorts, defaces and destroys them (i.e. sin, sickness, corruption and death itself), we should expect to find, and do in fact find, that often in the New Testament 'salvation' (and phrases like 'being saved') refer, not simply to people coming to **faith** and so being assured of **eternal life**, but to bodily healing and to rescue from awful plights (e.g. Acts 16.30–31; 27.44). Jesus' resurrection remains the foundation for a biblical view of salvation for the whole person and the whole creation, a salvation which, though to be completed in the future, has already begun with the mission and achievement of Jesus.

satan, the, 'the accuser', demons

The Bible is never very precise about the identity of the figure known as 'the satan'. The Hebrew word means 'the accuser', and at times the satan seems to be a member of YHWH's heavenly council, with special responsibility as director of prosecutions (1 Chronicles 21.1; Job 1—2; Zechariah 3.1f.). However, it becomes identified variously with the serpent of the garden of Eden (Genesis 3.1–15) and with the rebellious daystar cast out of heaven (Isaiah 14.12–15), and was seen by many Jews as the quasi-personal source of evil standing behind both human wickedness and large-scale injustice, sometimes operating through semi-independent 'demons'. By Jesus' time various words were used to denote this figure, including Beelzebul/b (lit. 'Lord of the flies') and simply 'the evil one'; Jesus warned his followers against the deceits this figure could perpetrate. His opponents accused him of being in league with the satan, but the early Christians believed that Jesus in fact defeated it both in his own struggles with temptation (Matthew 4; Luke 4), his exorcisms of demons, and his death (1 Corinthians 2.8; Colossians 2.15). Final victory over this ultimate enemy is thus assured (Revelation 20), though the struggle can still be fierce for Christians (Ephesians 6.10–20).

scribes

In a world where many could not write, or not very well, a trained class of writers ('scribes') performed the important function of drawing up contracts for business, marriage, etc. Many scribes would thus be legal experts, and quite possibly **Pharisees**, though being a scribe was compatible with various political and religious standpoints. The work of Christian scribes was of initial importance in copying early Christian writings, particularly the stories about Jesus.

second coming

When God renews the whole creation, as he has promised, bringing together **heaven** and earth, Jesus himself will be the centre of it all, personally present to and with his people and ruling his world fully and finally at last. This Christian hope picks up, and gives more explicit focus to, the ancient Jewish hope that YHWH would in the end return to his people to judge and to save. Since the **ascension** is often thought of in terms of Jesus 'going away', this final moment is often thought of in terms of his 'coming back again', hence the shorthand 'second coming'. However, since the ascension in fact means that Jesus, though now invisible, is not far away but rather closely present with us, it isn't surprising that some of the key New Testament passages speak, not of his 'return' as though from a great distance, but of his 'appearing' (e.g. Colossians 3.4; 1 John 3.2). The early Christians expected this 'appearing' to take place, not necessarily within a generation as is often thought (because of a misreading of Mark 13 and similar passages) but at *any* time – which could be immediate, or delayed. This caused a problem for some early Christians (2 Peter 3.3–10), but not for many. For the early Christians, the really important event – the **resurrection** of Jesus – had already taken place, and his final 'appearing' would simply complete what had then been decisively begun.

son of David

An alternative, and infrequently used, title for **Messiah**. The messianic promises of the Old Testament often focus specifically on David's son, for example 2 Samuel 7.12–16; Psalm 89.19–37. Joseph, Mary's husband, is called 'son of David' by the angel in Matthew 1.20.

son of God

Originally a title for Israel (Exodus 4.22) and the Davidic king (Psalm 2.7); also used of ancient angelic figures (Genesis 6.2). By the New Testament period it was already used as a **messianic** title, for example, in the **Dead Sea Scrolls**. There, and when used of Jesus in the **gospels** (e.g. Matthew 16.16), it means, or reinforces, 'Messiah', without the later significance of 'divine'. However, already in Paul the transition to the fuller meaning (one who was already equal with God and was sent by him to become human and to become Messiah), is apparent, without loss of the meaning 'Messiah' itself (e.g. Galatians 4.4).

son of man

In Hebrew or Aramaic, this simply means 'mortal', or 'human being'; in later Judaism, it is sometimes used to mean 'I' or 'someone like me'. In the New Testament the phrase is frequently linked to Daniel 7.13, where 'one like a son of man' is brought on the clouds of **heaven** to 'the Ancient of Days', being vindicated after a period of suffering, and is given kingly power. Though Daniel 7 itself interprets this as code for 'the people of the saints of the Most High', by the first century some Jews understood it as a **messianic** promise. Jesus developed this in his own way in certain key sayings which are best understood as promises that God would vindicate him, and judge those who had opposed him, after his own suffering (e.g. Mark 14.62). Jesus was thus able to use the phrase as a cryptic self-designation, hinting at his coming suffering, his vindication, and his God-given authority.

soul, *see* life

speaking in tongues

In many religious traditions, people who experience certain types of ecstasy have sometimes found themselves speaking, praying or even singing in what seem to them to be languages which they do not themselves understand. Sometimes these turn out to be actual languages which are understood by one or more listeners: this is what is described in Acts 2, and there are many examples from subsequent periods including our own. Sometimes they appear to be a kind of babbling semi-language corresponding to no known human tongue. Sometimes the speaker may be unable to decide which it is. Paul was well aware (1 Corinthians 12.1–3) that phenomena like this could occur in non-Christian contexts, but for him, and for millions since (not least in today's pentecostal and charismatic movements, though much more widely as well), such prayer was and is powerful in evoking the presence of Jesus, celebrating the energy of the **spirit**, and interceding for people and situations, particularly when it isn't clear what exactly to pray for (see, perhaps, Romans 8.26–27). There is however no good reason, within early Christian teaching, to suppose that 'speaking in tongues' is either a necessary or a sufficient sign that the **holy spirit** is at work in and through someone's life, still less that they have attained, as has sometimes been claimed, a new and more elevated level of spirituality than those who have not received this gift. To be sure, in Acts 2, and also in Acts 8.17 (by implication at least), 11.46 and 19.6, 'tongues' is a sign that the spirit has been poured out on people who weren't expected to be included in God's people. But there are plenty of other times when the spirit is powerfully at work without any mention of 'tongues', and equally every indication (e.g. 1 Corinthians 12 and 14) that praying in tongues is, for some, a regular practice and not merely an initiatory sign.

spirit, *see* **life, holy spirit**

Temple

The Temple in Jerusalem was planned by David (*c*. 1000 BC) and built by his son Solomon as the central sanctuary for all Israel. After reforms under Hezekiah and Josiah in the seventh century BC, it was destroyed by Babylon in 587 BC. Rebuilding by the returned **exiles** began in 538 BC, and was completed in 516, initiating the 'second-Temple period'. Judas Maccabaeus cleansed it in 164 BC after its desecration by Antiochus Epiphanes (167). Herod the Great began to rebuild and beautify it in 19 BC; the work was completed in AD 63. The Temple was destroyed by the Romans in AD 70. Many Jews believed it should and would be rebuilt; some still do. The Temple was not only the place of **sacrifice**; it was believed to be the unique dwelling of YHWH on earth, the place where **heaven** and earth met.

Torah, Jewish law

'Torah', narrowly conceived, consists of the first five books of the Old Testament, the 'five books of Moses' or 'Pentateuch'. (These contain much law, but also much narrative.) It can also be used for the whole Old Testament scriptures, though strictly these are the 'law, prophets and writings'. In a broader sense, it refers to the whole developing corpus of Jewish legal tradition, written and oral; the oral Torah was initially codified in the **Mishnah** around AD 200, with wider developments found in the two Talmuds, of Babylon and Jerusalem, codified around AD 400. Many Jews in the time of Jesus and Paul regarded the Torah as being so strongly God-given as to be almost itself, in some sense, divine; some (e.g. Ben-Sirach 24) identified it with the figure of 'Wisdom'. Doing what Torah said was not seen as a means of earning God's favour, but rather of expressing gratitude, and as a key badge of Jewish identity.

tongues, *see* **speaking in tongues**

the Twelve, *see* **apostle**

word, *see* **good news**

YHWH

The ancient Israelite name for God, from at least the time of the **Exodus** (Exodus 6.2f.). It may originally have been pronounced 'Yahweh', but by the time of Jesus it was considered too holy to speak out loud, except for the **high priest** once a year in the holy of holies in the **Temple**. Instead, when reading scripture, pious Jews would say *Adonai*, 'Lord', marking this usage by adding the vowels of *Adonai* to the consonants of YHWH, eventually producing the hybrid 'Jehovah'. The word YHWH is formed from the verb 'to be', combining 'I am who I am', 'I will be who I will be', and perhaps 'I am because I am', emphasizing YHWH's sovereign creative power.